Teacher Unhinged

Teacher Unhinged

Annalise Garcia

Prince & Ava
Publishing L.L.C.

Prince & Ava Publishing L.L.C.

CONTENTS

CONTENTS

CONTENTS

CONTENTS

I dedicate this book to the memory of Pedro Padilla. He always missed his mama.

First edition

Editing by Joseph Crumb

Cover art by Jett Vitali

This book was professionally typeset on Reedsy.

Find out more at reedsy.com

ACKNOWLEDGEMENTS

I'd like to acknowledge Georgina for her guidance in writing. Cheers to Laurie, for being an invaluable writing partner and friend. And thank you to Joseph, who's a better editor than any proofreading app out there! I also give gratitude to my mom, Chris, Bella for being my home base, Ezequiel and Esther Lopez for teaching me to work on weekends, and Teal, Babs, Amber, Ernie, Laurita, Brigitte, Kelly for their life support. I'm glad to have all my sisters and brothers. I love (all of them). I'm also grateful for my therapists. And I'd like to confess that my colleagues helped me daily through this thing called *life*. Thank you for healing my heart by being you. You are the wittiest and smartest people I've ever known. I have so much love for you all.

And Readers, I hope to connect with you.

How Did I Get Here?

I haven't always been what society would call a "homeless loser," staying with friends in Los Angeles for the past few years. I did earn my bachelor's degree and learned a trade in radio while going to the University of New Mexico. After graduating from college, I moved to Chicago. I got a job as a social worker, working with pregnant women and babies. But after five years of living in Chicago, I couldn't stand the winters any longer. Below zero weather is not for me. I'm more of a sun-worshiper. I do miss the food in Chicago though. When living in Chicago, my boyfriend at the time asked me if I wanted to move to L.A., so we did, in the summer of 2005.

I abruptly broke up with that jerk less than six months later. My boyfriend had gotten some gigs DJing at a few clubs in Hollywood. We had a routine of me dropping him off and picking him up. There's nowhere to park in Hollywood for free. One night, when I picked him up, he was drunk. He started asking a barrage of questions about my friends who were visiting earlier. They were in town to check out a college. He asked about when they left and then accused me of lying. It got heated FAST. I pulled over because I didn't want to wreck or for him to grab the wheel. We were on Vine near Santa Monica Blvd. We were yelling at each other. Then out of nowhere, he showed his teeth, growled and barked at me a few times and attacked me like a wild dog, biting me. The top of his head hit the ceiling of the truck, turning the dome light on. He lunged toward me, bit my shoulder and tugged at my windbreaker, pulling the seams apart. At some point, I think he hit his teeth on the steering wheel, because the horn honked. There was blood on the steering wheel, on his lips and on my jacket sleeve. I felt like I was the end of the Michael Jackson Thriller video, it was surreal.

He grabbed my car keys from the ignition, opened the door and tossed them over a locked gate on the side of a church. I ran after them, jumped over the gate without any difficulty to retrieve them. My adrenaline was pumping. He got his DJ equipment out from my back seat and started walking. I grabbed my keys, lept over the gate again, and booked it back home. I packed up all I could. Load after load, my stuff brimming out my Jeep Cherokee. I got a text from him:

"You'd better be the fuck gone by the time I get there." I was planning on it, but I thought he'd be in apology mode by this time. This was not the first time he was violent with me since we'd moved here. One time we were arguing in bed and he pushed me up and out. My head hit the wall. I was in such pain, but he didn't give a shit. Another time, I found a letter to a woman and he snatched it and backhanded me. It happened so fast that he busted my lip and the shock made me fall to my knees. It was so unexpected. That time he was apologetic. He fell to his knees crying, embracing me, rocking me and begging for my forgiveness... I forgave him out loud out of fear, but not really in my heart.

I kept packing. I wished I could take my bed. I just needed my audio equipment. He walked into the courtyard as I was walking out with *almost* my last load.

"All your stuff better be out of here," he said. I didn't' say a word. I kept walking, got in my truck, and WENT.

I was freaking out. I didn't know what to do. It was 4 am. I would have had to drive back home to Albuquerque in one night. Luckily my cousin, Joy, had recently moved to L.A. from Colorado. I called her.

"GET OVER HERE," she says to me. Thank God, because I didn't know anyone else out here. I was driving to North Hollywood when my now ex-boyfriend called on the other line. I let it go to voicemail. He left a message. He said he was putting my speaker monitors outside. He's insane! I turned back. My audio equipment were my most prized possessions. Someone would pick them up in minutes! I raced back on the 101 back to Hollywood. There they were. My subwoofer weighed a ton.

When I got to my cousin's, she and her boyfriend let me crash on their couch.

My windbreaker was torn and stained with his blood. My cousin took a picture of me a few days later when the bite mark on my shoulder turned green. She sent the picture to me, but I deleted it, I didn't want to be reminded of what an idiot I was.

My cousin let me stay with them for months with no guilt or weirdness. I will never forget how open their hearts were to me. There was no better gift in the world than people you can trust and would do anything for.

Then I got a job in radio operations for the largest broadcast company in the country and I got a place of my own.

I don't know, maybe I still would have done it all over again, just to get out of Chicago and be in Los Angeles. I couldn't have moved by myself. It would have been too expensive and I didn't know anyone in L.A. like he did, to help us find a spot. Maybe I knew it wasn't going to work out, but I did it anyway.

After living in L.A. for two years, things were going great. I had engineered audio for L'Oreal commercials with Penelope Cruz. I had made friends with music artists and producers. I was producing three nationally syndicated radio shows. In 2007 one of my music producer friends took me to the Grammys!

I came to L.A. to be a successful radio producer. I felt like I achieved that, but I realized it didn't pay nearly as much as I thought it would. I considered being a talk-show radio host. I learned that was where the money was. But I wasn't willing to act a fool or to be controversial for the sake of controversy. I felt like that would be selling my soul. I admire people like Casey Kasem, Dick Clark and Ryan Seacrest. My secret dream was to be an in-demand pop music producer. It's my *secret* dream because I'm still learning the art. And I keep it secret is because part of me feels like spending time on music production is selfish. My boyfriend had left his kids in Chicago to come to L.A. to become a music producer. My father spends his life having fun composing music instead of taking care of his kids. I loathed them both for that. Aside from having to move out abruptly from living with my boyfriend, my life was on the up-and-up.

...Until the housing bubble and the economic downturn of 2008. Starting from around 2006, people were no longer able to pay for the mortgages on their homes. About 10 million people lost their houses in foreclosures. With that, small businesses started closing down. Those small businesses had to lay off their employees, and there was a snowball effect. There were layoffs, after layoffs, after layoffs.

The radio networking company I worked for laid off 4,000 people. They did it on President Obama's Inauguration Day, January 20, 2009. The layoffs were on the last page of a few newspapers. Word on the street was, the company chose that day strategically, to not be in the news. None of the radio hosts on the network breathed a word of it.

I got laid off from that job and then fired from another. The firing was from an NPR affiliate in Encinitas, near San Diego. I was doing voice-over work. My good friend from high school, Jade, let me stay with her in San Diego until I got situated. Things were going great for a year. Then the Director found out that I was going to be a contact person for the new union that was voted in. The Director and my supervisor had told me on my first day that they didn't think the union was a good idea. They started writing me up almost every week. They wrote me up for things like "five seconds of silence between elements," or "breathing too loudly on-air." I was walking on eggshells. I was soon diagnosed with fibromyalgia around my neck and shoulders. I had horrible pain with all the stress. I had to go to a masseuse because at the end of each week my trapezius muscles felt like rocks. It turned out that the Director had turned up the high frequencies on my mixer. The mixer that "no one is supposed to touch," according to them. So, it made my breathing sound loud on-air. I had a feeling I was going to get fired. I started having panic attacks, crying and hyperventilating. I learned that when someone wants you out, they get you out.

I started losing my hair, not sleeping, and getting female infections. Two years ago I wanted to be successful, now I just wanted to be able to sustain myself. I felt like I was reaching the end of my rope, getting to the end of my savings. What was I going to do if I couldn't put a roof over my head or feed myself? I had done all the hard work that I was supposed to. I *had* the determination. All for nothing.

I started thinking about how I could kill myself that wouldn't cause anyone trauma. Like, I couldn't hang myself and have a friend find me. That's awful. They would never get that memory out of their mind, ever. Or blow my head off, yuck, all that blood. I thought about drowning myself in the ocean, but breathing is so instinctual, I didn't think I could actually do it. Then I thought of jumping off of a steep cliff. But what if it's not high enough and I live with broken bones and horrible injuries and medical bills? It wouldn't be worth the risk. I thought about drinking myself to death, but I saw the movie *Casino*, it takes a hell of a lot of drinking to do that. Pills might be a good option. But I didn't know where to get them. All my friends and I are hippyish and refuse to take pharmaceuticals.

I would exhaust myself from searching for jobs, not hearing back, crying and thinking of ways to kill myself. Then my friend Olive would come home from work. I lived with Olive in her apartment in Hollywood on Fountain St. It was near the police station. We would produce digital music together. She had some lyrics written already and ideas for the melodies. We spent night after night for about a year working on one song in Logic Pro. We even had her record the vocals at my producer friend's professional studio. She has raspy-Jazzy type vocals. The song is great, but I couldn't get the E.Q.'s right on the bass. I didn't know what to do except for post it on SoundCloud.

Right now I'm at my friend Ernesto's. I'm getting ready for my dead-end part-time job selling men's skincare at Bloomingdale's. I know Ernie from working together on a show that airs on Sirius Satellite Radio. I just got out of the shower and checked the time on my phone. I noticed I had a missed call from my dad. He left a message. I had left him a message earlier asking to borrow some money.

I hate, and I mean *hate* asking anyone for money. It's the last thing I would want to do on this earth. But I had no choice. There's a problem with my paycheck. I haven't gotten it. I've moved so many times, it could have gotten lost in the mail or sent to an old address.

I don't want to ask my dad for money, but I'm definitely not asking my mom, she's done enough. She gave her life for me when she got pregnant with me at the age of seventeen, and my father was twenty-eight. My mom sometimes held down three jobs, but she managed to make ends meet. She's my role model and mentor, my Wonder Woman, my heroine. I've learned a lot from her. She was always confident and fearless. I got the drive to be a hard worker from her. I decided not to repeat the cycle of having babies young and living in poverty. Well, she did pound that into my head, anyway. My mom functioned as both parents. And I tend not to forget that my father didn't pay child support for the first few years of my life.

My so-called "father" is in his late sixties. His name is Jose. My half-sister Joselin and I were each named after him, except she spells her name with an "i," and I spell mine with a "y." Our father is a singer-songwriter. He's never been married and has five children from five different women. Our names and years of birth are:

1. Marcella - 1970
2. Joselinda (Joselin for short) - 1974
3. Toby - 1974
4. Joselyn (me) - 1975
5. Angelica (Angie) - 1985

Marcella was given up for adoption at birth. Joselin was second, and then Toby was born ten days after her. I was born seven months after them. "Papa was a-rollin' stone." He was donned "New Mexico's Native Jewel," by his fans... or maybe by him? He was born in Las Cruces, New Mexico. The black-haired, green-eyed guitarist makes the women of New Mexico swoon over him. When he sings his Spanish melodies, they are drunk with lust, and have sex with him without condoms!

Marcella lives in Arizona with her husband and family. She is a foster parent, like the couple who adopted her. Toby lives in El Paso, his mom is from Juárez. We've only seen him twice. Dad stopped talking to Toby. Dad said he "had had it with him" when Toby started getting in trouble with the law. I thought it was strange that our father had given up on him and stopped calling him. I thought, "Parents are allowed to do that?" Angie is about ten years younger than the cluster of us and grew up in Albuquerque, like Joselin and me. The one thing we all had in common was that our father didn't raise any of us. I could never understand how he could abandon us all.

I met Joselin's mom when I was hospitalized for surgery at the age of four. Her mom worked at the same hospital and visited me. My father visited me while I was there too. He gave me a big grey and white rat stuffed animal.

A stuffed rat. I wish I would have known what "foreshadowing" and "narcissistic" meant back then. It would have given me a lot of insight into who my father was. I mean, how egotistical do you have to be to allow *two* women to name their daughters after you? Wouldn't you say, 'I already have a daughter named Joselin?' How hard is that?

Joselin and I met each other when we were ten years old. It was then that my father's girlfriend at the time encouraged him to start seeing his kids. Our father was raised by his aunt Linda because his mother had passed away when he was two. He was living with his dad for a while, but my dad's stepmom was abusive towards him, so he didn't want to stay with them anymore. Joselin and I were both taken to aunt Linda's funeral by our mothers when she died. At the gravesite we bowed our heads in prayer and joined hands.

Joselin and I look a lot alike. We're about the same height, with dark, thick curly hair, beige skin that tans, and brown eyes. She has her mother's smiling eyes and a few happy freckles. I have more almond-shaped eyes and age spots. We used to spend some Sundays together, before we got boyfriends.

Joselin discovered our oldest half-sibling when she was planning her wedding to Francisco. She found out that Francisco was a cousin to Marcella through Marcella's adopted family.

That's when I wrote a letter to my father to ask him honestly how many brothers and sisters I had. We met at a park. He focused straight in my eyes and said I didn't have anymore half-siblings. That's when I realized my father was a liar.

I listen to his message on my speakerphone and set my phone down on the windowsill so I could put on my makeup.

I had told Joselin I was afraid I might have to have to sleep in my car because I wasn't going to have enough money for gas. I wondered if she told him?

I didn't want to ask my sister for money because she had already helped me get my jeep out of impound for parking tickets. L.A. tickets will be the death of me! Is it even worth living here?

I listen to my father's message:

"A-hi, *hita*. I was just waking up from a nap. I've been sick for the last three days. I took two naps. I haven't been able to sleep. I went to the V.A. Hospital, and they took blood. So yeah, I want to make sure it's not the prostate cancer coming back. I'm just tired all the time. I had them check me for diabetes. I'm always thirsty and tired. Or I don't know, maybe it's my cancer? I apologize for not answering your call. I listened to your message, and what really hurts me in this is that no one is taking care of me."

Taking care of? He acts like he's bedridden and can't do things for himself!

"You've never taken care of me. I'm tired of arguing. It causes me anxiety and stress. I talked to Joselin about my kids, and she said that you lost respect for me." I crinkle my eyebrows and look at my phone. Well, even if she did say that, it *is* true. "But you know what she told me?

She said 'I've got your back, dad, don't worry.' My eyebrows go up. Is he trying to pit us against each other? "I don't want to go on and on leaving messages. I do love you, I do love my daughters. I just feel used." My jaw dropped to the floor.

"I understand you're having a hard time. I can't figure out why you can't get it together. I'm going to send you some money, but you said some cruel things to me and me to you. It's been hard for me. I don't know how much I can send. But, if you want to go back, then I can go back too. Your mom said it was safe, Joselyn. And when women have lied to me, I don't know if it's revenge, but it just gets to me. And me getting back to them hurts the children. Three out of five women said it was safe." I roll my eyes. "But you came into this world anyway, and you're the one who ended up paying for it, bottom line. Women who have lied to me, one way or another, I make them suffer. Sometimes, or all the time, or most of the time, the kids end up suffering because a woman lied to me. And I'm not blaming you, but if you wanna go back all the way to those days, I guess I could do the same. The important thing is, I'm either not going to get respect from you, and you're not going to get respect from me. Or maybe we can find a way to respect each other. We've both made mistakes. Let's discuss things in a sensible way. I'll send some money out. Love you, *adios*."

I grabbed my phone from the windowsill. I went into the bedroom and threw it at the mattress and pillows as hard as I could.

"I cannot *believe* this guy! I can't believe he admitted to taking revenge on five women! He *knew* what he was doing! He did it for 18 years to five kids! He has no conscience, no guilt, no feelings! He must be a sociopath." I felt sick to my stomach. I never wanted to hear that message again. But I didn't delete it either.

I finished getting ready for work and packed up my things.

In the past year, I've filled out about two thousand online applications. Enough to make me want to throw up. Doesn't my father know that I'm a go-getter... because of *him*? We had to be, because he wasn't there. My mom and I had to do everything to stay above water. I was working by the age of 14 so I could buy my own clothes. I thought by earning a degree and having skills in radio, I would always have a job. But I was wrong. I'm not a moocher. I'm just having a tough... decade.

How could he not be there for me when I need him the most? *Oh!...* like he did when I was a baby! *I'm* the idiot. Why would I think the man who abandoned his five kids would help me when I needed him? I thought he'd come around and want us there in his old age, after surviving prostate cancer, but no. I had given him opportunities to redeem himself, to be there, to be needed. But he interprets that as me using him. I'm tired of trying. He has to show effort to have a relationship, and he doesn't. He's so... shallow. We never talk about anything meaningful. He doesn't ask about things that are important in the world or in our lives because he doesn't pay attention to what's going on. He doesn't try to get to know any of us. I'm not sure if he has feelings or emotions. He hugs, but his hugs aren't warm. He says he loves us, but he doesn't show it. I can't do it anymore. It's not worth what I get in return- disappointment and loss.

If his point was to not argue, he failed at that, he took his jabs. If his goal was to show me love, he definitely failed at that. If it was to show respect, he crushed the possibility of that. How could I respect someone who takes revenge on women, at the cost of his own children? I could never forgive him for that! What kind of person takes revenge and then is stupid enough to admit it?

"You're relieved of your fatherly duties!" I yell. "You're off the hook, Jose! You obviously don't want to be a father! But I take my presence and my love with me!" I had to say it to him and the ether.

I pick up my stuff and head out the door. It's about three o'clock in the afternoon on a clear day. It's 2016, and Christmas is approaching. I hate this stupid job at Bloomingdale's, but it's all I've got for now. It's a long drive to Newport Beach and my Jeep is a gas-guzzler. I'm going to have to cut corners and sleep in my car tonight instead of using money on gas to drive back to L.A.

2

Drive to Newport Beach, California

I navigate onto ever-crowded I-405. I take the 405 South from L.A. to Newport Beach. It's congested with Long Beach traffic, *again*. So tired of it. I drive an hour and a half for a part-time job selling expensive men's skincare in the perfume section. It's a gamble because I suck at sales. Luckily, a friend that let me stay at his place gave me the job.

On the drive, I keep thinking about my life.

It's going to be a year that I've been driving from L.A. to Newport Beach. I recently qualified for SNAP food benefits, so that helped. At least I wouldn't starve. I could fill up on avocado sandwiches and oranges for pretty cheap and they would keep in my car.

After my layoff in 2009 I lived with Ursula in North Hollywood. I survived on unemployment. When that ran out, I lived with Betty in Sherman Oaks.

Ursula, Olive, and Betty were supportive of me. They were real family. They didn't judge me. They backed me, supported me, asked me questions, remembered what I said to them, and vice-versa. Growing up as a Hispanic female in New Mexico, I was used to feeling discriminated against by white people. This new family contradicted all that. They made me learn to judge people individually, by their character, as Martin Luther King Jr. told us we should do. I would have revived those thoughts of drowning in the ocean, had it not been for these women.

Ursula ended up moving to Oregon.

Betty was energetic, always doing things for her kids. Making them homemade lunches for school and dinner. Forcing them to go on road trips to San Diego or Big Bear. She'd do things like letting her kids get a new pet, (often), or painting in a tutu and heels.

When we ran together, she would dance off-beat at a stoplight so she wouldn't lose her heart rate. She was never embarrassed about people staring, and I was never embarrassed to be her friend. We cooked, ate, ran, talked about our goals and drank together. I started drinking wine with Ursula and Betty every evening when we lived together back in 2009. After I got laid off.

...Oh, no, there's a slowdown on the highway in front of me. I don't want to be late. It's usually forty minutes from here. I hope it's not an accident. ...It doesn't seem to be.

I go back to thinking about my dad. I remember when I met him. I was about four. Someone knocked on our trailer door when I was playing in my room. I heard my mom talking to a man, but I didn't recognize his voice. My mom calls me.

"Joselyn, come meet your dad."

'My *dad*?' I think to myself. 'Who's my dad? ... I have to see *this*.' I walk into the living room and see a tall light-skinned man with a dark afro. My mom introduces us and tells me I'll be going with him today. I cry 'no!' and hold on to the end of the couch with dear life. I'm not going with this guy! I've never seen him in my life! My mom turns to my "dad."

"I don't think she's going to go with you today," I hear her say. Oh thank God. She's not going to make me go. He came by some other times and my mom went with me the first couple of times. We went to eat at Furr's once and the second time we went to Uncle Cliff's Amusement Park. After the second time my mom told me I'd have to go with him on my own. I guess if she said it was okay, it would be. I trusted my mom. I don't remember seeing him much after that until I was about ten.

Most people like Jose Martinez, after all he's famous around here. Some people may think he's a great singer and that he has a healthy relationship with his kids. He's done things like call us girls on stage and brag about us. People love it when he goes to parties and funerals of fans, (but it's really for the free food)! He's friendly enough, and folks think he's a great person. People may even think it's cool that he gives out his CD's or articles about himself as gifts, but I noticed it all has to do with him. Everything is about him. He doesn't seem to be in tune with people or their feelings.

He could be worse. He's not a monster. He never beat us. He doesn't drink, smoke or do drugs. For years, I was fascinated by him, his creativity, and his ability to make music. I wondered if I had any of his talents of playing the guitar or writing a song. But he never taught me how to begin. I took a guitar class, but I stopped after my fingers got callused.

How he got away with having five children out of wedlock and not caring for any of them, I don't know. I guess because he wanted to and because no one stopped him. His career allowed it. Jose was a singer and a musician who was working on his career! You can't take care of five children and work on nine albums, come on! When you're a musician, aren't women always throwing themselves at you? Everyone allowed him to do whatever he wanted. His parents weren't around to scold him or tell him to knock it off. Jose had one sister, a good and decent woman. He didn't listen to her. She passed away last year. Unfortunately, I was sick and couldn't make the funeral. My mom's parents told him he didn't have to marry my mom, but he would have to take care of me. That's as much as anyone stood up to him. But then my grandmother would invite him over for breakfast. She would make him eggs, beans, chile, papas, and coffee; all the things he loved. Sometimes she would make him enchiladas, and later he would complain about how much onion she put in them. Rude.

I've seen him cry three times. When the aunt who raised him died, when his father died, and then when he was going to father Angie. He was fifty back then, crying, feeling sorry for himself, alluding to suicide.

He said something about being too old to have kids. He said he didn't know what he was going to do, and that maybe he should just end it. I couldn't believe he was having this conversation about his daughter, as if we were all like a disease or cancer. I wanted to tell my own father to man up. I felt sorry for my soon-to-be sibling. She was going to have this poor pitiful father. ...And he tells *me* to get *my* shit together.

I remember how hard it was to learn what the word "bastard" meant when I was young, and that I was one. I had a hard time when I would see little girls with their daddies. I'd get jealous when fathers would call their girls "princesa," or little girls would call their dad's "daddy." So jealous.

It hurts to know your own parent doesn't love you or only loves you when it's convenient for them. I have to give up. He will never be the father that I need him to be. He can't fix the past, and he could care less about changing the future. My standards for a father are high. My grandfather set them. And my dad's efforts are low. I have to let this whole thing go! This time, my grandmother isn't going to convince me to talk to him anymore. I've been through this since I was 14. I can't remember what made me decide I didn't want to see him anymore, but my grandmother on my mom's side pressured me to see him... for the rest of my life! The rest of my life, until now!

I hate to admit that I'm like my father in lots of ways. I have his black curls, his nose, same color of skin. We're both stubborn and prideful. But I'm done with him.

It took me an hour and a half to get to my destination. I take a right from Jamboree to Santa Barbara Drive. You know you're getting close when you see more manicured grass on the sides of the roads. The outdoor mall is an oval "island" surrounded by green grass and palm trees in Newport Beach. It's walking distance to the Pacific Ocean. I put my black silk smock on, freshen up my makeup, and check at the time. No time for a snack! I get out of the Jeep, wearing all black and dreading going through the perfume department.

"Time to make the donuts!" I tell myself as I take a quick gulp of vodka from a miniature I had. I chase the vodka with a sip of coffee, followed by a stick of gum. I hide the skincare products in my smock pockets and throw away the miniature bottle before walking in.

3

Late Night Police Stop

Bloomingdale's is open until ten tonight because Christmas is the day after tomorrow. After work, the only food place that was open, and that I could afford was Del Taco. I bought a couple of burritos at the drive-through, and parked in the back of the parking lot. It was a lovely night, about 62 degrees. I was about to turn off the engine when I decided there was too much light in the parking lot. Instead, I park in the residential area behind the Del Taco. The side streets were darker. I could talk on the phone and smoke a clove cigar in peace without being under a spotlight.

12:20 am, officially Christmas Eve. I check my gas tank, then my wallet and my bank app. When I finish my food, I light up a thin cigar and call Olive.

"Ha-llo?" Olive answers with a weird accent.

"Hey, how's it going?" I say with my phone on speaker and put it down on my middle console.

"Good. What's up with you?" I imagine Olive is outside on her balcony. She was probably smoking a cigarette, playing solitaire on her phone when I called.

"I'm not going to have enough gas money to go there tonight and come back tomorrow, so I'm going to crash in my car again tonight. I'll get showered for the day before my shift at the gym." I have a membership for Planet Fitness, and there is one in Newport Beach.

"Are you sure? Do you feel safe?" Olive asks with doubt in her voice.

"Yeah, it's safer than any place in or around LA," I say as I scan around at the McMansions in the neighborhood.

"I don't know... you're so vulnerable in a car," Olive says in a whiny voice, like your mother, lecturing.

"I feel safe that I can lock the doors." I usually put my sunshade up in the front, and little black blankets around the side windows. I make sure no one is out when I put up camp. I glance up at the pin-clips on each corner of the SUV's ceiling fabric. I use them to hold up the black blankets around the windows.

"Besides, I have my revolver, if I need it," I remember I should take it out from under the backseat. In a Jeep, you pull the back seat up from the crease then pull the bottom up and over to access under the seat.

"Well, be careful," Olive says.

I spot a police officer driving slowly towards me from the opposite direction. He has a spotlight on and proceeds to shine it on me.

"Stay on the line. A police officer is slowing down," I say.

"Whaat?" Olive still sounds like a mother.

"Listen, don't talk," I say to Olive. I put my cigar out and put the phone on mute.

Ever since camera phones came out, there's been an uptick of people of color videotaped dying at the hands of police officers. The latest casualty was Tamir Rice. He was an innocent twelve-year-old African American boy playing by himself at a park with a toy gun and was gunned down by police within seconds. If something was going to happen, I wanted a witness. Olive was on the line for a while, but the connection was lost.

The police officer parks his car across the street and approaches my vehicle. He's tall and white and has glasses on. He asks me what I'm doing and asks me for my license and registration.

"Did I break a law, sir?" I ask.

"License and registration, please," is all he says. I want to argue, but decide it's in my best interest to comply. I fish them both out. The police officer takes my documents and goes back to his police car. After a few minutes, he returns.

"Are you on probation for a DUI?" The officer asks. His voice is deep and severe.

"Yes. I have an interlock in my car. It's a requirement for New Mexico for a year." I motion with my hand where it is, and he sees it.

"Uh-ha. But you're also on probation in California," the officer follows up.

"Yes, I got a DUI in New Mexico on a California license," I explain. "So, I have to pay in both states."

"Yes. Your probation restricts you from being anywhere except home, work, or AA."

"I just got out of work from Bloomingdale's. I was getting something to eat before I went home," I say.

"Can I search your vehicle?" the officer asks, as he sweeps his flashlight around my jeep.

"What? No," I respond.

"Why not? What are you trying to hide?" The officer probes and continues to wave his flashlight inside my vehicle.

"I'm not hiding anything, I just don't want you to. It's my right," I say as I sit up and put my hands on my steering wheel.

"Because you're on probation, officially, I could impound your vehicle and search it that way. But, that might cost you about $500-600," the officer threatens.

"Oh wow, fine, search it," I say with disdain and sweep my hand up.

The police officer radios another police officer to come. It's pretty dark, other than the street lights. The new police officer is there in minutes. The first police officer goes to the second police officer's car and they talk to each other in private. From across the street, the first officer tells me to step out of the vehicle. They tell me they are going to search me. I comply. I can't see what the second police officer looks like because the first officer's flashlight is shining in my eyes. All I can tell is that he is Anglo European along with the other guy. I have a hoodie on over my smock. The police officer asks me to pick up the bottom of my hoodie and turn around in a circle to check for weapons. I do as he says, and he makes me pull out all my pockets. Then he directs me to sit on the other officer's car bumper. This is when my heart goes from somewhat nervous, to a full-blown wallop attack. I do as I'm told, and my mind floods. I keep a four-foot container with clothes, blankets, and shoes in the rear cargo area, and a loaded revolver under the back seat. Since living with Betty and her kids, I didn't want the gun to be accessible to the children. It's loaded with five hollow-point bullets. They're called "cop killers" because they can penetrate through a bullet-proof vest. That's why they're illegal. My heart is beating, but I don't want my breathing to indicate that I'm panicking. I might have to go to jail tonight for violating my probation and having a concealed weapon.

The police officer starts with the driver's side. His flashlight is going through the front and through my middle console. He notices the phone and asks me who Olive is. I say she's my best friend. He says she's calling. I told him our phone call got disconnected. Then the officer moves to the front passenger side of the vehicle. He finds my cigars. My heart is racing. He goes to the back seat and sees nothing. I yawn out of nervousness. He goes to the back and opens the hatch. The police officer finds my clothes in the black bin. My legs start to shake as if it's cold outside, but I know it's not that cold. I wish I had a cigar, to do something with my hands. I yawn again and then try to chit-chat with the other officer. The first officer goes around to the back driver's side and finds the door locked and stuck. It has no button to push to unlatch the door; it broke off. I know there is no button and I hope he skips it. I have to reach in from the driver's side to the back to open it from the inside. It's where the gun is. At this point, My heart is about to pound out of my chest. Can the police officer watching me see it? The first police officer shines his flashlight into the window, comes back over to me and says,

"Why do you have me thinking you're doing something bad out here?" He says in a low enough voice, for the other officer not to hear. "You should be careful where you hang out," the officer says.

"What? I was ..." I stopped. I didn't want to argue with a police officer.

He gave a nod toward the other officer.

I didn't understand and surveyed the neighborhood again. I parked at what appeared to be the backside of a house. It had a dirt backyard and a chain-link fence. It was hard to tell if it was under construction. It was the strangest house on the block. All the other homes were modern McMansions with grass lawns. This one was old and had trees completely obstructing the view of the house. Are they trying to hide something? Odd. Was it a drug house? I suppose it was what the police officer meant. I parked there because it was dark and no one from inside would come out and yell at me for parking there.

The police officers were gone in seconds, and I thanked my lucky stars that I'm not a felon! No tonight! Whoo-hoo!

I call Olive back from a gas station. I tell her what happened and promise her I will find another neighborhood to sleep in, farther away. I'm pretty sure that California law gives a year in jail for each hollow-point bullet, and there were five in there. So lucky! Gracias a Dios. I'm going to buy a couple of miniatures to calm me down, so I can pass out.

4

Night Doula

For the new year, I complain to my best friend. We're in her roomy apartment in Sherman Oaks with dark cherry wood floors, littered with Husky dog hair.

"Betty, this January makes it a year that I've been working this dead-end job! I can't find any real work for shit! I've sent out over 2,000 résumés this year to places I want to work and even places I don't! It's ridiculous. I've never had trouble finding a job like this in my whole life! Now that everything is digital, no one sees your face at all. I haven't been called for *one* interview."

"Gurrl, you should take the Birth Doula class I took. I charge on a sliding scale. You can get paid $300-$3,000 for each birth. I think you can get a scholarship, too. Text you the number," Betty said while getting dressed. Betty is skinny but thinks she's skinny-fat. She holds Hollywood standards on herself. She stands at 5'7" tall, with blonde hair and big blue eyes. She has light skin that can tan, a small nose, and always red pursed lips. Betty also has boney, tanned shoulders, thin arms, and runner's legs.

I tried to imagine myself as a birth doula. Could I do it? I had only seen one birth. The birth of my baby sister. It was pretty amazing, but that was almost twenty years ago. And what about all those fluids and odors? I have a weak stomach. Things like vomit and bodily fluid trigger a gagging reflex in me. I have trouble with it at least once a week. I don't know why. It would be very unprofessional of me to run out to throw up while trying to work. I'm not sure if I could handle it, but it's the only reasonable option I have right now.

The next Monday I called the school and asked about the scholarship. I communicated back and forth with them and submitted an application. I was approved and was able to take the next class. I spent several full days getting trained. There were lots of earthy hippies from all over the world. The best part about training was that the school was on the next boulevard to where Betty and I lived. It was walking distance! It was a strange old, wood, two-story building with small rotundas on the corners and stained glass. It mimicked a mini castle.

Soon after I'd gotten trained as a birth doula, Betty and I were in the kitchen. She opens a bottle of wine.

"Would you be interested in working as a night doula, like me? You could pick up the overflow from Carrie and me?" Carrie was the business owner who got referrals from the doctor she had when she gave birth to her two children. She'd been working as a night doula for fifteen years.

"I charge $35-45/hour, and a minimum of 12 hours, from 7 pm to 7 am," Betty explains.

"That's more than $400 bucks a night!" I estimate the math in my head.

"Yeah, not bad, huh?" Betty nods and smiles.

"And what do you do?" I ask sitting at the kitchen table.

"Cuddle with babies at night and take naps. Feed them, do sleep training. We'll have to train you on that." Betty gets ingredients out for dinner. She usually sticks with a vegetarian or vegan diet. I love staying with her because she's not as lazy as me and cooks for her kids daily from scratch.

"Hmm, sounds nice," I say, as I consider it.

"Ya." Betty starts dicing potatoes. "What are your thoughts?" I envied her meticulousness for cutting vegetables, especially since *I* was the vegetarian.

"Yeah! It sounds like cheating! I can cuddle with other people's babies and not have any kids at all, yay! Sounds fantastic. All the benefits, low responsibility, and high pay. I'm in." I pause. "Takes care of baby urges?"

"Or creates new ones!" Betty winks. She talks about having more babies, but I don't believe her. I have no children. I never felt like I was in an ideal situation to have them.

Betty talked to Carrie about adding me to the team and trained me on sleep schedules and what to do when a baby wakes.

My first clients live in Manhattan Beach. They live in a two-story glasshouse, two blocks away from the ocean, close enough to hear the waves crashing. It's frosted glass, where you can see out, but you can't see in. I arrive on time and check myself in the car mirror. From the driveway, there is a ramp to the front door. I can see my reflection in the house, I'm wearing maroon scrubs. It's the recommended uniform, even though we're independent contractors. I ring the doorbell and the heavy glass door opens. A tall, young handsome man opens the door and invites me in. He's holding the baby and bounces him up and down as I walk in.

We introduce ourselves, and I ask where I can wash my hands. We sit to talk about the baby. Milestones, eating, pooping, and sleep patterns.

The baby begins to cry, and the father stands up to bounce the baby, but he cannot comfort him. I ask if I can hold him. This was the moment of truth. I've never worked with babies before. Was he going to quiet down or cry more? This could be the defining moment for me. The father hands the baby over. I hold him and cuddle him a bit. I hold my breath. The blonde-headed baby looks slightly confused but stops crying. (Whew) I take a breath and keep him close. The father frowns with jealousy.

The couple shows me the baby's room downstairs. The mother tells me that I can stay with the baby there and if he wakes up hungry, just knock on her door. In the room, there's a crib, a plush chair, and a fuzzy oval rug in the middle of the carpeted room. The mother gathers some blankets and a stuffed elephant for the baby and tells me she'll get a bottle. I sit down with the baby on the chair. Soon, the mom returns with a bottle and leaves. As I feed the baby, his eyes get heavy and he falls asleep. After a while, my arms get tired. I put the baby down in the crib, and he starts to cry. I pick him back up again. I can't have him crying on my first day. I sit down, and he fusses, so I stand. After my arms feel like they are going to fall off, and the baby's breathing steadies, I sit again. He stays quiet. Thank goodness. I get to rest, but not comfortably.

I sit and think of how crazy this couple is to let a complete stranger into their home to stay with their baby. They didn't even do a background check on me. I probably would. If I was rich. Yeah, these people don't even know if I'm crazy! I could walk out with this baby, and they would not be able to find me. I mean they could, through Carrie, but if I didn't want to be discovered? IF I was crazy and wanted to steal a baby.

It's dark, but I try a second time to put the baby down in the crib, but he wakes up the moment his body touches the mattress. I'm so tired. I heard I hated the crib when I was a baby too. Must have not been fond of bars. I can't stand it. I need to get some rest. I take the baby upstairs to the living room and stretch out on the gigantic sectional. I hold the baby next to me close. I wake every twenty minutes or so to shift with him, but I'm able to get a little rest. He wants body warmth, like in the womb.

The baby wakes every few hours, and I'm completely exhausted by the time the sun starts to light the house and the sky. I take a few photos of the ocean view. It's stunning. The location itself had to have cost millions, not including the three-story glasshouse. I wonder how they have so much money? I don't know what the father does for a living. Whatever it is, it's lucrative. This couple looks in their late twenties.

The baby cries right before my shift ends, so I give the baby to her so she can nurse him. She tells me goodbye and I tell her I'll see her tonight.

I'm happy with how the night went. It's challenging, sleeping lightly, and not getting much shut-eye, but it's a pretty easy job, I thought to myself.

I took back those words after working a week. I was sleep-deprived and disoriented.

I made it a routine to get coffee and take a walk on the beach before driving to Betty's so that traffic could die down.

I finally have a job that pays enough to live!

After a few months, I saved about $6,000. I saw myself buying an RV and outsmarting everyone in LA; living rent-free. I imagined myself piling up my cash in the back of the RV to buy a house. It was the perfect plan. Eexxcellent...

5

Tiny House

I enlist the assistance of my good friend Carter when I decide to buy an RV. I've known him for about ten years. By trade, he's a car guy; he buys and sells classic and expensive vehicles all over the country. He's the sensitive, affectionate type that will cry about anything. He's usually cheerful unless you talk to him about politics. Carter's a considerate guy who will help you with anything.

We search online for some RV's in the area. I make appointments with people to see the rigs in person.

It's "June Gloom" in LA. That means throughout June, the day starts cloudy and gloomy. Sometimes later, the sun breaks through, but sometimes not.

I checked out one RV; it was nicely redone on the inside, but when I see it in person, it's a rust bucket, and it's too long. I passed on that.

I am going to meet Carter at the following appointment. When I get there, Carter is already there. I can see him inside the RV, sitting, chatting it up with probably the owner. Carter is a medium-skinned African American man from Alabama who spent most of his life in Hawaii and LA. Carter always wears a hat and looks like he walked out of the 70's band The Commodores. He wears a long afro and hippy jewelry. He and his family have a background in music.

I walk up the driveway. The house was probably built in the '80s. There's another RV in the backyard on the other side of the wood fence. I peek inside the RV and step up two steps to get in. I give Carter a nod and search his face for an expression, his demeanor is excited and happy and carefree. Then I extend my hand to introduce myself to the owner of the RV. He's a white man, average height, big belly, sandy brown hair, and is wearing a cap. The owner shows me the front "living area." The middle area has the bathroom and shower, and there are twin beds on both sides in the back. He shows me outside to the generator, runs it, and then shows me how to pull out and retract the awning. He shows me the motor, and he turns it on. He sets wood blocks up to drive off the curb and go for a test drive. The engine sounds good. It has get-up-and-go, even uphill. When we come back, the owner returns the RV into its spot. I ask him if I can have a few moments with my friend to discuss it.

The owner says, of course, and goes into his home. Carter's eyes sparkle.

"Jo! This is a good deal! Did you hear the engine? It's only got seventy-five thousand miles on it!" I scan around. It could use a slight facelift. Some new curtains and new seats? I could resell it if I want to.

"So, it sounds like you're trying to convince me to get it. I like it. The toilet could have been cleaner, but if you think the engine is in good condition, I'll make an offer. I only brought half with me, though," I said, concerned.

"That's fine, give it to him as a down payment and tell him you'll bring the rest tomorrow. I'll bring you here, and you drive her back. You should call her 'Wilma.' Bring Wilma back with you," Carter says with giddiness and adventure in his eyes.

"It's settled then!" I step out of the RV and knock on the owner's house door.

6

No Parking!

I park the R.V. near Betty's apartment in Sherman Oaks. Betty lives in an expansive complex with vast manicured lawns and big trees. It's beautiful, but those lawns get manicured at 6 or 7 in the morning sometimes. I hate the noise. There are lots of squirrels and doggy stations.

I bust into the upstairs apartment to invite everyone to come to see my new R.V. Carrie gets a smile on her face and brings along a few summer beers. Carrie is about 5'5" with a slim yet curvaceous figure. She has naturally blonde wavy hair and blue eyes that smile.

I take them to "Wilma," and they all crowd in one at a time, 'oohing and ahhing' at the retro style of the late '70s.

"I can't wait to get one. I used to talk with Mark about fantasies I have of traveling on the road cross-country," Carrie says.

The kids leave, and we women stay laughing, drinking and joking for another hour. We have all the windows and doors open for air.

"We're going to have to take it to Venice for the 4th of July!" I say. The 4th was in a month. June-Gloom usually clears by the holiday. "Oh yeah! That's a good idea!" Betty says.

"I think you can't be drinking and parked on the street in L.A. I think you can get a D.U.I," Carrie says as she tilts her beer towards us.

"Oh, that's the last thing I need is another D.U.I," I whisper. "I've had enough fines and A.A. to last me for the rest of my life."

"I thought A.A. worked for people?" Carrie asks.

"Yeah, if you're into coffee-drinking, cigarette-smoking Catechism cults. I don't know. I couldn't connect to the idea of the first step of being "powerless against your addiction." I think that's a bad way to start. I always imagined fighting addiction was about feeling empowered."

"Sounds Jesus-y," Betty says.

"Although, there were a lot of good-looking gay guys at the West Hollywood A.A," I remember. "Who don't want anything to do with me."

When the sun starts to set, Carrie leaves to tend to her children and husband. Betty and I stay a while longer. When it gets dark, I tell Betty I'm going to grab some blankets and try my first night in the R.V. I want to see how it feels. Betty is excited for me, but before we get to the steps, someone knocks at the door. The outside light is on.

"Yes? Can I help you?" Betty says through the open window. A man in his 30's, White, slightly balding, waves and ducks his head.

"Yeah, I just wanted to meet my neighbor." He's under the street-light, where bugs have gathered and are bumping into one another.

"Your neighbor?" I question.

"Yeah, I live across the street. I'm Neil," the stranger says. "Oh, hi Neil, well, I'm not staying, so I'm not really going to be your neighbor," I say while deciding to move the R.V. that second.

"Oh? Where ya going?" The stranger acts as if we're friends. "Down to San Diego." I pretend.

"Oh, that will be fun. Well, have a good trip!" The man waves and crosses the street.

"Is it me, or what the fuck is he doing knocking on my house? I wouldn't go knock on his door. It's nine o'clock at night. It's already dark. Who the fuck does that?" I say.

"I don't know what that was," Betty agrees.

"Was it a passive-aggressive way to say 'Don't stay here?' Is this an R.V. thing? I don't know what just happened."

"No, that was weird." Betty nods her head.

"Right? It's really weird," I had to confirm. We walk down the street together. A waxing moon was already visible.

"Why don't you stay on that other block tonight, on the other side of Riverside?" Betty points with her thin arms and skinny fingers.

"Yeah, I don't want him seeing me around." I hurry back before it's really dark. I park on an adjacent main street. I notice the RV swings with the passing of each vehicle. At first, I struggle to go to sleep, but after another beer, I finally doze off.

In the morning, around 8:45, there is a knock at my door. I hold my breath. If I get up, the R.V. will swing back and forth, and whoever is outside will know someone is in here. I scan for any shadows against my walls or around the curtains. They knock again. I barely breathe. I know it's not someone I know. I'm not expecting anyone. No one knows where I am. I wait until I can hear someone walk away, and it sounds still again. Why on earth would someone knock on an R.V. door that is parked on a public street? I cannot figure out why people feel at liberty to knock at my door! This is going to be very stressful if this is what R.V. living is like in L.A.

After an hour, I get up out of bed. It gets too hot inside. You can't run the air conditioner without plugging it in or running the loud generator. So I learned that an R.V. is a thin wood box. I park somewhere else and go about my day, spending my time out. This time I parked across Riverside in a different residential area. That night I slept in peace.

The following day is a Sunday. I go about my errands in my Jeep because it's faster, and it has air conditioning.

When I return to the R.V., there are six yellow legal-size papers posted on almost every window marked, "Do Not Park Here!" I'm beginning to feel unwelcome.

I know I'm not going to be able to stay in the same parking spot because of the parking laws. There's "street cleaning" once a week on each side of the street. If you are parked there during street cleaning, you get a $75 ticket. I've collected enough of those. Rule #1 when in L.A.: Read the parking signs! That's the only rule for being in L.A. Now I have two vehicles to worry about.

After finding another parking space, I spend time at a little coffee shop. It's cooler than my R.V. I'm on Facebook and Jade posts a picture of one of our good friends, Pedro. It says "RIP Pedro Padilla" and some other text, but it all got blurry with my tears. I go out to the sidewalk and call Jade immediately.

"Hello?" Jade answers. Jade is one of the three people I still talk to from high school. She's a beautiful Latina with notably large almond eyes and a curvy figure.

"What.. What did you post? Where did you hear this?" My eyes well up with tears, and my voice goes high.

"His brother posted it just a minute ago. We're friends online."

"No, no, no! ..How?" I say as tears fall. My mind reels. He could have died from anything like getting hit on his bike, to alcohol and drug poisoning. Pedro liked to party.

"He was alone at home. They found him on the kitchen floor. He choked," Jade says. I take in a breath and sit on the nearby bench.

"Do you think that's true?" I say. Jade and I knew Pedro well. "I don't know. That's the news that came from the family," she says.

"Do you know anything about the services?" I ask. "Not yet. I'll let you know," Jade tells me.

"Thanks."

"Talk to you later, *hita*." Jade and I call each other "*hita*," and I call her kids "hito." It means "Mi hijo," "my son," or "my daughter" in Spanish. New Mexico families use it as a term of endearment.

I grab my laptop from the coffee shop and go to my Jeep to cry.

7

New Mexico

On sort of a whim (sort of, it had been on my mind), I decided to move back to New Mexico to see if I could find work. It was the end of July. I felt like L.A. was pushing me out, after living in my R.V. I would've stayed forever, but the night doula work dried up. I was making good money, sleep training babies, but I hadn't gotten work in more than a month. And there was no word of any coming soon. Anyway, I'm sick of the traffic. That was never-ending. There was also trouble with Aliso Canyon nearby. The Aliso Canyon "leak" was more of a massive natural gas blowout, Northeast of Los Angeles. The leak was discovered by SoCalGas employees in late October of 2015 from an underground storage facility. But because of weak regulations, the gas company didn't have to do anything about it. It became a gas blowout in May of 2016 and has been the single worst natural gas leak in U.S. history. It's having a horrible impact environmentally. Reporters were discovering layers of incompetence and cover-ups by Governor Jerry Brown. It was unearthed that his sister was on the board for SoCalGas.

The company said the leak was plugged, but residents still complain of methane odors, headaches, skin rashes, and pets, and birds dying. One day Betty's son woke up with a strange rash on his hands. We lived about 18 miles away. It was causing me anxiety. In addition to the blowout, I absolutely *loathed* the leaf blower noise at the butt crack of dawn. Oh, and let's not forget the lack of free parking. Plus, everything is so dirty. Piss on the sidewalks, who knows if it's human or dog? Either way, gross. Not to mention how expensive everything is. I got so tired of it all.

I plan to drive the R.V. to Albuquerque first, then would have to take the train back to L.A. and drive my jeep later. I parked the Jeep at Betty's, in her gated parking space, so I wouldn't have to worry about parking tickets.

On my drive, I get excited to pass the Arizona/New Mexico border. I roll through Gallup, then Grants. The site of casinos makes my stomach get little butterflies. It's about 8:00 in the evening by the time I arrive in Albuquerque. The orange light from the sun setting peeks from the west, under the clouds. It starts to rain. I roll the windows down, and I smell it. New Mexico rain is my favorite scent in the world! It feels fresh and earthy. I park the R.V. in front of my mom's house and honk the horn. HONK! HONK! My mom and stepdad come out of their house with huge smiles on their faces. They wave their arms, surprised to see the monster R.V.

"Oh! You brought the rain!" Pete, my stepdad says with a smile as he pulls on a suspender and walks over to hug me. Rain is good luck and always welcomed in the desert. Pete is in his '60's, about 5'10", has a round face, wears round-framed glasses. He has curly salt and pepper hair along the sides and back of his head. He's always been good to me, ever since he married my mom when I was eighteen. He's retired and passes his time playing 70's rock music on his guitar.

I'm not sure what I'm doing back home. I haven't lived here for so long, almost 20 years! I hope it's not a mistake.

I set the parking brake and get out of my rig. My mother, Clara, and Pete invite me inside. Pete lingers outside for a few moments, letting the rain fall on him.

My mom, my stepfather, my baby sister, and I gather in the kitchen to catch up.

"You want some chicken?" My mom asks me.

"Noo, mom, I'm still a vegetarian," I say and shake my head. I've been a vegetarian for about seventeen years but she never fails to offer me chicken when I come to her house. We talk into the night. I was raised as an only child. My baby sister Alexandria "Alex" wasn't born until my senior year of college. She's always been the apple of our eyes. She's 5'6" with long blonde curly hair and will be graduating high school this year. Time sure goes by fast. Now in her teenage rebellious stage, she's decided she wants to change her name to Andromeda... but we can call her "Andro" for short.

My mother opens her refrigerator searches for something for me to eat. She is a small woman, about 5'4" with a light complexion and salt and pepper hair. She's always put together, with makeup on as early as 7:30 in the morning.

"Do you want some cereal?" She closes the refrigerator door.

"No, thanks." My mom has never been much of a cook. Luckily, Pete is the chef of the family.

Before I go back to my R.V. to sleep, my mom gives me an envelope from my cousin Marcy, Pete's niece. She lives in Santa Fe, and we have always gotten along. She is a couple of years younger than me. When we get together, we laugh a lot. The envelope was holding a birthday card. My birthday had been a few months past. I open it up. Besides a card, I'm stunned to find a check for $100. Wow. I had been worried about food. This will hold me over for at least a week! I wonder why she sent this now? In the card, she thanked me for letting her stay with me in Chicago back in 2001 and for taking her to a Bulls game. She had been a Bulls fan for at least a decade since Michael Jordan had been playing with them. Jordan was no longer playing with them when we went, but it was remarkable to go anyway. I can't believe her timing! She has no idea how I need this money right now.

I'll be staying in my R.V. on my parent's property until I can find a job. It's beautiful outside tonight. I say goodnight to my mom and go into my R.V. and open the windows. At least I have them, and I'm safe.

8

Job Call-backs

After getting my undergrad degree in 1999, I wanted to get a master's degree. But I got rejected by the Community and Regional Planning Department at the University of New Mexico. So I ended up moving to Chicago.

I had a fourth or fifth cousin living out there. He was super supportive of his wife traveling around the country to do union organizing work. He was a retired sociology professor and took care of their youngest daughter who was still in high school. He made Terry breakfast before school, took the snow off her van and warmed it up. He was supportive of me advancing myself. He was an example of a Latino male that I had never seen before. He was the feminist father figure I had never had. He lectured me with his accent every morning about politics. I didn't want to cut him off, but he would almost make me late for work. I loved his lectures.

After moving to Albuquerque, at the end of July, my sister Joselin emailed me a link to a website that posts jobs for non-profit organizations. I prefer to work for the community rather than for a capitalist. I get started sending out résumés right away.

After a couple of weeks, I found a message on my phone from a charter school that I applied to. The job is for a part-time Educational Assistant position for *math*. Still, I call back and agree to go to the interview anyway. I also get calls for two other interviews. The first scheduled interview is for an intake person for the Rape Crisis Center. Heavy. Possibly too heavy.

The Rape Crisis Center interview goes well. It was with three people at their main office on the second floor. My only concern was how triggered I would get if I took the job. The second scheduled interview is with the charter school.

When I drive to the interview, I discover it's in the worst part of the city, known as "the War Zone."

The principal, Simone, meets with me in her office to talk about the position. She's a tall lady with straight shoulder-length blondish-white hair. She has a fair complexion, a narrow nose, and thin lips. She doesn't wear makeup and has big blue eyes. She uses glasses only to read. She's seated at the head of the long table and has a very gentle tone. She thanks me for coming and explains how the school is a credit-recovery school.

"Here at Dolores Huerta High School we are different, in that we work in quarters instead of semesters. This allows students to make up credits that they may have lost at other schools," she tells me.

"Students will earn participation points for engaging in class. If the student is not here 80% of the time, they can make up participation points by getting tutoring for lunch. If, for example, they don't finish 70% of their work or 80% of their participation points, the teacher can give them an Incomplete. The student will have another quarter to finish."

"Sometimes we get true freshmen. If they take six classes a day and pass all of their classes, it's possible for them to graduate in two years," Simone explains.

Bob Lombardi, the math teacher, introduces himself. He tells me everyone just calls him "Lombardi." He explains how this population of students struggles with attendance. He explains that we have blended classes with mixed grades in each class. Lombardi gives me some practice math questions to take home.

"What we're asking is how would you explain these problems to a student?" Lombardi says. He has a thin, lanky build, green eyes, salt and pepper hair, and a five-o'clock salt and pepper shadow. They tell me how the population of students they serve have huge issues with attendance, so it's hard to teach a unit. The math department serves more as tutors for whatever level the student is in.

At the end of the interview, Simone asks if I want a tour of the school.

"Sure!" I say. She shows me the front office, which has a long front desk that has the school name painted on it. The mascot is a quetzal bird. On the opposite side of the front desk are some round tables and chairs.

As we walk down the hall, a man is walking in our direction. Simone introduces me to Jim Herbert.

"Jim is the Dean of Students, President of Facilities and Master of Technology. He wears several hats," Simone says. Jim is a little taller than me. He has blue eyes and a brown beard with a few white hairs and dark brown hair on his head. He's wearing a flannel shirt, jeans, and black shoes. We shake hands and smile.

Simone and I walk to the staff lunchroom. There are two doorways from each hall.

"The staff lunchroom is also the staff workroom," Simone says. It lies in the middle of the school and has walls halfway up from the floor. From mid-way, up, there are windows. Anyone walking down the hall or in the student commons area can see into the staff lunchroom. It's kind of a fishbowl. I see one long table in the back that is stacked with printer paper on the bottom shelf and paper-cutters on the top. To the right of it is a shorter table with laminating machines. Behind the work-table are a shredder and a copier. In the corner is a shelf of organized colored papers. Besides the lunch table, is where the staff mailboxes are. There's a kitchenette opposite the work-table. In the middle of the room, perpendicular to the worktable is another long table for eating. At the end of the long eating table, a small round table.

"This is the 'free food table'," Simone says and grabs a couple of pita chips from it. We continue to walk down the hall, and when we reach room 2, Simone stops.

"What's your degree in?" Simone asks.

"English," I say.

"A new full-time position has come open. The old English teacher took a position in Rio Rancho closer to her father, who she takes care of. That's a full time teaching position. Would you be interested in something like that?" Simone asks me.

"Full-time? But I have no teaching credentials," I say. She explains the provisional license and what the requirements would be. She finishes the tour of the school and walks me back to her office.

"We could start you off on a waiver. Within the year you would have to take five exams. Each one costs about $100. You will have to take one class, which is cheaper at the community college, to get your endorsement. You can get endorsed in Language Arts or Reading. The more endorsements you have, the more marketable you are for teaching jobs. Within your first two years, you would have to put together a dossier. That means you would have to create a lesson plan, teach it, gather the student work, and analyze it. You would have to reflect on the lesson plan and what you learned or what you would do differently. You scan all the documents and upload them to the New Mexico Public Education Department. There is a fee to make the submission, and to pay for the Level I license."

My head was swimming. It sounds like a lot of stuff to do, but this lady seems to have the attitude that anything can be done easily... and within a deadline. I never in my life dreamed of becoming a teacher, much less a high school teacher. All these fees made me wonder if it's even worth it. The application processing fee for each endorsement is $95. Maybe I'm biting off more than I can chew?

"Let me review this information and let you know if I would prefer the full-time position by tomorrow," I say.

"Sounds good, call my cell phone," Simone says.

"Oh, and you'll have to undergo a background check."

"Oh, okay," I say as if it's nothing. But inside I cringe because of the DUI on my record.

Before I leave the school parking lot, I check my voicemail. There's a message for a part-time teaching position. It's for a non-profit organization that teaches business to adults. It would probably be easier to teach adults, but I need a full-time job.

I take the side streets to my mom's house. Off to one side of the school, near the sidewalk, is a white cross bedazzled with trinkets and flowers. That means someone died there, a *descanso*. Hmm... Did they die *in* the school?

My mom recently retired from being an Educational Assistant. She worked in early education for the past twenty-five years. She encourages me to take the teaching job. I'm super reluctant.

"What about my DUI?" I ask her.

"I think as long as you don't get a DUI *while* you're a teacher, you should be good," my mom says. "But you might want to ask her about it before you take the job. My stomach drops like I'm on a roller coaster. There's nothing that makes me feel more like a loser than that stain on my record. It's my biggest regret.

I can remember getting fingerprinted like it was yesterday. I was bawling my eyes out. The lady asked why I was crying. I never wanted to have a record.

"Be-cause-now-I'm-in-the.. sys-teeeem!" I sob in syllables. The lady glances at the other correctional officer suspiciously.

"Why, what are you trying to hide?" she asks, as if I'm some sort of murderer. I stop crying and peer at her like she's crazy. As if this wasn't bad enough. Jail is the worst place on earth. They treat you like a dog.

Luckily, the cousin I had been drinking with saw me get pulled over and called my mom. My mom bailed me out the next morning. When she picked me up downtown and saw me step out of the paddy-wagon, she started waving her arms yelling,

"Lindsay Lohan! Lindsay Lohan! Over here!" How can you not love this crazy woman?

Jail definitely makes you appreciate your freedom.

I call Simone the next day and tell her about my most embarrassing DUI. I ask her if that would disqualify me for the position. She says she'll have to ask the lawyers and will get back to me.

When Simone calls me back a few days later and tells me the DUI was long enough ago that it's not a problem. I decided to take the teaching job.

God help us all.

9

My First Day

The first day of work for me is the second week of August. It's an "In-Service Day" with just staff and teachers. The day is filled with meetings, training sessions, and little time to prepare for the quarter. We gathered in the lunchroom because Mr. Smith, the guitar teacher, brought doughnuts.

I read in the handbook that tattoos are not supposed to be visible, so I wear slacks and a collared, button-up shirt. I want to hide my phoenix tattoo. The bird is on my left shoulder blade. Three of its feathers sweep over my shoulder to the top of my shoulder, chest and bottom of my neck. Button-up shirts with collars become my basic "uniform" for work. I usually wear black, brown or grey dress shoes, depending on what colors I'm wearing.

At about 9:05 a.m. the principal asked us to gather in the commons area. Each round table has different plastic zip folders of every color.

"Welcome, welcome everybody," Simone announces as individual conversations settle down. "I'm so happy to see all of you. You will find your agendas inside the packets at each seat. Feel free to pick whatever color you want. There are writing utensils inside.

"So, about five years ago we used to be a 'packet' school. Students would be given a packet for a particular subject and they would work at their own pace. When they finished the packet, they would finish the class. We got 'C' grades by the state since then. But because our school got a 'D' grade last year, we have to come up with an 'Improvement Plan.' This year we are going to incorporate Mindset Lessons once a month. You can do this however you want to. It can be a Bell Ringer, a writing prompt, a video on someone who had a positive mindset or some reading material. Whatever you see fit to teach the students that having a positive mindset goes a long way. Document your lessons and send them to me each month. If you have questions you can ask me, or talk about it in your PLC meetings," Simone says. I learned that PLC stands for Professional Learning Community. It's something you do with your peers to improve your teaching.

Simone told us this was going to be our last year of using the PARCC as a standardized test for graduation. The new governor was changing the company. She said it's been difficult for teachers to prepare students for this test due to their attendance. Our school has to keep an enrollment of 200 students to keep a certain amount of funding for the fiscal year. When a student doesn't come for ten consecutive days, we have to drop them from the enrollment and enroll more.

"We've hired a couple of new people this year who I want to introduce you to. Please welcome Jocelyn Martinez." Simone claps, and others follow suit. I stand, wave my hand, and smile.

"Jocelyn will be our new English teacher. She's going to take over the new Leadership class." It's something the principal and I agreed upon in my contract previous to today.

Linda Doyle asks if I can send a class description, so I make a note.

"And we have Kimberly. Kimberly is our new Guidance Counselor." She has a big beautiful smile and big bouncy brown curls and waves to everyone. Simone motions toward Kimberly and claps, and we do too. "Let's go around. Introduce yourself and talk about a positive thing that happened this summer." Simone starts with herself. "I struggled to leave work behind, but once I got out of town, it helped me release a lot of stuff and get grounded." Simone scans the room for someone else to share. "Martina?"

I begin to go through one of my folders and inside of it is a calendar with a lot of events. There are papers about school procedures, Child Abuse Awareness, Suicide Prevention, and a list of about 60 deadlines!

I open another folder titled, "Emergency Safety Procedures." I shuffle through it. Inside of it:

- Closing of School - in cases of power or water malfunctions, (things of that matter)...
- Unscheduled Early Dismissal Procedures - snow dismissals...
- Evacuation Plan - for fire or fire drills...
- Shelter-In-Place - In case of an external risk situation...

Martina is talking but I'm not paying attention. I keep going through the emergency plans:

- LOCKDOWN Imminent Threat Response
- Course of Action: RUN-HIDE-FIGHT

The recommendations had illustrations of characters running, hiding, and fighting back.

"Umm... Pam." Martina picks on Ms. Baker to answer the question next. Ms. Baker is a short white-haired lady. She introduces herself as the science teacher then starts talking about her summer.

I keep reading the "LOCKDOWN Teacher Guidelines: Imminent Threat Response."

"The positive was that my grandson and I spent a lot of time together this summer."Pam's voice drowns out.

The paper about teacher guidelines has bullet points:

"1. If you become aware of an immediate physical threat to life or physical safety, all-page "LOCKDOWN." Communicate the threat to as many people as possible, as quickly as possible. This will increase everyone's reaction time. Seconds save lives!" I start to feel uneasy thinking about the possibility of a school shooting. I continue to read:

"2. Quickly get yourself and others to a safe place. Leave the threat area. Have a long paper with tape ready by your door window, so you can block the shooter's view of the inside the classroom." I start to freak out. How likely is a school shooting?

"3. Once in a safe place, keep a roster of students and find the students with special needs." Another bullet-point says, "-BEWARE OF UNSCHEDULED FIRE ALARMS." I realize this must be regarding the last school shooting. The one on Valentine's Day at Marjory Stoneman Douglas High School in Florida. and tears well up in my eyes and I try to hold back the tears, but realize I won't be able to. I jump up and run to the bathroom with tears in my eyes. I don't know if I can do this!

I take some moments in the bathroom taking deep breaths and wiping away tears. I gather myself. I may be too sensitive or emotional for this stuff.

When I go back to the meeting the principal lets us go our separate ways to prepare our classrooms.

I went to my new classroom to check it out. I noticed I didn't really have any official English textbooks. I asked Jobin Jones if he had history textbooks, he pointed to them and said,

"Yeah, but I don't use them. They're from 2009."

"Wow," I say.

"I just create lessons for the students using more up-to-date articles."

"Ahh, I see."

I went back to my room and spent a couple of hours doing something calming. I cut out butterflies with a stencil to make a huge sign I found on Pinterest. In the middle is an open book and the butterflies look like they are flying out of it. Above the butterflies reads "Discover the magic of reading." It turned out nice!

10

Jump Start Day

After ten days of inservice, we have "Jump Start Day" for students who are new to the school. We put out interactive displays in the commons area of cool classes that we offer. We do icebreakers to get to know one another, kids go to their classes and get to know who their teachers are. It's a condensed school day. It's a time for teachers to check for engagement and disengagement. Who do we need to work on, in terms of positive experiences with our school? Tension and nervousness are high all around.

Things go fine in my classes. I go over the syllabus and introduce ourselves so the new students can get to know us. We do icebreakers like "Truth, Truth, Lie" I give them a short demo lesson of what we would be doing. I have them search for independent reading books they may be interested in and let them read for a little while. I assign workbooks and create files in the filing cabinet for them to leave their books in. We don't have lockers. I pass out notebooks and folders to anyone who needs them. We are a Title I school, and most of our students can't afford lunch or school supplies.

During third period, I hear voices from outside of my classroom, kind of loud. I hear them again, still unintelligible, but even more vehement. I listen. One raised voice says "BITCH!" Oh-oh! A fight! I run to the commons area, but everything echoes in there. I glance around and see the Dean of Students, Jim, go toward the science room. I run in the same direction. I see a cluster of students with their phones out and their cameras recording. I can't see who is in the middle because it's a tangle of hair.

"Let go! Let go! Jasmine!" Ms. Baker yells. Ms. Baker is in the middle of two girls holding on to each other's hair.

"No!" one of the girls yells back. Jim pulls one student in one direction, and I pull the other student the other. I hope all the hair gets untangled! Arms were grabbing and reaching. Jim manages to get one kid untangled and out of the room while I hold the other one back. My heart is racing, and my hands are shaking. My breath is out of control. The principal comes in to take the other student to her office. She's about five inches taller than me and quite a bit bigger. My heart is still out of control. It was like everything was slow-motion when it's happening.

Take a breath. Wow! When I get home, I'm having a glass of wine!

11

First Day of School

Tomorrow is the first day of school, and I have to fill seventy minutes of time for five classes. I have no idea how to do it. I have a syllabus and a basic curriculum of the course to go over. We were encouraged by the principal to do an icebreaker with the students, to get to know one another. Before leaving for the day, I print some icebreaker examples.

On the first day, maybe I could go over Mexican-American history and how to take back Aztlan?

"It could be counted as 'vocabulary,'" I say out loud to myself as the glow of my laptop lights my "bedroom" in my RV. Teach them what colonization means and what Manifest Destiny is all about. Well, maybe not on the *first* day.

Instead, I do the icebreakers and go over the syllabus and class expectations.

I noticed the staff was mostly European-American. The students were about eighty-five percent Mexican-American. I think Catalina and I are the only ones who speak Spanish. The rest of the students are European-American, Native American and African-American. I'm surprised at the segregation. But when I think about it, the only diverse school I went to was the one on the military base. This school is close to the base, but in the poorest neighborhood in Albuquerque.

I was nervous, but attendance was low on the first day, so I wasn't as nervous as I could have been. Attendance was just like Simone and Mr. Lombardi warned me about. There were about six kids at the beginning of first period, with a roster of eighteen. Students began to trickle in all during first. Fewer students were tardy for second, but they appeared to be more scared than me, so my anxiety didn't go up. The maximum classroom size is 18, but there were only about ten students.

My first thought is blame. Who the hell is not bringing them to school? Why are they not attending? What are they doing when they don't come? The principal had already warned me, but this is unbelievable. Is school not valued at home? When I asked Mr. Leblanc he said a majority of these kids have parents from Mexico. The parents probably have a minimal education and most don't speak English. Most of these parents have not graduated high school. They can't help the students through their studies. Another issue is that these families are poor. If they have children at home, sometimes they make their high school kids babysit while they work. Sometimes the teenager is supporting the family. This is the definition of a disadvantaged family.

As I go through my plans, I see a couple of kids with their heads down or with facial expressions of not understanding. I realize they aren't ready for a lot of the vocabulary I'm using. I'm approaching this class like a college course. These kids may be reading more at a middle school level. Some of them say they don't like reading!

One boy during third period is not staying in his seat. He walks around the room then peers out the door. It makes me nervous, not knowing what he's up to. He tries to get the attention of kids outside of class by giving a 'ghetto whistle'. Gang members usually do this to get their homie's attention. I know because I grew up in the projects. He has his hoodie on, and hoods were not allowed. He's Latino with short hair, sagged down jeans with a belt, and a red shirt and shoes that have white and red. I don't know if I'm dealing with kids in gangs or not. It is the roughest neighborhood in the city. Are there still Crips and Bloods, or are they different names now? I have no idea. Am I supposed to let it go or tell him something? I ask him to sit down and take his hoodie off. He sits for a while, then gets back up and starts circling the room again. Finally, the bell rings and class ends. Whew, I survived that class!

There was a quick forty-minute lunch break, fourth, then fifth. It was go, go, go! No breaks, no stopping, no chill time. For passing periods, teachers stand outside their classrooms to monitor the hallways. I think it's for in case a fight breaks out. No time to even use the restroom! You present a lesson... again, again and again. I'm not sure if I have the stamina for this.

I don't understand why people bad-mouth charter schools. The maximum population is two hundred students. I wouldn't trade my classroom size for the world! I heard from my mom that Albuquerque Public School classroom sizes are 23-32 students. That constitutes cruel and unusual punishment for teachers! I wouldn't ask an administrator to watch, much less *teach* 20 students. I would protest that ..or just not be in the field, which I guess is where a lot of people are with the profession. There's no way I could handle 30 students in one class. Who could manage that?

It's the last period of the day. Sixth period is my prep period. "Prep" is teacher-talk for a class period to prepare for the next day, like for making copies or lesson plans. Sometimes, it's a time for sitting in the lunchroom for a break to stop your mind from spinning before you go insane. Quiet time. Take a breath.

"This is too much," I tell myself. I text my mom: "This is the hardest job I've ever had, hands down." My mom replies with a laughing emoji.

I go into the lunchroom and find Mr. Jones in there. Jobin Jones is our only history teacher. He teaches all the histories, World, U.S., New Mexico, Government, and Economics. Not sure how he prepares for all those classes. That's got to be insane.

"How do you have the energy for this? This was only day one and I'm exhausted!" I say.

"Eh, you get used to it," he says.

"I don't know how you do it," I say and get some water. My prep feels like no time, and the bell rings for the end of the day. I gather my things, walk to my car, and sit down.

"I earned every penny I made today." I take another deep breath and drive home.

When I get home, I open the garage door and realize I have to do the process all over again. I'm going to have to plan for tomorrow, teach five classes, sometimes grade papers, then do it all again. Plan, teach, grade, repeat. Plan, teach, grade, repeat. Oh. My. God. This job goes beyond working the day. This is all-consuming! I set down my things, and realize I'm going to have to think of a "Bell Ringer."

First, I pour myself a glass of red wine.

A Bell Ringer is a question that is on the board when the bell rings. It has a student-friendly learning goal. These learning goals are supposed to coincide with the "Common Core" standards. These are national standards for public schools. I have the standards up on my wall on a big six-foot-long poster with a ten-point font. They *have to* be posted up in the classroom. It's so hard to read, not just because of the small font, but because of the technical over-exaggerated language. Edu-speak. They're divided into subjects and grades. But because my classes are blended with different grades, I wasn't sure which ones to use. I read at the 9th grade one.

"CCSS.ELA-LITERACY.RL.9-10.1 :Cite strong and thorough textual evidence to support analysis of what the text says explicitly as well as inferences drawn from the text." How do you enjoy literature if that is the outcome you're deeming for? Where is the exploration and fun in learning when your goal is to get kids to, "CCSS.ELA-LITERACY.RL.9-10.4: Determine the meaning of words and phrases as they are used in the text, including figurative and connotative meanings; analyze the cumulative impact of specific word choices on meaning and tone (e.g., how the language evokes a sense of time and place; how it sets a formal or informal tone)?" No wonder kids hate school.

The Bell Ringer can be a writing prompt. Students start on the Bell Ringer so the teacher can enter attendance without leaving the students waiting. Teachers are supposed to register attendance as soon as possible. Otherwise, we get a friendly reminder from the Attendance Coordinator. The Bell Ringer should be some thought-provoking question. I struggle with thinking one up. It has to be something that the students will want to answer and be engaged in. I planned the rest of the class but still couldn't think of a Bell Ringer. I fall asleep, with my laptop still open. I have dreams of walking into class unprepared, with no lesson. Nothing for the kids to do. I keep trying to think of what the students could do. I remember I can put them on computers for the reading program. But in the dream, the kids couldn't log on to the program. The system wasn't working and I didn't know how to fix it. I remember it's a Reading class and have them read while I troubleshoot the computer issue. When my alarm rings, I wake up in a cold sweat, still unable to think of a Bell Ringer question. I finally Google "Bell Ringer questions" into my laptop and find some writing prompts.

"Thank you, Internet!" I shower in my mom's house and get ready for work two hours ahead of time, to make sure everything is set. Luckily, this charter school has an alternate schedule, compared to other schools. Classes start at 10 a.m. I'm more of a night owl, so it suits me way better than 7:45 a.m. That's ridiculous about public schools. Studies have shown for decades that teenagers need more sleep. Why do we torture people in our society?

I get ready for work and start all over again. Breathe.

12

Lunchroom - I Do Not Think It Means What You Think It Means

There are doughnuts on the free food table when I walk into the workroom in the morning.

"Ooh, who brought doughnuts?" I ask.

"Oh, Mr. Smith is usually the one who brings in doughnuts," Mr. Jones responds and Mr. Smith smiles.

"Thanks for bringing those in!" I say to Mr. Smith. He's the guitar teacher and only works in the morning. I believe he's the oldest staff member and a self-proclaimed staunch Republican. Mr. Smith walks out of the lunchroom with his guitar and a bag.

David Ridgeway is seated at the far end of the long table. He's one of the three English teachers. He's half White, half Hispanic, from Long Beach, California. He has short black hair, brown eyes, a black beard and mustache. He has a build like Popeye, but with darker skin. Mr. Ridgeway wears teacher clothes, like button-ups with a pattern. He's married to a beautiful Latina woman who is a neonatal nurse. They have a newborn and a two-year-old. It's endearing how he talks about his family all the time.

Mr. Jones is making copies. Mr. Jones is taller and more significant than Mr. Ridgeway. He has the build of a guy you want to hug. Maybe because he tends to wear Hawaiian or floral shirts? He's a White guy with a round bald head, brown eyes, a reddish-brown handlebar mustache, and beard. Mr. Jones has the kind of presence that fills up the room and has a booming voice. I like Mr.Jones for the same reasons as

Mr. Ridgeway, he's smart, quick-witted and a dedicated husband and father. Mr. Jones's wife is a short Latina woman with short brown hair and huge, emerald brown eyes. She's a yoga instructor.

"Hey, have any of you done this dossier thing, for your teaching license," I ask. Everyone shakes their heads.

"No, but I'm supposed to," Mr. Jones says.

"I've searched on the Public Education Department website, but it's not very user-friendly. I can't find what I'm supposed to do.

"Well, you can try calling, but they usually never answer," Mr. Jones says.

"Ah, great," I say disappointedly.

Mr. Ridgeway finishes signing some insurance papers for the business office.

"Wham, bam, thank you, mam!" Mr. Ridgeway says while straightening his papers on the table with a few taps.

Pam Baker glan up from her phone, scowls, then goes back to scrolling. I turn to I trun to give Mr. Ridgeway a confused facial expression like, "Did he say what I thought he said?" Mr. Jones turns toward Mr. Ridgeway from the water cooler.

"I don't think you want to say that out loud, at work, or with women in the room," Mr. Jones says as frankly as possible.

Mr. Ridgeway pulls his phone out of his pocket.

"I'm going to look up the etymology of that phrase." He feverishly taps on the screen of his phone.

"Of 'wham, bam, thank you, ma'am?'" I ask.

"Yeah," Mr. Ridgeway says, with a confused expression on his face.

"Yeah, that's probably a good idea!" I say, my face in the refrigerator. Mr. Jones laughs and shakes his head. A moment later, Mr. Ridgeway says

"I didn't think it meant *that*!" There's a look of disgust on Mr. Ridgeway's face. Ms. Baker finally looks up from her phone.

"Well, I was wondering," she says and we laugh.

"I thought it meant..." Mr. Ridgeway tries to explain, brushing his hands together, as if he's finished with something.

"You thought it meant like, "Badda bing, badda boom?" I ask.

"Yeah.. more like that. Like, 'Done!'" Mr. Ridgeway says.

"Well, *kinda*," I say. We chuckle. The warning bell rings for first period.

13

Typical Day

First period was fine, but lots of students came in 5-20 minutes late. I realized the first thing in the morning is not the time to explain how to do anything important. I end up having to repeat myself several times to explain the assignment to the late folks.

Second period I had to write up Alejandro. He came to us from Desert Hills, a behavioral health residential treatment center. I have never had an appropriate conversation with Alejandro. I'll say hello to him and he'll tell me he's going to go on a drive-by, will use inappropriate language or put up gang signs to me. I've talked to Jim about what to do. I could send him to the Dean and write him referrals all day but it seems like he wants to be removed from class. Jim encourages me to keep him in the classroom, if I can. The only good thing about Alejandro is he's usually soft-spoken and does not burst out with anger. I was working with him one-on-one. When I glanced up, some girls were talking during silent reading, so I redirected them to get focused. Alejandro glares at them, puffs his chest out and says,

"Yeah, Bitch." I don't know if the girls heard him, but I didn't want the girls to feel threatened by him, so I sent him to Jim.

During third period, Jayson asks me for a pencil. Jayson started last year as a freshman and he and his brother are supposed to be in Special Education (SpEd). Laina thinks Jayson's mom removed her three kids out of SpEd because she had to go to so many meetings. So although they are not officially in Special Ed, they need accommodations.

Jayson's brother Keven is also in my class. They are both remedial readers.

Keven tells me his brother is on his phone, which I thought was funny. I tell Jayson to put his phone away and he does. Then after a few minutes, Jayson has his phone out again. I ask him to put it in my drawer and he tells me 'hell no,' so I tell him that is inappropriate language and send him to Jim.

Lunch came and went quickly.

During fourth I hear a lot of loud talking in the commons area. I walk out there and Mr. Leblanc is there. Mr. Leblanc is about 6'2", has salt and pepper balding hair, wears glasses. He works for the local newspaper, the Albuquerque Journal, as a copy editor. He has excellent grammar and editing skills. He's trying to manage Jayson, Keven and Alejandro. They are being loud and refusing to go to class or ISS, (In-School Suspension). I give up and go back to my classroom.

I have given my class an assignment to work on but Vincent is drawing. I redirect him a couple of times but he just keeps on drawing. I take him out into the hallway to have a private conversation with him. I ask him what's wrong and he just shrugs. I tell him he can't have his head down in class. He shrugs again. I tell him he has a choice, either work on the assignment or go to ISS. He chose to leave.

Fifth period was running smoothly, then Alexus came in, about twenty-five minutes late. When students are more than thirty minutes late, we are to mark it as an absence. I get her started on what we're doing, but then twenty minutes later, her friend comes to my door and Alexus says she has to go. I told her she just got here. She stares at me with a confused look on her face, but continues to walk out the door. I tell her she has to have an adult sign out for her.

"I'm going to church," she tells me. I don't believe her. She and her friend walk down the hall like I didn't just tell her she needs to be signed out by an adult. Crap, now I have to call her guardian.

What a day. Where is my wine?

14

Lunchroom - Paint Night

It's a mild September morning. When I get to work, one of the math teachers, Linda Doyle, is in the lunch workroom, along with Mr. Smith. Lombardi walks in soon afterward.

"Who brought doughnuts?" Lombardi asks as he unpacks his reusable grocery bag.

"Mr. Smith," Linda glances at Mr. Smith with a smile. She has a crumb on the corner of her mouth.

"Have some!" Mr. Smith says.

"I'll just have one," Lombardi says but is probably lying. I've seen him, he has a sweet tooth. Lombardi takes bread, turkey, a jar of mayonnaise, and a jar of pickles out of his bag and lays it on the table. Then he takes a chocolate doughnut. I take a knife, and cut a quarter of a doughnut and eat it. I don't have a big sweet tooth and can't eat a whole doughnut. I just like to have the taste of it. I prefer salty foods and have a habit of adding salt to all my savory food. If anyone comments about it, I tell them it's fine, I have low blood pressure.

Lombardi transfers his food to the refrigerator while he chews.

Ms. Baker walks in, followed by Mr. Ridgeway and Mr. Jones. Ms. Baker turns to Linda, "Hey, do you want to join Martina and me for Paint Night?" Ms. Baker is a brilliantly artistic lady.

"What's Paint Night?"Linda asks.

"Paint night?" Mr. Ridgeway mouths to Mr. Jones with a question on his face.

"It's where you go out to a venue, sometimes dinner, and they have supplies for painting, and you do a painting project! They have events like this around town. We can do a Girls Night!" Ms. Baker says.

"Oooh, 'Girls Night,' Mr. Ridgeway says while he turns toward Mr. Jones with his eyebrows up. Mr. Ridgeway puts his arms up and shrugs,

"You want to wrestle in the yard?" Mr. Ridgeway asks Mr. Jones. And Mr. Jones nods his head yes. They both put their arms up in a wrestling position.

Lombardi has put his lunch ingredients away and turns to take a second doughnut. I smile.

"I don't know why these kids wear those ripped jeans," Mr. Smith says.

"Oh my gosh, you sound like my grandma. Those jeans have been around since *I* was in high school. It's been the style for decades. It's time to get over it," I say. Mr. Smith appears to be surprised at my response but I don't care.

"I think they do it to be sexy," Mr. Smith says.

"No. They don't," I say even more annoyed.

The warning bell beeps for first period.

15

Get Out of Class! Go to Class!

First period goes well. Second period I need to pee, but I'm not supposed to leave the students alone in the classroom. I call Charlie, the Attendance Coordinator.

"Charlie, can you cover for me, I need to run to the restroom."

"No," he tells me. I know he's joking, but it's not funny.

"Come on Charlie, before I pee my pants."

"All-riighht," he sighs. I wait, but he doesn't show up. I call the front desk.

"Catalina, can you find someone to cover me while I go to the restroom?" I ask.

"Let me see if I can find someone," she says. I wait another few minutes. Nothing. Forget it, I've got to go. The students are reading. I whisper to the kid nearest the door.

"I'll be right back. I'm gonna go to the bathroom," I say and they nod. I see Felicia, the social worker in the hall.

"Felicia, can you please watch my class for a second? I need to pee badly!" She nods her head and stands by my door.

For third period Laina and the Principal spent 15 minutes trying to get Felipe out of my class. When he walked in, he said, "Fuck you," to whoever told him to put his phone away. When I gave the class directions for the first assignment Felipe put his earbuds in and started rapping loudly. He was distracting everyone. I tried to get him focused on what we're doing, to no avail. He just registered recently and it's only his second day in my class, but I have to send him to ISS.

While Simone and Laina deal with Felipe, I get the class going on their Bell Ringer.

"You have a few questions for your Bell Ringer. 'Who are the antagonists in our class book, *1984*, and how would you describe them? *And*, who are the antagonists in *your* life, and why do you say so?'" I pause. "When you finish that, you can read independently for 15 minutes. Then we're going to continue with the Bill of Rights. After that, we'll keep reading in *1984*. Okay?" I can see the students thinking about the question.

After what seemed like forever Felipe *finally* goes with Simone and Laina. He was driving me nuts! If someone tells you to leave a room, isn't it hard not to?

Once Felipe leaves it's easier to teach. We go over the 4th Amendment and for some reason, the students are very interested.

"You mean I don't have to let a cop search my car?" one of my students asks.

"No. You can tell them you have a right to privacy. But remember, some police officers may say they smell weed from your car. That would mean they have 'probable cause' to search it. What is 'probable cause'?" I ask. "What does the word 'probable' look like?" I write it on the board.

"Probably," someone says.

"Right, like you 'probably' did something illegal. Now, do you have to explain anything to the police officer?" I ask.

"No," Josue says. "You have a right to remain silent."

"Right. The 5th Amendment protects against self-incrimination. As a minor, it's in your best interest that you wait for your parents to get there and you don't incriminate yourself." I begin to wonder if I'm making smarter criminals. But either way, the class goes well.

The day went quickly and my prep finally came. I talked to Jim, the Dean of Students, about Felipe. He told me he had to tell one of Felipe's friends to stop calling him "Crackhead Felipe." The student who called him that said that's been his nickname for years! The dean said Felipe wasn't phased by the name at all. The social worker told me he has impulse control issues.

When I return to my desk, I get a call from Charlie. We have caller ID on our phones.

"Hey, Charlie."

"Hey Joselyn, I just got a call from Joshua's mom. He didn't come to school today because he's in the hospital. He was leaving for school when he got into a fight with his neighbor. And the neighbor is some crazy guy on drugs and threw a stick at Josh and it lodged in his neck."

"Oh my gosh!" I can't believe what I'm hearing.

"Yeah, so can you just mark him as excused in your grade book? He won't have to make up participation points while he's out."

"Yeah, of course."

"Alright. I don't know how long he'll be out, but keep marking him as excused until he comes back."

"Kay, will do." I sigh and hang up.

I get up to make copies in the workroom and when I'm walking back to my classroom, I see Jose and Victoria. They are the couple I always see out of class, walking around or eating McDonald's. Outside food is not allowed, I was told, because if we let them leave they would never come back.

When they walk past me, Victoria has her phone out. I put my hand out to take it.

"Phones are not allowed, Victoria, you know that," I say in the hallway. Victoria does not put away her phone, but instead, she smiles and holds her phone up higher, where I can see it. I'm not about to grab a student's phone out of their hands. The student has to give it up willingly for me to take it. That's my own rule. Victoria smiles and keeps her phone out right in front of her face and peers up at me with a smirk.

"You think you can do whatever you want with no consequences, don't you?" I say.

"And what are you going to do about it?" she says, smiling even bigger, holding her phone. I have never hit a child in my life, but I can imagine myself slapping the shit out of this smart-ass right now. I turn back to the Teacher's Workroom.

"I'm going to write you up first of all." I bee-line it to the referral sheets in the bin but can't find a pen anywhere. This is often the case in the Workroom. One of the teachers making copies hands me her pen. I sit down at the table to scribble the referral while complaining about how entitled these two kids are. The people in the room agree while I write angrily.

I start to think to myself: And now what do you do? Think about it. Why are *you* mad? Who's day does that ruin? Only my own. Victoria's mission is accomplished. Don't let her do it. Who's the adult here? Breathe. Oh, my gosh, can I do this job?

I show my teeth and growl, mad at myself. I finish the write-ups and shove the referral in Jim's mailbox. I think about how soon I can go "home" to my RV to make a drink.

Now that I'm getting paid, I've made arrangements to move in with my friend this weekend. We used to work together at the college radio station. He just recently got a divorce and bought a big beautiful three-bedroom house. He has an eighteen-year-old son and a ten-year-old daughter. The son decided to live with his mom permanently. The daughter goes back and forth due to shared custody. I'm taking the son's room. I'm excited to be getting back on my feet again. Living in the RV has been a bit cramped. All I really do is watch Netflix off my stepdad's Wi-Fi. Now I'll be able to watch Rachel Maddow, Stephen Colbert, John Oliver, Trevor Noah... and.. tonight's Zozobra! Old Man Gloom can take with him this feeling I have of not being successful. Burn it up.

16

Baggies

First and second periods are probably my favorite. First period kids are too sleepy to give me problems and second just has decent kids in it who do their work and try hard.

Third period Jayson asks me for a pencil. Again.

I'm in the middle of a lecture, and when I glance down, Cesar has a line of about five piles of tiny empty plastic baggies in a line. Tiny baggies that drug dealers put meth or crack in. My eyes get as big as tortillas and I try to shield what I see from the other students, but it's impossible. I put a pause after every word and whisper, "What-*are*-you-*DOING*?"

"What? ...These are for skittles, Miss. They're for a piñata." Cesar tries to lie.

"Put those away this *second*." I grab some as proof for Jim. I tell the kids to get started on their assignment and rush to my computer to ask Jim to come A.S.A.P. What the hell is this kid thinking? You're just going to count your drug bags in my class? Why can't you do this in math class? Jim comes quickly and takes Cesar and his backpack.

I continue with the class and everything else goes fine.

For passing period Mr. Jones tells a group of boys to put their phones away. All of them do except for Keven. I say loudly,

"Oh, who's phone's going to be taken away?" I walk toward the group. Keven still doesn't put his phone away, so ask for his phone.

"No, Miss." He turns his back to me. Oh, these kids are going to be the death of me. I have to write him up now.

I do love my fourth-period Leadership class. I have a really smart Muslim girl student named Basma. She's made friends with a very "woke" African American student named Raya. Both of Raya's parents have passed and she and a few siblings are being raised by their oldest brother. Basma and Raya both made friends with my teddy-bear sweet Mexican-American student who loves his mama. Sometimes I wish I could adopt Raya. She writes songs about her mother's death and makes me weep.

My second-period student Joanna walks in to ask me if she can turn in a reading log late.

"What are you doing in here Joanna?" We have a policy that the teacher has to call before sending a student to your class. "You already know you can turn in work late. I'm trying to teach a class right now and you are disrupting it."

Joanna looks at me sheepishly and I scan around the room and see her boyfriend. "Are you in here checking in on your boyfriend?" I ask her.

She peers down and doesn't answer. "You know, I found the bathroom pass of mine that you lost yesterday. It was in your boyfriend's second period. This has got to stop Johanna. Go to class." I feel bad for my tone, but she has to get her own life! She is so codependent on her boyfriend.

Her boyfriend has his head down. I go over to him to try to get him started on the assignment, but he doesn't budge. Just goes to show how much control I have over my classroom. I sigh and check in with the kids who are doing their work.

I'm excited for the end of the day because I'll be moving this weekend.

17

Buzzing Bracelet

It's a crisp September day outside. The sunlight is flooding into my classroom from the high East facing windows and warming my face. It's first period and Angelo has ants in his pants that do the boogie-dance. He's a true freshman, and struggles with staying in his seat. I ask him to get started on his work about five times before I get tired of repeating myself. I often tell him not to throw things in class, but he throws a pencil to someone.

"Can you *not* throw things please? Someone can get hurt," I say. But not five minutes later, he throws a snack-pack of cheese. Ugh.

I need to pee. I try to get someone to watch my class while I go to the ladies room. I call the Attendance Coordinator.

"Hey Charlie, can you come cover my class while I run to the ladies room?"

"No," Charlie says abruptly.

"Come on, pleeeeease."

"Okay, be there in a minute," Charlie says.

"Thanks," I say and hang up. I wait. And wait. I go to the door and peer down the hall. I see no one. I can't wait.

"Manny, I'll be right back. I'm going to the restroom," I whisper.

"Ah-aight Miss," my student replies.

When third period comes along, I'm at my desk checking emails when I hear,

"Miss?" The juvenile convict's voice is so recognizable to me, it often makes me bristle a bit. I look up. He's a Hispanic kid, a little taller than me with dark brown hair that is shaved on the sides and brushed back on the top. He has excessively bushy eyebrows. The most jarring thing about him, though, is his ankle bracelet. It's to monitor his location since he's on house arrest. He and his delinquent friend beat up a homeless man while he slept.

"How many segments do I have to do in Read 180? I finished one." Mario asks in a low voice. I stand up and take a few steps out of the sun to see him. He walks closer to me from his desk.

"Two. You have enough time. I'm sure you can do it!" I say, encouraging him.

He leans his head back and squints.

"Why don't I give you like... seventy bucks, and you'll say I did it?"

"Mmm.. because that's not how we earn credit?" I act as if I have something to do at my computer again. He's testing me. He turns to go back to his desk. "It'll be easy. You know you can do it." I sit back in the sun and focus on my computer screen.

He sits down and starts talking to someone else. I'm not quite sure how serious he was. Maybe next time I should joke and say 'Add a zero to the end of that,' and laugh. It takes time to get to know each other that well. We aren't there yet. He has to at least know he can't bribe me.

After a few minutes, his ankle bracelet starts buzzing. I try to ignore it, but I see him sit by a computer in the corner of the room to charge it.

I question my decision to take this job, but then I remember how difficult it was to get jobs these past ten years. I guess I can tough it out, for now.

At the end of the day I take home some papers to grade. When I sit to read them I'm stunned. Some of these kids don't know how to capitalize the first letter in a sentence. There are run-on sentences, terrible spelling, no names on papers. One student capitalizes the first letter of each word! Holy moly, we have a lot of work to do! One student's Bell Ringer writing prompt response says,

"If I was able to design a society it would be more important to have more communitetion of Freedom of Choice it's to let them keep there own babies and every one to get ther owe job."

18

Lunchroom - West-Wing Wong

The crew is in the staff workroom for lunch, and Mr. Leblanc is unpacking his salad. Mr. Leblanc is one of the three English teachers. He's trilingual, he can speak Spanish and French.

"Is this Committee Friday, coming up? Or PLC (Professional Learning Committee)?" Leblanc asks.

"Committee," Mr. Ridgeway responds, without glimpsing up from his phone.

"Oh, so there's a staff meeting?" Leblanc continues.

"Yes," Mr. Jones answers. Mr. Jones is standing by the microwave. He's waiting to heat his homemade enchiladas with red chile on them. They look delicious.

"Oh, so they should be passing off the Wong Award," Leblanc says excitedly. The Wong award is referring to Harry Wong, an educator, and author. His books and videos about how to be an effective teacher are on the shelf by our mailboxes.

"Oh, you mean the 'West Wing Wong'?" Mr. Jones says.

"Whaat?" Ms. Baker asks. Laughter breaks out in the room.

"Yeah, haven't you noticed? It only goes to people on the west side of the building." Mr. Jones puts his lunch in the microwave. On the west side of the building is the math team. We Humanities teachers have an understated rivalry with the math team. Mostly just banter.

"Really?" Ms. Baker sounds surprised.

"Monique, You, Theresa, Coach." Mr. Jones puts out a finger with each person as if he's counting.

"I've been here for eight years and haven't ever gotten that dang award!" says Mrs. Doyle, the math teacher, whose classroom is also on the west side.

Have you taken all your tests, Joselyn?" Mr. Leblanc asks me as I pick out the cranberries from my Trader Joe's pre-made salad.

"No. I've taken the English test, the Reading test, and the Readiness Assessment. I passed all of those but I know I need to study for the math test," I say. "It's a lot of money to spend for something I'm not sure I want to stick with."

"You're not sure if you want to stick with teaching?" Leblanc asks.

"No! You all do so much! I'm not sure I can keep up!" I say. Leblanc nods in agreement.

"Well, I think you should!" Mr. Leblanc tries to encourage me. "We need people like you in the field. How about, I pay for your math test."

"What, no. Why would you do that?" I ask.

"Well, my teaching mentor paid for mine and I want to return the favor," Joe says.

"Joe, I'm grateful that you are mentoring me though teaching, but that's enough! You don't have to pay for my test," I insist.

"I just want you to stay in the profession," Leblanc urges.

"I'll think about it," I say.

The time for lunch flies by and the bell beeps, indicating lunch is over. Here we go again, go, go go!

19

Calm, for a Crisis

It's the last week of September and Mr. Jones, Mr. Ridgeway, and I are in the staff lunchroom about an hour before classes. Ridgeway often comes in before the sun comes up. Mr. Jones and I regularly get there about an hour early to prepare for the day. Mr. Leblanc usually comes in as the bell for first period is ringing. I guess you can do that when you've taught for ten years? I pour some hazelnut creamer in my coffee and begin to stir. My student, Marlene, knocks on the door, opens it, and asks to speak to Mr. Jones.

Marlene is from the Apache Pueblo. She's eighteen years old, short, medium brown skin, with long black straight hair. She often wears her hair up in a tight twisted bun and usually wears a lot of makeup. She has beautiful Native features with high cheekbones and big almond eyes. She's usually fairly quiet and is engaged in class.

I'm halfway finished with my cup of coffee when Marlene returns to the lunchroom and asks for me. I walk out into the hallway, and she asks for school work because she's going to have to leave for a family emergency. We walk together to my classroom as she explains the situation.

"My older cousins have been on drugs, and they didn't want to take care of their daughter, Samantha. I told my mom that I would take care of her, so we took her in. After a while, I moved out into an apartment on my own and brought Samantha with me. My mom moved in with her boyfriend. This morning I heard Samantha in the bathroom, and when I found her, she had cut herself. There was blood all over. I had to take her to the hospital. I stayed there for a while until I knew she was going to be okay. Then my grandma got to the hospital and told me to go get cleaned up because I had blood on me. I came to get some work," Marlene explains to me calmly. I'm in shock. I can't believe how she's holding herself together at the moment. I'm sure I'd be a mess and in total distress.

I put my coffee cup down and get Marlene a reading log. She thanks me and leaves. I walk back to the workroom, stunned.

I don't know if I can handle all that comes with this job. And I'm sad just because my father doesn't love me. It would suck if both my parents were on drugs and straight-up didn't want me.

That has to be painful.

I'll go home to a glass of wine or two to cry about this tonight.

The warning bell rings for first period and the teachers stand outside their doors.

One of my students is walking fast with a purpose, past me. He goes over by the breakfast line and straight-up clocks a student in the face.

"THAT'S FOR POINTING A GUN IN MY FACE LAST NIGHT!"

"Oh shit," I say and several teachers and I go to break up the fight. We get them separated. The principal takes one student and the social worker takes the other. The bell rings.

"Well that escalated quickly," I tell Mr. Jones.

"Yes, it did." Mr. Jones agrees and we go into our classes.

At the end of the day, the social worker calls me to tell me that the boys quashed it and are friends again.

"Say what?" I'm confused.

"Yeah, I don't know. Jose said he understood why Cameron got mad," Felicia says.

"Wow, I don't think I'd be that forgiving if you pointed a gun in my face," I say. Felicia sighs.

"Yeah, well, Joe and Cameron were still put on a Peace Contract. So if you can just keep an ear out for any nasty talk about fighting again," Felicia tells me.

"Yeah, sure, no problem. I'll let you know if I see anything," I say.

"Oh, and one more thing. Cameron got his girlfriend pregnant, so she will be going to prenatal visits. I'll let you know when to excuse her absences."

"Oh, okay," I say, shocked, yet again. We hang up.

So ready for a drink!

Lunchroom - Don't Try Everything

When I walk into the lunchroom, Lombardi, Jones, and Ridgeway are sitting at the table. There are doughnuts on the free food table.

"Mr. Smith bring these?" I ask. Mr. Lombardi nods his head. I see a little glazed frosting on his beard.

Mr. Lombardi is practicing German. He does that now and then.

"I regret that when I went to Germany, I didn't try any beer," I say.

"Oh, that's a sin!" Lombardi calls out.

Mr. Jones shakes his head. "No, That's good!"

"What? What do you mean that's good?" Lombardi a puzzled expression.

"You don't have to try everything. Yeah, go to Germany... try a little Naziism..." Mr. Jones says as he moves his hand in a way that imitates like he's shaking a cigar. We all sit there, looking at each other with eyes wide, nodding, and not saying anything. I cut a piece of a doughnut with a butterknife and shove it into my mouth.

"I don't drink beer anyway." I shrug with my mouth full.

Mr. Smith walks in and the warning bell for first period rings.

"Is it time to get naked?" Mr. Smith asks.

"No, Mr. Smith. Definitely not," I say with anger in my voice, walking out.

Professional Learning Community

Every other Friday we have a staff meeting and either a Professional Learning Community meeting, or PLC's before school starts. My group members are the Humanities crew, Mr. Leblanc, Mr. Ridgeway, Mr. Jones and myself.

"Who wants to 'debrief?'" Mr. Leblanc, the note-taker asks. I've learned that "debrief" is code for decompressing or venting.

"I'd like to," Mr. Ridgeway says. "Michael comes to class every nine days. He'll check his phone and then go to the bathroom with his backpack. I think he's dealing drugs" We all shake our heads.

"There are a few kids who know that they'll get dropped from the school after ten days so they come every nine days. Then there's the problem with the drug dealing. Have you let Jim know about your suspicions?" Mr. Leblanc asks.

"Yeah, I'll send him an email when I see him doing that, but Jim always seems to be dealing with a crisis situation," Mr. Ridgeway says.

"Hm, do you have more to debrief?" Mr. Leblanc asks. Mr. Ridgeway shakes his head.

"No, that's it."

I say I want to debrief. I tell the group about Cesar and his baggies and how Sergio was searching AK-15's online and how I had to write them up. They frown and shake their heads.

"Don't worry, Sergio doesn't last long. He'll stop coming soon. He does it every year," Mr. Leblanc says, then continues.

Joe goes next: "Well, I'm frustrated with the staff meeting today. We have enough on our plates with planning and grading and teaching. Now we have to turn in Mindset Lessons every month! All this documentation takes away time that we could be using to come up with quality lessons! Not to mention alerts every two weeks and then incorporate student-led lessons!"

Alerts are emails that are to go out from each teacher to the mentor. They eat up a lot of planning time. The purpose is to fill the mentor in on the student's attendance and progress. Student-led means lessons that the students want to do or have content that they're interested in. "I'm just wondering if we are going to see any changes in the students with these alerts. The students who don't come to school, don't come to school. We teachers get blamed for bad attendance. But some don't come because their families or homes are unstable. Those things are out of our control, you know?" Leblanc flips his hand up.

"Yeah," we all say in unison.

"We have to send out alerts every two of weeks. Then submit grades every four weeks. We have to keep track incomplete grades, which creates so much more paperwork. Then we have to shift gears to plan out what we're going to teach the next quarter. It's just *too* much!"

"I don't know how you all do this. I don't know if I can keep up," I say for the umpteenth time.

"And then those fucking mentee files!" Mr. Leblanc's at his edge.

"Oh, man! Those mentee files are rough!" I say. We keep track of ten mentees. Their files include report cards, grades, credits, Incompletes, Incomplete Contracts, Attendance Contracts, Next Step Plans and test scores. My files are a mess.

"Middle school is a wasted time for them. They don't retain anything! They might as well work on the farm," Leblanc says.

No one else needs to debrief after that and we get down to what we're going to do for our PDP's. PDP stands for Professional Development Plan. Your plan has to focus on measuring student improvement. Then you meet with the principal about how you are going to improve your teaching. You come up with a strategy or use some sort of learning tool and write about how you'll use it in the classroom. You check in with the principal about how your PDP is going at some point during the year. At the end of the year you reflect on how it went, and report about what you did and what you might do differently. It's just another level of hell.

After about an hour Mr. Jones says,

"I'm PCP'd out." I laugh. He means "PDP'd" but he often uses word-play to make jokes. We wrap up and start the school day.

22

Lunchroom - Doughnut Etiquette

"I can't finish this," Mr. Ridgeway says with a doubtful expression on his face. It's lunchtime, and he's sitting at the long table with a bowl of peppers, cheese, and cured meats in front of him. Ms. Baker, Mr. Jones, and Lombardi are all in the room. I see Mr. Smith left doughnuts for everyone.

"You don't have to finish it," I say to Mr. Ridgeway from across the table.

"You don't have to finish it," Mr. Jones repeats while shaking his head. "It's like cutting a doughnut in half." Then he glares at me from the corner of his eye.

"Ohhhh..." I laugh because I know he's talking about me.

"Yeah, who does that?" Mr. Jones smirks, then Mr. Ridgeway cuts in.

"Some of you, I noticed, don't even cut it in half. It's like you put your fingers in it..." We laugh.

"HA, HA. THAT'S NOT ME," I say, shuffling through the papers that I found in my mailbox.

"Or take out like a spoonful. It's like rats got into it," Mr. Ridgeway continues. "It was like someone said, 'I'll have a little bit of every dough-nut on one plate.' By the end of the day, you've had a full doughnut. So just eat the doughnut!"

Martina, the computer teacher walks in.

"We need some doughnut protocols around here," Lombardi says with a stern expression on his face as he pounds his fist on the table.

"Doughnut etiquette!" Mr. Jones stresses. "Ya touch it, ya, take it!" His pointer finger goes up.

"Ya eat it!" Lombardi adds.

"What if you didn't technically touch it?" Martina asks.

"A doughnut has a hole in it, therefore you're not eating the entire pastry, so eat the whole thing! Mr. Jones play-yells.

"It's a hand-held pastry!" Mr. Ridgeway throws in sound reasoning why you *should* touch and eat the whole doughnut.

"Is that like eating pizza with a fork?" Ms. Baker asks.

"Oh, that's a sin," Mr. Ridgeway says with conviction.

"Who does that?" Lombardi asks.

"Ooh, I do! Chicago deep-dish. You gotta eat it with a fork."

"Naw, you don't," Mr. Ridgeway insists.

"Yeah, if you're not eating your deep-dish with a fork, it's not deep enough," Mr. Jones says. As I take a sip of my coffee, I go off in my own world reminiscing about when I used to live in Chicago and how good the food was. After a moment, I whisper to myself,

"Mmmmm.. Chicago deep-dish." I reach for the salt for my salad.

23

Drowning

The T.V. is on when I'm leaving for work this Thursday morning. My roommate must have left it on.

The Christine Blasé-Ford testimony is on. Ms. Ford is getting sworn in. I won't be able to see any of it because I work from 10-6. Though when I get in my car, I find it being broadcast on the NPR station. Mrs. Ford is going to testify to Congress about how Brett Kavanaugh sexually assaulted her when they were in high school. It's significant because Brett Kavanaugh is about to be approved by the Senate to serve as a judge on the Supreme Court, a life-long position.

I don't foresee this going well. It seemed not to matter when Anita Hill testified against Supreme Court Justice Clarence Thomas in the '80s. She said that he had inappropriately touched her and sexually harassed her at work. He's *still* on the Supreme Court. And no one in this administration seems to care about sexual assault. Or rather, they brag about it.

It's September 27th, and it's chilly and bright outside in Albuquerque, and the air is crisp. We got snow a few days earlier, but it melted pretty quickly in the city. I listened to the testimony on my ten-minute drive to work.

'I'll have to check the news later to find out what happened,' I think to myself. I force myself to stop listening when I park in the school parking lot and turn off my car. I zip up my jacket and brace myself for the cold. I run for the school doors. When I get there, I open the lock with my key and pull the heavy door open. I walk forward down one hall, take a right, and walk down the other hallway to my classroom.

I open my classroom, and it's cold. I don't have a temperature control unit in my class. My classroom is controlled by either Mr. Ridgway's or Mr. Jones's. Either way, something is wrong with the heater. I change from the coat that I'm wearing into the long grey sweater in my closet. I typically wear that in class because it's always a bit chilly in here.

"It's a beautiful day in the neighborhood, a beautiful day in the neighborhood, would you be mine, would you be mine?" I sing to myself when I put my sweater on. I hear the Christine Blasé-Ford testimony again, loudly. I follow the sound next door to the history teacher's classroom. No one's in there. The class has desks clustered into four, and Youtube is up on the display board. I grab a stool in the back and watch.

"...I remember the boys laughing as they ping-pinged down the stairs," Mrs. Ford says. I feel heavy, stuck to my chair.

Suddenly I remember how Robert had laughed at me after raping me in the back of his truck. He told me to get the condom afterward. Shame swept over me and I felt humiliated. Christine's words were bringing me back to high school, 1992 Spring Break, Elephant Butte, when I was a junior. I remember some things clearly, like Robert giving me and Jade shot after shot after shot of vodka. Jade knew Robert from sports. Jade was a cheerleader, and Robert played baseball. I remember Jade and I were sitting in the back seats of someone's van, and the van doors were open. Robert was hanging in from the outside. He's about 6'1" and has a square build. I was never sure how many shots of vodka we had, five, I think. I had promised my mom that I wouldn't drink while I was there, but we were about to leave, so I didn't see the harm. I had never had more than a couple of sips of a margarita before, so after so many shots, some things completely blacked out. I only remember being in the back of Robert's truck, with him on top of me. Then blacking out again. I remember him driving me back to my friends, drunk. When I got home, the room was spinning ... back then ... and now.

I realize I'm in Jobin's room, and I feel a sinking in my stomach and my heart starts beating hard. I feel heavy, like I can't breathe. Like I'm drowning. Dizziness falls over me and I feel a hot sweat on my back. I can hear my heartbeat in my ears and start to breathe faster. I have to get out of here. I walk out of the classroom and down the hall to the front of the school. I burst into the closest girls' bathroom. It's about an hour before first period, and I'm having a panic attack. No one's in there, thank goodness. I'm sobbing, crying, short, quick breaths, heaving. My hands are shaking uncontrollably. I can't talk myself down, and I can't catch my breath. I go into the first stall to get tissue for my eyes and runny nose.

The secretary, Catalina, walks in. Catalina is a few inches taller than me, she has her hair highlighted blonde and wears it straight. She has six kids, some of whom have attended this school. She's worked here for the past thirteen years. She's bilingual and priceless to the school's operations.

"Estas bien?" Catalina has a concerned look on her face and holds her arms out to hold me up. I try to talk, but I don't make sense. I'm sobbing words and not full sentences.

"I... was... watching... It... was... It.. just." I suck in more sobs of air.

"Slow down. Just breathe." Catalina holds my arms, moves my curly hair back from my shoulders, and shows me how to breathe slowly with her.

"It... just... reminded... me." I try to continue, but I'm crying. "It... just... made... me..." I'm not making sense.

"Breathe. It's okay. Have you talked to anyone about this?" Catalina asks.

I nod my head and start to steady my breathing a little.

"Just... to... a... friend."

"Maybe it's time. Ask Felicia for a referral, mmkay?" I nod my head, yes. I've confided in Felicia in the past, about student-related stuff. I nod my head again. She's as reliable as you can get.

"Do you want to take the day off? Get a sub?"

I usually try to tough everything out, but yes, absolutely, I want a sub. Maybe we should chalk this up to a mental health day?

"I'll order a sub for you. Don't worry about it. Are you okay?" Catalina asks before letting go of my arms. I nod my head again.

Catalina leaves the bathroom to get me coverage for the day. I grab more tissue and check myself in the mirror. Mascara is smeared all over my eyes. I try to clean myself up before walking out. Thank goodness I can go home. Who knows how this would have affected me in the classroom. I try to steady my breath to breathe more deeply. Then I hear Christine Blasé-Ford's voice in my head again. I flashback to being in the back of Robert's truck. I take a breath, but then my breathing becomes shallow, like sobs. My heart starts to race again, and I spiral downward. I rush outside of the bathroom to the outside of the building to get fresh air. I peer at the snow-covered mountains and breathe. I try to focus on the mountains instead of the past. I breathe the cold air steadily.

When Felicia comes into work, I meet her at the front door and tell her I need some help. She walks me to her office and gives me a website to When Felicia comes in to work, I meet her at the front door and tell her I need some help. She walks me to her office and give me a website to look up therapists that take our insurance.

I keep breathing. I leave sub plans, gather myself, and then my things.

As I drive from the school to where I live in the Northeast Heights, I'm grateful I do not live in the crazy neighborhood where our school is.

When I get home I make myself a drink. I'm so glad I was able to leave work. I spend the whole day, off and on, sobbing, crying, mourning, grieving, heaving, and drinking. It feels like my entire body is weeping, and it lasts the whole day. I hold on to the kitchen table and hunch over and cry. I hold on to doorways, eyes red and puffy. Wrenched with grief, I lie down, but can't feel comfortable. I get up and go to the backyard to smoke a clove cigar. I have never felt this way. I don't know what's happening. I do know what is happening live on T.V. Right now, Brett-The-Frat-Boy KavanaUGH is testifying to Congress. I dared not turn it on. I would have a more significant breakdown. I hate that something happening outside of myself is having such a strong physical and emotional effect on me.

The Republican-led Senate is going to push this self-entitled rapist through as a Supreme Court Justice. This administration who, without words, are saying, "Rape is ok! You can rape in this country and get rewarded with power from the SUPREME COURT!" They're saying, (without saying), 'You can be successful and powerful in America, AND you can rape!' 'We get our way. We push our way through, even if we're not wanted!' - just like rapists do. It is pure patriarchal corruption. The agenda is to rid America of life choices for women. They want to control access to contraception and abortion to keep us poor and disenfranchised.

It goes on like this for hours. I go outside for fresh air or drink cold water to try to relieve myself in some way. I put the bottom of my iced drink on my puffy eyes. The whole day, my body wrenches and cries and weeps to the point where I feel like a dead carcass. Vacant. Cried out. Maybe Catalina's right. Maybe it is time to get professional help.

I search for therapists online, make a few phone calls, leave a few messages. I spoke to a few different therapists and began to talk myself out of it once I understood I'd have to dish out $75 a session. I start to tell myself it isn't worth it, but then realize it is. I made an appointment with a Licensed Professional Clinical Counselor named Sharron. Her profile says she works in "Mindful Therapy." I'm not sure what that is, but it sounds progressive. If it doesn't seem worth it after the first appointment, I won't make any more appointments.

I get a text from my cousin, Marcy, who is currently in a lawsuit with the city of Santa Fe. She's suing them for not transferring her from someone who was sexually harassing and stalking her at work. Marcy asks if I'm watching the Kavanaugh testimony. I text back 'no' and make another drink.

"He's acting like an entitled little frat boy!" Marcy texts. "It's disgusting." I sob some more in another room and stare off. I cannot understand why I'm feeling like this. I've never felt this horrible, not even after my own sexual assault.

But then again, I tried to deny it happened. I tried to forget about it, but a few days later, I had green bruises on the inside of my thighs. Proof of what had happened. I thought about how I was forced to see the asshole who did this to me at school for another year and a half. I got through it, though.

Why is my body aching like this? I've been depressed before, but it didn't feel like this. This was different than anything I had ever felt. It was like someone had died. Something did die: my belief in justice.

I lay down again to take a nap. Can't sleep. I go back to the kitchen, get some water, then outside to the backyard again to breathe. There is unmelted snow from the fluke snowstorm. The fresh air feels good, but I still can't fully catch my breath. The sun warms my skin. I take pictures of Winter, my roommate's black cat, who loves to roll in the dirt. He's black with yellow eyes and loves to escape the backyard, so I have to watch him. His hearing is pretty bad, and he knows nothing of the 'hood life.' He couldn't make it on his own.

He's a great distraction.

"Don't pee in the garden!" I run over to chase him away.

24

Therapy Session 1 - Juvenile Delinquents and Secondary Trauma

After work, I walk through the school parking lot to my car and inhale the fresh early October air. The sun is setting.

I use Google Maps to find my new therapist's address once I'm in my car. It seems like she works out of her home. The address is in a residential area.

Her directions are perfect, down to the mailbox with the hearts on it. Go down the dirt driveway, she said. I park my car. It's unclear where her property ends, and another begins. There are some old cars parked further back and then some horse stables. I put my knitted hat and scarf back on and knock on her door.

She opens the door and smiles.

"Joselyn?" She asks. She's older than the photo online. She's a petite woman, about five feet tall, with short salt and pepper hair and wrinkles on her face. She's probably in her sixties. She's wearing a sweater with a scarf, jeans and some short brown boots.

"Yes, Sharron?" I say and smile back. She invites me inside. The room is short on one side, but long on the other with wood floors and a kiva fireplace in one corner. There's a maroon velvet love seat that has two hand-sewn pillows on it to my left and a brown reclining chair to my right. The room is decorated in Southwestern style. Sharron gestures for me to sit on the love seat opposite her. She gets a file and a pad of paper from a table next to her chair. She sits on the plush reclining chair and we settle in.

"So tell me why you're here," Sharron asks.

"Well, I've been dealing with a few different issues all my life. I think the one that is the most pressing is that I think I have PTSD or secondary trauma or something. I work in a high-risk high school in the worst neighborhood in the city." I wring my dry hands.

"Okay, tell me more," Sharron urges.

"I have a student who's on an ankle monitoring bracelet, and I read what he did in the paper. It makes me nervous to have him in class because I don't know if he's the type to lash out. There's a part of me that is afraid of him. There's another part of me that wants to give this fifteen-year-old another chance in the world. Hopefully, to make his life right. He's doing well. He's focused in class, he gives effort. Sometimes his bracelet beeps in class. I want to avoid talking about why he has it at all costs." I start to warm up and take off my coat.

"Why, what did it say in the paper?" Sharron interrupts.

"He and an eighteen-year-old beat up a homeless man while the man was sleeping by a cafe."

"Oh, yes, I can see how that can be a little unnerving," Sharron remarks. She writes something down.

"Yeah, and so the real question I have for myself is if I'm even in the right profession. I feel like my life has gone off course. I was working in radio and doing tons of voice work. Then the economic downturn hit. I was laid off and am barely recovering financially now, if you can call it that. I was pretty much homeless for a while. Staying with friends for about two years, sometimes sleeping in my truck. I feel I'm hyper-alert because of sleeping in my car and an incident at work with a guy who came to our school on a motorcycle."

"Wow, yes. Now, you said some other things have been bothering you. What are those things?" Sharron says, prodding for more information.

I clear my throat before talking.

"Well, I know I have daddy and family issues, but those are tolerable because I don't talk to my father." I shift in my seat and put my hands between my legs for warmth.

"Alright, and anything else?" Sharron wants the whole enchilada.

"Um, yeah, and I suffered from sexual abuse as a child and a sexual assault or, um, survival incident. For some reason, it came up during the Christine Blasé Ford testimony the other day. Before they confirmed Brett Kavanaugh for Supreme Court Justice. It bothered me so much that I had such a severe reaction. I would like to keep control of my own emotions. I don't like that the government had such an effect on my emotions that day." I sound as if I know what I want, but don't know how to get there.

"Did you ever grieve your sexual assault?" Sharron asks.

"I talked to a friend about it, but grieved? No, I don't think I grieved." I respond with wrinkles on my forehead. Sharron writes something down and then asks: "So, you would like to work on the work-related stuff first?"

"Yes, I feel like it's the most pressing. It's what causes me the most stress," I say, a bit eager.

"I see. Well, I like to work more often in the beginning. So you can process things and think of new ways of breaking through into the healing. Visualize yourself into the purposeful-catalyst role. I want you to think of those instances when you have the most fear and stress. Then imagine the best results possible. Can you meditate on that for a week?"

"Yeah, sure," I reply. I can do this. I pretty much already do.

"I'll give you a print-out of the instructions, in case you forget." She hands me a sheet of paper. "We have time, would you like to tell me about the guy on the motorcycle?" Sharron coaxes.

"Yeah, might as well get it out. So, if you can picture our school parking lot, it goes in a loop. There's an entrance going one way, to drop kids off at the front door and an exit at the opposite end of the parking lot. We let out at 6 p.m and I was leaving around 6:15. When I got into my car, I noticed an old man on a motorcycle driving very slowly in front of the school, starting at it. I drove from my parking spot to the exit. I stopped to think about if I was going to cut in front of him or wait for him to pass. Since I was at work, I decided to wait for him. But he came in through the exit right in front of me. I was suspicious because he went into the parking lot the wrong way. And who picks up a kid on a motorcycle with no helmet? Something didn't seem right. I drove out of the parking lot into the street and tried to keep an eye on the guy. He lingered over in the corner, by the dumpster, where I couldn't see him. I stopped in the middle of the street since no one was driving behind me. Then he rode up to a female student." I paused and used my hands to show where the motorcycle guy was and where I was. "'OH HELL NO,' I said, and I drove through the entrance. There were only two students left. One female, who he was talking to, and one male. I drove up to him and rolled down my window. He drove up to the male student and said something to him. The male student said, 'I don't fuckin' know you! You don't need to be talkin' to me!' I started laying on my horn, trying to get attention from inside, but it didn't work. The guy turns to me and says 'What is your fucking problem?' I told him *he* was my problem and he'd have to leave. He told me he didn't see any 'No Trespassing' signs. I told him I did and he needs to go NOW. While I called 911 the male student's mother came for him, picked him up and exited the exit-way. The guy on the motorcycle exits from the entrance and meets their van in the middle of the street. 911 is ringing and ringing and then there's a recording that tells me to hold. Finally, someone answers and I tell them what's happening. I'm watching the altercation from across the parking lot but I can't see or hear exactly what's going on. I heard later from the male student that the guy on the motorcycle threatened to kill his mom. That's when my student popped out of the passenger side. He told the biker, 'You'll have to kill me first!' The mom had to stop her van suddenly when her son jumped out. The student reported to me that the guy had pulled out a black ten-inch blade. From across the parking lot, I see my student kick the motorcycle. It takes the guy all his strength to keep up his Harley. When he steadies his bike, he takes off, and my student and his mom leave. The police called me when they had gotten to the school. It was 9:30 at night. Everyone had already left! I talked to the young girl afterward. She said the guy on the motorcycle had asked her what she was eating and if she liked ice cream. That was when I pulled up." I feel some nervousness in my chest.

"What most bothered you most about that whole incident?" Sharron asks, peering at me.

"I felt helpless. I couldn't figure out a way to keep the students safe." My voice breaks.

"I'm going to have you learn an exercise called 'See Out,'" Sharron says. "Practice this exercise ten minutes a day. Sit or walk and allow your attention to see or feel or hear whatever is around you. Say 'see out' or 'hear out' or 'feel out,' depending on what your attention is on. I'll demonstrate." Sharron allows her gaze to wander while repeating the phrases. She's noting where her focus is. Then she asks me to do it. Sharron warns not to allow time to lapse between each thing noted. Otherwise, your mind wanders. The exercise is to remind us to be and live in the moment, allow emotions to pass while being "distracted" by the now.

"I'll give you time to practice it," Sharron says in a peaceful, non-pressing tone.

"So, see you next week, same time?" I give her cash for the appointment.

"Yes, sure." Sharron finds a change bag and makes the change for my transaction.

"Thanks." I felt like I had purged a little toxic crap. I felt a little lighter.

The North Valley was getting colder at night, the air was changing. Winter is coming early. I notice it's darker in the valley. I turn on my car and ponder the session the whole drive home. It was worth the money. I don't know if I want to tell her about my drinking.

25

Lunchroom - Missing Kids

It's October, and Mr. Ridgeway and Mr. Jones are in the staff lunchroom when I get to school. Mr. Jones is drinking black coffee, and it smells so good, I make myself a cup. Mr. Ridgeway is sitting at the head of the long table.

Ridgeway folds up the Albuquerque Journal.

"Yeah, so, I read this morning that Muhammad is missing," he says with a concerned expression on his face.

"I saw that article, is that one of our students?" I ask and Mr. Ridgeway nods.

"One of them is. I think the other kid goes to Highland. I read they were near Hoover Middle School. Apparently, it was some drug deal gone bad. The police say there's a Snapchat video showing the boys beaten, bloody, and with broken bones," Mr. Ridgeway says with his eyebrows peeking together.

"That's terrible," Mr. Jones sits, with a glazed stare over his face, like he's sick.

"When's the last time you saw him?" I ask and stir my coffee.

"It's been about three weeks since he's come to class." You can see him searching into his memory banks as he talks. "Every time he comes to class, he looks high as a kite. Sometimes I wonder if he's hallucinating," Mr. Ridgeway says and takes a sip of his coffee. It's nearing the first bell, so I gather my coffee, water flask and keys.

"I hope they find them," I say. The bell for first period beeps. "The kids and whoever did this to them."

We all get up from the table and hold the door open for each other, sigh somberly and shuffle to class.

"I still don't know how you guys do all this," I say before we go out into the hallway.

26

Therapy Session 2 - Missing Kids & Father Abandonment

For my second therapy session, I was a little reluctant that we weren't going to do anything productive. What could we possibly talk about only a week later? Sharron invites me in, and I sit on the love seat.

"There's a student that has been in the news that goes to our school. He's been missing," I burst out.

"Oh, I'm very sorry to hear that," Sharron says sincerely.

"Yes, and there's a video that showed up on social media that shows him and some other kid bloodied, with broken bones. Our student is on probation, and there is a warrant out for his arrest. So police don't know if he's trying to lay low, or if he's missing... or worse. These kids don't understand. And they think we don't care, or worry about them. They think they're invincible and don't realize the dangers of gangs and drugs. Police arrested another person suspected of killing one of my other students. He stopped coming to school quite some time ago. He died over $40 worth of marijuana. I thought it was going to be at least a few pounds. No, he got shot in the face for a bag of weed. The guy they arrested is a suspect in shooting someone else in the face and paralyzing another." I guess I had some verbal vomiting to do.

"I'm very sorry to hear that." Sharron still has a very grave expression of concern. "Do you want to talk about that some more?"

"No, it was just on my mind. My mom just sent me an updated video from the news." I shook my head as if to shift gears.

Sharron reads the paper in my file.

"Do you want to work on your grandmother, your father?" she asks.

"My father," I say decidedly. I cross and then uncross my legs.

"What would you say is the real issue?" Sharron's eyebrows go up, and then focuses me.

"Abandonment." I don't want to waste any time.

"And so what did you tell yourself as a result of this abandonment from your father? What did you start to believe about yourself, due to your father's abandonment?" Sharron asks, with her hand on her chin, giving me her full attention.

"That I wasn't good enough to be loved," I say, with some difficulty and a sob.

"Alright, now we're going to work on a positive mantra that you can remind yourself about this abandonment. What would you like it to be?"

"Umm.. that I am worthy of being loved?" I say with little hesitation and a shrug.

"Would you like to add a little something like 'and I love myself,'" Sharron asks. "Is that okay? Do you agree with that?"

"Yes, okay."

"Here, write it down on this card and take it with you," Sharron says as she hands over a pen and a 5 x 7-inch card to write on. I write it carefully, not in my usual messy writing. "On a scale of 0-10, how much do you believe that statement, that you deserve to be loved? Zero being, you don't believe it's true, and 10 being that you feel it is true," Sharron asks.

"Oh, about a six, I guess. I mean, I know it's true," I say.

"But how much do you *feel* is true?" Sharron asks.

"Yeah, I guess about a six." I *want* to confidently say ten, but I can't, not today.

"And what about your father's abandonment was so difficult?"

"My mother having to struggle so hard as a single mother just to provide," I say. "My mother had three jobs at one point, and I would only see her for about five minutes a day. Then I would go to *Tia* Rosi's, across the street. *Tia* Rosi would watch me every day, before and after school, then on weekends."

"Assign an image to that pain or that struggle. It could be a memory or a picture in your mind."

I can only think of the street on Griegos and 4th Street. I would cross it every day back and forth from our trailer to *Tia* Rosi's apartment. I could remember the ugly trailer we lived in at that time, the green and white one that got broken into. Still, my memory of the street seemed more vivid, crossing toward *Tia* Rosi's.

"Once you have the image in your mind, tell yourself the mantra, that you are worthy of love, and you love yourself. And do it with a smile on your face. There is something about the neurological way we remember things. It will be stored in your memory as something positive. Try it with your eyes closed."

I begin to repeat the mantra.

"I am worthy of being loved, and I love myself. I am worthy of being loved, and I love myself. I am worthy of being loved, and I love myself." I picture the street.

"I am worthy of myself and ..." I broke out in tears because that time was so hard only seeing my mom for minutes a day.

"Now go back to the exercise of See Out. Do that until the emotions subside, and your disturbance level is zero," Sharron gently says.

I go back to visually noticing the things around me, the rooster outside, and the plants in the room. My breathing becomes more regular.

"Are you back to zero disturbance?" Sharron asks and I nod.

"Let's go back to the image of your father's abandonment and start saying the mantra to yourself again," I repeat the process and break down in tears again. We repeat the See Out exercise until I've calmed myself down.

"When you feel overwhelmed, where do you feel the pain on a physical level?" Sharron asks.

"It's more in my chest," I say.

"Do you want to go back to the 'See Out' exercise, or continue with feeling the emotions?" Sharron asks. I take a few moments to consider.

"I want to continue with feeling the emotions."

"You're very brave to do that." Sharron's positive feedback, makes me feel more courageous.

I close my eyes and hold the image of the street and repeat the mantra. At about the fourth time, I didn't believe myself, and I started crying again.

"Where's the pain?" Sharron asks again. I move my hands further down from my chest to my stomach.

"Alright, now continue with the See Out exercise until you are back to zero disturbance."

I take less than a minute to regulate my breathing again, focusing on the present, and I become calm.

"Are you back to zero disturbance?" I nod my head.

"Our session is nearing an end, but I want you to continue to use the exercise twice a day for ten minutes, and as needed." Sharron gives me a script of the instructions and says we should schedule a time for two weeks later. We complete our financial transaction, and again, I say good-bye, feeling that the money was not a waste.

I step out to face the cold October air and take a breath. It smells like it's going to snow. I could use a drink.

Fall Break - Found on the West Side

It's Saturday morning on our four-day Fall Break in October. My very first thought when I opened my eyes was 'coffee!' I hadn't even sat up yet, and I was jonesing! I decided to make some herbal tea instead. When I open the door to my room, the house reeks of bacon. 'Ew, it smells like burning carnage.' I think to myself. My housemate must have made breakfast for his daughter. I hurry and make my tea and go back to my room.

I had a text from my mom.

"They found the two boys." She's talking about the boys that went missing, one of them our student. I immediately Google the local news on my laptop. The remains of both boys were found in shallow graves on the West Side. That's where bodies are often found in Albuquerque because there is a remote mesa out there. There's no housing and the earth is very sandy. I lay back on my bed, stunned.

I'm partly relieved that they found the boys. It's terrible that they're dead, but I'm sure their families couldn't sleep with them missing. At least they can have closure and have their bodies be laid to rest. I don't want to think about the torture they endured before they were killed. Whoever is responsible for this is still out there. This city is never safe. Never has been. My heart goes out to their families.

I sit back up. Should I go to the services? I haven't gone to any funeral services for any of our students. How many times I'm going to have to do it once I go to the first one? I know I'm in denial by not going, and not acknowledging the deaths, but for now, I'm okay with that. "He wasn't my student," I tell myself. I didn't even know him. I'll see when the services fall, and if other staff members go, I think, guiltily and lay back down.

Tears and Coffee Withdrawals

Today is a Monday In-service day, and the staff has meetings. We're back at school from fall vacation and we've gathered in the lunchroom first.

"What's today, Committee Friday or PLC Friday?" I ask Mr. Ridgeway. He sits there with his eyes closed but doesn't say anything. "Are you ignoring me on purpose?" I ask him.

"No," Mr. Ridgeway says, still with his eyes closed. "I need to reset." I assume he's imitating being a student.

"Do we need a seating chart?" Jim, the Dean of Students, asks with a devious smile. We laugh.

"What's your new class book this quarter?" Mr. Ridgeway asks me.

Refugee, I say. "Have you read it? It's kind of new."

"No. How's it going?"

"Great! The reading level seems just right and there's a lot of action. It's really interesting," I say. "You?" I ask.

Bless Me Ultima. Mr. Ridgeway replies while peering down at his newspaper.

"Oh, I like that book," I say.

Kimberly is talking to Ms. Baker about how her doctor wants her to go in every week for an ultrasound.

"Why?" Ms. Baker asks.

"Because I'm borderline 'old' and pregnant." I think she's in her mid 30's.

"Ah, just tape a Fitbit to your belly and download the information," Ms. Baker suggests. We laugh and walk across the hall to Mr. Ridgeway's class for our meeting. Dave's class is configured with four groups of four desks, and Simone, the principal, is at the front of the room.

"Welcome back, everybody. I hope you are rested from the short break," Simone announces. Her hair looks like it's still damp. "I'd like to start by going around by sharing a struggle and a positive that we had over the break. Go ahead and share with a partner, and then if anyone wants to share out afterward, we can have volunteers." Simone tags someone as her partner, and the room begins to fill with low murmurs.

After we share with partners, Mr. Leblanc shares. He speaks in a low, calm voice.

"My biggest struggle is shifting gears from Quarter 1 grading to Quarter 2 planning. That's always a rough change. My positive was the snow. I love the snow, and it was really unexpected."

I'm next to share.

"Laina and I are going to take a book-writing workshop. The instructor suggested we quit coffee, so I did. My struggle was the withdrawal symptoms. They ranged from headache and irritability to neck and muscle stiffness. When my roommate's daughter's sleepover included incessant piercing screaming, my thoughts moved toward homicide. When I realized I couldn't kill children, my thoughts then moved to suicide. Then I Googled how to quit coffee, and I learned that I have to wean myself off with black tea. My positive is that the worst of my coffee withdrawal is over! .. but I'm really excited about this book-writing workshop!"

Ms. Baker raises her hand. She has a strange pause before she begins to speak:

"I'm going to try to say this without crying. Through the break I kept wondering if the police were going to find Muhammad. Then I got the news that the bodies were found. And I can't help it, as much as that kid drove me up the wall, and was such a stinker, I... I miss him." Ms. Baker's voice cracks.

"Yeah, I'm sorry, I didn't want to be the one to bring him up at the start of our meeting," Simone admits while biting her bottom lip. We look at Ms. Baker to say more, but she can't. Mr. Ridgeway speaks up from another side of the room.

"Yeah, I had been thinking about him during the break, too, wondering if they were going to find these kids. Then I was here yesterday grading and ... I got to some of his work ..." Mr. Ridgeway pauses to keep himself from crying. "It just sunk in that ... he's ... gone." Kimberly reaches for a box of tissues and passes it down to Mr. Ridgeway. I am so grateful that the men here are not embarrassed to cry. To me, showing vulnerability is a sign of strength, especially in our society.

"I plan to have an assembly tomorrow during 2nd period to address the deaths of Muhammad and Adan. Adan was a student of ours who was gunned down this year from a drug deal gone bad. We are going to have a floating sub for coverage. If you or if a student needs to take a moment for yourself, or would like to talk about it. You're not required to play social worker. Listen, validate their feelings. Don't go into the speculation and graphic, gory details about the video, or the drug dealing. Just refer them to Felicia. We don't want to sweep our feelings under the rug. Questions?"

"Yes," Laina asks with her hand up from the other table. "Is there more we can do to stop the drug dealing?"

"You know, we do what the law allows us to do. We never caught Muhammad red-handed, so our hands were tied. His parole officer knew he was dealing. We do what we can." Simone continues, "We had another incident with a couple of students last weekend. The word is that Eddie was playing with a gun and accidentally shot Isaiah in the neck. Someone from the base heard the gunshot and called it in. Isaiah is at UNMH and is recovering. Jim and I are going to visit him in the hospital if anyone would like to join us. We are going to talk to both students and their guardians to see if they can return." There are low murmurs in the room and disappointment.

"So, we'll break out individually to plan today, and then we'll meet back to reflect and share out. Sound good?" The principal glances at the clock and keeps to the schedule.

I go into the lunchroom to fill my water canteen. Mr. Leblanc asks me,

"So, what is your book going to be about?"

"I'm going to call it 'Teacher, Unhinged,'" I smile.

"So it's a memoir?" Mr. Leblanc asks, but Mrs. Doyle answers instead of me, with a naughty smile on her face,

"No, it's actually a biography... about *you*, Mr. Leblanc!" We all burst out laughing.

"HA! HA! Good one, Linda!" I can smell the fresh pot of coffee.

"Oh, that coffee smells so good!" I say.

"It's terrible. You wouldn't want any Joselyn. It's poop coffee." Mr. Jones purses his lips out and shakes his head.

"Thanks, Jobin." I decide not to get any.

"I've been writing more lately," Mr. Ridgway tells me.

"Really? Cool, about what?" I ask.

"I'm kind of writing these journals to my sons. There are some things about growing up with my father that I don't want to repeat," Ridgway says.

"Oh! Well that's awesome that you are being cognizant of your parenting! I wish my dad cared about how he treated his children," I say, feeling moved.

At the end of the workday, I'm at my desk checking emails. There's an update from Felicia that she got a hold of Muhammad's mom. According to Muslim tradition, he was buried as soon as possible. So there will be no services. There will be a candlelight vigil at Oso Grande Park a week from today. I forwarded the email to my personal account, so I would have the name of the park. I think I'll go.

29

Heart-to-Heart With the Kids

When the kids come back from Fall Break I make a point of talking to them about Muhammad and Adan. They had both been killed by drug dealers. Apparently there was a Snapchat video. People said that you can hear someone telling the boys, 'Say you fucked up! And Muhammad is crying, 'I fucked up! I fucked up!' The video reportedly showed the boys bleeding from his joints. Savage.

When the bell rings I walk to the front of the class and sit on my tall stool.

"I'm glad to see your shining faces back from the break. I want you to know that there's going to be an assembly today. The gathering is to honor the lives of two students from our school who were both killed recently."

"I know there seems to be this natural dynamic between you and your parents when you become a teenager. You don't see eye to eye and you rebel against them and your teachers. But it doesn't have to be that way. Your parents and your teachers don't tell you 'don't do this and that' because we hate you. It's because we love you, and we're trying to protect you and prepare you for the future. I grew up in this city. I know what it is like. It's a dangerous city with a high crime rate. Your parents and I have been there. I went to Van Buren Middle School. One day I borrowed someone's jacket because it got windy. I borrowed it from a kid who was not using his because he was playing basketball. I put my hands in the pockets, and there was a little gun in there! I've been to the parties where there was drinking, drugs, and people with guns. Sometimes those people with guns pull them out and shoot, and bystanders get caught in the middle. This is not a safe city, so please know that we are on your side. We are here because we want to help you learn, so you can be successful in whatever you want to do. Whatever makes you happy, okay? Please remember that."

"On a separate note, the NRA, the National Rifle Association, says that schools would be safer if teachers packed heat. What are your thoughts? Would you want your teachers to carry?" I see lots of shaking heads.

"Noooo..." one student says out loud.

"Why not?" I ask.

"Cause, what if they got mad at you and pointed it at you?"

"You think we would do that?" I ask. "You know we've passed background checks?"

"Maybe! A teacher could be like, 'Why didn't you do your homework?'" He says with his fingers pointed like a gun.

"Oh my gosh, I don't think anyone would actually do that, but I wouldn't want to carry a gun at school. I'd be afraid a student would try to take it away from me," I say. "Alright, just wondering what you thought."

"This quarter we're going to start a new class book. It's called "The Secret Life of Bees by Sue Monk Kidd. It's my favorite book. But first, let's get started with your Bell Ringer..."

30

Therapy Session 3 - Abandonment and Elephant Butte

At the end of lunch, I admit out loud to my colleagues that I'm not looking forward to therapy tonight.

Mr. Jones hands me some coloring book printouts of the holidays to color. This is how we've been dealing with our stress lately. We often change the images to make them dark, murderous or crazy, with alcohol or drugs. I take the printouts and start sifting through the pile to find one. I change my mind and stand up.

"I'm going to tell Felicia," I say restlessly, and I walk out of the lunchroom.

I walked toward Felicia as the guidance counselor walked away from her.

"Felicia?" I say

"Yeah?" Felicia turns toward me.

"I'm dreading going to therapy tonight," I say anxiously. Felicia and I have a pretty open dialogue about everything.

"Oh, what is she having you do?" Felicia gives me a concerned expression.

"She has me hold an image in my mind of the worst part of my trauma, then say a mantra. I bawl my eyes out, then she has me go back to a mindfulness exercise until my disturbance is zero. Then we start all over again." The bell rings for the end of lunch.

"Oh, that sounds like Cognitive Behavioral Therapy."

"Yeah, whatever it is, it's hard. It's emotionally taxing!"

Felicia says something, but I can't hear her over the kids and have to go unlock my classroom.

"Tell me how it goes!" Felicia says louder.

"Yeah, I will!" I yell.

"It's good that you're doing that," Felicia says. I smile back.

At last, the bell rings for the end of 6th period at 6:00.

The kids leave for the day. A few say, "Bye Miss," as they hurry out the door.

I gather my things and rush out to my appointment. The sun starts to go down soon after six. Daylight Savings is coming soon when the sun will be down by 5:00. I hate that. It's the middle of October and it's always pretty darn cold. I get to my therapist's address on time as the darkness begins to envelop us. Sharron opens the door.

"Hi Joselyn, how are you doing?" Sharron says, smiling.

"Hi, good, good, thanks. Ooh, it's so cozy in here." I smell the fire going. I sit on the couch and take off my coat.

Sharron opens a file and reads one sheet of notes from our last visits.

"You did very well last time. Would you like to continue? Are you comfortable with that?" Sharron asks gently. I nod my head. She writes something down in my file.

"Yeah, I'm fine with that," I say, with some reluctance.

"Go to the exercise of having the image in your mind of the worst part of your trauma. While you do that, state the affirmation 'I'm worthy of being loved, and I love myself.'" Sharron smiles.

"Alright," I say, seated in the middle of the love seat. I close my eyes, take a breath, and repeat the mantra about fifteen times. Sharron interrupts.

"How did that feel? How much do you believe in that statement, on a scale of zero to ten?" Sharron asks. I keep my eyes closed.

"Umm, about an eight," I say, then open my eyes.

"Good! That's really good. Okay, now let's go to a positive image. Think of a time when you felt loved, and you also loved yourself." Sharron brightens up when she talks about it. I think for a while and then tell Sharron I have an image ready in my mind.

"What's the image of?"

"I remember a birthday party my friends had for me in LA. All of my good friends were there. We had such a good time, and I felt their love," I explain while moving my hands from between my thighs to each side of me.

"Hold that image in your mind and repeat the mantra again." Sharron guides me by repeating the mantra. I close my eyes and begin to say the mantra, and then tears come.

"I got an image of my friend who passed away back in May. I was thinking about him earlier. I miss him," I say while reaching for some tissue.

"Oh, I see, and did you grieve for your friend?" Sharron looks at me with concern again.

"Yes, I grieved," I confirm. "It happened in the summer."

"Did you have anything unresolved?" Sharron asks.

"Yes, I hadn't seen him in years. We were supposed to get together, but he got called into work. I miss him." I wipe away more tears.

"Let's go to the Feel exercise, where you close your eyes and say 'hear, feel, or see' depending on what you focus on." I do the exercise until my disturbance is zero. "Good, now let's go back to the exercise with the positive image. The one of your birthday. Repeat the mantra."

I close my eyes and say the mantra about twenty times. I picture my friends, Ursula and Betty, smiling and toasting. We lock eyes for every toast. I see my friend Mando, kissing my cheek while pulling me in for a picture. This is the second birthday party Mando makes it to. Steve is there. He's the one who organized the shindig and bought the dress I'm wearing. It was a beautiful dress, black with ruffles and bright colors. It reminds me of Frida Kahlo. I maintain these images of my friends. Wanting to feel their hugs. I miss them.

"Now how much do you feel like that statement is true on a scale of zero to ten?" Sharron asks.

"I'd say a nine," I say with my eyes still closed. Then I open them. Sharron smiles.

"That's good! Let's try it again." I'm able to repeat the exercise. I maintain the image in my mind, with only good feelings from it. Sharron asks me again how much I feel on a scale of zero to ten. I tell her I'm at a nine.

"Is there anything from keeping you from feeling a ten?"

Sharron asks, looking at the paper in front of her while tilting her chin toward me.

"No, it's the difference between knowing it and feeling it. I know it's true, I just don't feel it one hundred percent." I feel stuck.

"Alright, we have about twenty minutes left, is there anything else you would like to work on in that time?" Sharron asks me directly.

"How about the sexual trauma?" Sharron asks gently.

"Sure." I will never show anyone that I don't have the courage, even though inside, I don't want to talk about it.

"Tell me what happened, and I will check in with you about your disturbance level."

"I was seventeen, and my friends and I went to Elephant Butte Lake for Memorial Day weekend. My mom made me promise that I wouldn't drink and I agreed. We spent two days there. On the day we were leaving, we were gathering our things when Robert invited Jade and me over to a minivan. He gave us shot after shot after shot of vodka from a gallon bottle. I had no idea what my limits were. I had only had sips of alcohol before then. He flirt-chased me around the beach until we fell together in the sand kissing. He got me to the back of his truck, and I passed out. In my drunken stupor, he helped himself to me. I don't remember much, only waking up a couple of times with him on top of me. I can't understand how he could enjoy someone who was unresponsive? Unconscious. He ended up taking me back to my friends. My friends drove home to Albuquerque while I lay in the bed of the truck with a tarp over us. I don't even remember who was in the bed of the truck with me. I was still spinning when I got home. I threw up several times in my room."

"How did that experience make you feel?" Sharron asks.

"Worthless. I had planned on only sleeping with one man for all of my life. I planned on marrying my first love. He had joined the Army and was stationed in Germany. I had been faithful to him and Robert threw all of that away. I felt dirty and used. He took away the purity of my relationship. After that, I was sure my boyfriend wouldn't want me anymore. I told my best friend that Robert had raped me during Spring Break and her first reaction was to laugh. She didn't believe me. I ended up going out with her and a couple of guys one night when she was house-sitting for her uncle. She went with one of the guys into a bedroom and I was left with the other guy in the pool room. We were making out and when he started taking my clothes off, I kind of didn't care, since I was worthless. But when he started having sex with me, I started to regret it. I told him to stop and he said, 'Wait.' He finished and I felt even more worthless because he didn't use a condom. I was sure I had HIV by that point."

"How is your disturbance level now?" Sharron checks in.

"Zero," I say.

"Good, keep going."

"Well, to make things worse, the next year, when I was a senior, I had the same English class as Robert. The teacher sat us alphabetically by the last name. One semester by A through Z, the next, from Z through A. Both of our names start with the letter 'm' so either way, he either sat behind me or in front of me all year. It was a constant reminder of what he did to me."

"Well, that's it," I say, shrugging.

"Well, there seems to be either no disturbance or you have really repressed things very deeply. So I'm going to check in with you on our next session, okay?"

"Sure."

"I'll see you in two weeks then."

"Let's schedule the next visit through email," I say.

"Okay."

I put my jacket on, walk outside into the chilly breeze, and pull up my hood. When I get in my car I tell myself,

"Hey! You did pretty well tonight, you deserve a drink!"

31

Sibling Surprise

It's a Saturday in mid-October and I'm at home cleaning. I got a text from my oldest half-sister Marcella in Arizona. She's the one who was adopted out to a family at birth. She's married to an Anglo guy she met from Christian school. They have two biological kids together, along with their foster children. They usually have two to five foster kids with them at any given time. Marcella home-schools the younger kids. She's about 5'7, and her skin is a little darker than the rest of us half-siblings. She has black hair and brown eyes and a very caring heart.

The text from Marcella says:

"I sent my DNA to Ancestry, and I found two more siblings! They are full brothers! Call me when you can!" I literally scream out loud immediately from the kitchen. My heart starts beating and I try to regulate it while I call.

"Hello?" Marcella answers. I put her on speakerphone. "How did this happen? Tell me everything!" I'm beside myself. I make a drink, get my long thick sweater that has a hood, and go outside while she talks. It's chilly out, but I need the fresh air to hit me.

"Someone gave me an Ancestry kit as a gift, and I sent it in. Six weeks later, I got an email saying my results were in and to check them online. It said I was 30% Native American 40% from the Iberian Peninsula, and I had a connection with someone. It was a close connection, so I reached out to him. The site has a place where you can message people. He said all he knew was that he's adopted and was born in New Mexico, and his father is a famous singer. Joselin, we have a brother named Felipiano, and he has a full brother named Alvaro! We emailed each other through the website and exchanged information. We later spoke on the phone. He said that Alvaro is the oldest, and he is living in Germany with his new wife. They have no children. Felipiano lives in Irvine, California, with his wife and two-year-old son."

Our father has to know about them, I think. My sister continues.

"The boys grew up together in California," Marcella explains.

"Wow. So the brothers aren't twins?" There was supposedly a letter found from our dad's ex-girlfriend about twins back in the '80s. I'm confused. I shake my foot and swish the ice in my drink.

"No, they aren't twins. They're a year apart. Would you like to talk to Felipe? Marcella was already shortening his name, like she had known him forever. "He's the only one I've spoken to so far since the other one is in a different time zone," Marcella says.

"Yeah, I guess I would. What did you think of him?" I ask.

"He's great! I'm sure you'll like him," Marcella says without hesitation. In a few seconds, I get a text from her with his contact info.

"Does Joselin know?" I ask about my other older half-sister. I would have expected this news from her, somehow.

"Yeah, she knows. I told her this morning," Marcella says.

"Isn't she out of town?" I ask.

"Yes, she's on her way back from California right now on a plane."

I'm so shocked. When I get off the phone with Marcella I call my sister Joselin. She's disembarking from her plane in Albuquerque and has to call me back.

Eventually, Joselin and I rehash all that was reported by Marcella. We're both shocked, but not surprised. We wonder if these are the "twins" from the letter found by my dad's ex-girlfriend?

This means our father abandoned *two more* humans. I finish my drink and make another, then go outside again for more air. Jose is so disappointing. The alcohol and the chilled October air is just what I need.

32

End of Day - Cat's Milk

At the end of the day, a lot of the staff stand in two cheerleading lines and say good-bye to students by the exit. All the students have left the building.

"What are you going to bring to the potluck tomorrow?" Mrs. Doyle asks Mr. Jones, who's standing across from her.

"Me? I'm not bringing *smack* to the potluck! I'll bring pickle juice!" Mr. Jones says defiantly, pushing his finger in the air while pushing his chest forward.

"What? Why?" Mrs. Doyle asks.

"I'm tired of putting my all into potluck dishes, and no one else puts any effort in!" Jobin complains.

"I *love* the dishes you bring!" Theresa, the third math teacher, says.

"Ha! Ha! So you're bringing pickle juice?" Mrs. Doyle cackles.

"Yeah, you wanna bring cat's milk?" Mr. Jones says. He's making a pinching motion with his fingers near his nipples.

"Cat milk? Like, milk from a cat?" I question.

"Cat milk? I actually *have* cat milk!" Kimberly exclaims.

"You mean cow milk, right?" I say to Kimberly.

"No, I mean cat milk. I mean, it's got to be synthetic, right? But you can give it to a baby cat!" Kimberly's voice is cracking all over the place, loudly.

"Kimberly's bringing cat milk!" I say. "I'm bringing Obama Juice."

"What's Obama Juice?" Felicia asks.

"It's government-issued orange juice," Mr. Jones interjects with a straight face, and then smiles and shakes his head 'no.'

"No0... it's what President Obama has for breakfast instead of coffee. Since I've quit drinking coffee, I drink 'Obama Juice.'" I explain.

"*Former* President Obama," Mr. Jones interjects again.

"Stop ruining my life, Jobin! I can have whatever President I want to in the morning!" I yell dramatically, but jokingly.

"What are you going to be for Halloween, Joe?" Mrs. Doyle asks Mr. Leblanc .

"He doesn't do Halloween!" Ms. Baker says.

"Tell me where you live, I'm going to go trick-or-treating over there," Mrs. Doyle asks with a wicked smile. "I know you don't live far."

"I'm very close," Mr. Leblanc confirms quietly with a smile.

"Do you give out Halloween treats?" Ms. Baker asks Mr. Leblanc.

"Well, they don't come to my house anymore," Mr. Leblanc waves his hand and raises his eyebrows.

"They know!" Mr. Jones says. "I'm the grumpy old man on the block! Turn off my lights!" We laugh and then go off in different directions to pack up.

33

Candlelight Vigil With No Candles

I race home to bundle up after work. The candlelight vigil will be at a park. We're nearing the end of October, and there's snow on the ground from the last surprise snowfall.

I knew I'd be late, but I was sort of glad. I'm hoping to get there after the candles are lit. If the family goes, I want to show them support from the community, even though they're not from here. The sun is already down, and it's dark. At the same time, I'm a little reluctant to go. Anything could happen at this vigil. It's Albuquerque.

I pick my mom up first. When we get there, we notice there's a local police presence. That's good. Through the darkness I see a big crowd gathered toward one area of the park, but there are no candles. We park as close as possible and walk arm in arm toward the crowd, our feet crunching on the snow in the grass. Five policemen are huddled together talking. The large group is silhouettes of people. When I see any of them close up, they look like teenagers. I can hear somebody talking, not so loudly, on a microphone. It sounds like a young girl, maybe sixteen years old. Most of it inaudible, except for...

"But we have tonight, and we're all here. Thank you for being here tonight," The young voice finishes. Another female voice announces that someone else wants to speak about Muhammad. I can see the silhouette of a cameraman from a news station. The camera doesn't appear to be on.

Then someone else gets on the microphone. It sounds like a teenage male.

"Yeah, I met Muhammad like a few years ago, and we just started hanging out all the time. I taught Muhammad everything he knows, like, everything. And I feel guilty now, you know, like maybe it should have been me?" The teenage voice says.

"Oh my god, are you serious?' Let's go. I can't listen to this." I whisper to my mother. My mom agrees. "If his family is here, I'm sure they don't want to hear that either. Yeah, whoever that was *should* feel guilty and should have kept it to themselves." I'm angry. My mother and I return to the car, arm-in-arm, still crunching in the snow. Our breath billows out from our faces. We get back in the car.

"Can you believe that shit?" I say with anger. "I can't even. I shouldn't be surprised. What does he think this is? 'Get shit off your chest night?' If he taught Muhammad to deal drugs and Muhammad is gone, then he *should* feel guilty and it *should* have been him!" I roll down the window, so the frosty air hits my face. I'm livid, and my mom doesn't protest. I have her temper. Despite my being hot-headed, I drive much more slowly than I usually do. I stop at my mom's and thank her for going with me. She invites me in.

I decide to go in with her and say hi to my stepdad. He's listening to one of my favorite artists on the Internet, Santana. I make a mental note to get him more Santana music for either his birthday or Father's Day. Over the past few months, he's been helping me with things like flat tires or shopping for speakers. I blew one out in my Jeep. Stuff that I would expect a dad to do. I realize he's a great guy. He comes from a big family. His mother and father are now passed, so I think he's cherishing family in a new way and appreciating his role as a father.

When I get home, I make myself a drink, flip open my laptop and start on the next day's Bell Ringer question. I've been spending 3-4 hours to plan every night.

34

Lunchroom - Jazmine-Centric

Ms. Rivera, the art teacher, is talking when I walk into the lunchroom,

"Well, when the world revolves around *you*, you know, you get up when you get up!" She's probably talking about a student.

"That's a good transition to like geocentric, heliocentric..." Lombardi says to Ms. Baker, the science teacher.

"Jazmine-centric?" Ms. Baker finishes.

"Jazmine-centric, there's a science lesson waiting to be taught there!" Lombardi finishes with a smile, and Ms. Baker and Ms. Rivera chuckle. I fish a Snickers Mini out of a massive bowl of Halloween candies. Today is Halloween.

"First, I gotta get her to stop talking about religion in science class," Ms. Baker says.

"Oh wow," I say.

"Oh, is she the one that said 'Jesus rode a dinosaur'" Mr. Jones quips.

"What?" Lombardi appears to be confused.

"She didn't say that," Ms. Baker says and laughs.

"Oh, she was thinking it," Mr. Jones smiles and winks. "Jesus had two raptors."

Ms. Baker continues: "We were talking about the age of the world. I was going around the room letting everyone guess. Jazmine said, 'It's four thousand years old, I know it!' I was like 'dear god,' in her world, the dinosaurs co-existed with man. She knows it because Jesus told her so!" Ms. Baker squeals.

"You just asked for it with that question," Mrs. Doyle says, and we all laugh.

"So did anyone say 4.6 billion years?" Mr. Jones asks while pouring more coffee into his cup.

"Mohsin was the closest," Ms. Baker says while fishing out mail from her box.

"'Cause he's a heathen," Mrs. Boyle says (we all know he's a sweet Muslim boy).

"Does he speak in a Russian accent in your class?" Ms. Baker asks me.

"Noo," I say, confused.

"It's funny when he says 'Jesus Christ,'" I say.

"Catholics say 'Allah,'" Mr. Jones offers. Some of the folks of New Mexico say it as slang, but I'm not sure of the origins, I've been wondering if the roots were Muslim.

The bell for first period beeps.

"I still don't understand why it's only *my* class that Mohsin is using the Russian accent," Ms. Baker says, while I shake my head we go out of the room from separate doors.

35

Therapy Session 4 - New Siblings, Abandonment

The forecast calls for a massive snowstorm tonight. I rush after work to get to my therapy session on time. The air's crisp, and temperatures are in the 30's.

Sharron opens the door,

"How are you?" I say, because I don't want to be impolite.

"Doing fine, thanks," Sharron answers as she settles into her chair comfortably.

"So, how was the week? Is there anything you want to report back?" Sharron always speaks in a calm, deliberate manner.

"Um, I practiced the See Out exercise. I like that one. I said the mantra in the mirror." I felt like I was being quizzed and had not done my homework.

"Good! How did it feel?" Sharron stares right into my eyes as she asks.

"Good, it felt good." I had only practiced that morning before my appointment.

"So what do you want to work on today? Do you want to continue with the negative image and the positive affirmation?" Sharron asks.

"Well, I've recently learned that my dad fathered two other boys that were given up for adoption. We found each other through ancestry.com."

"Well, that's interesting," Sharron says with a surprised expression on her face.

"Yes, he lives in Irvine, California, and the other one lives in Germany. He married a woman from there. I'm so glad my sister found them," I say. "But it makes me angry that my father abandoned yet two more children. It's disturbing and infuriating. He abandons kids like we're puppies!"

"Would you say this is related to what we were working on?" Sharron asks.

"Yeah, it compounds it," I admit.

"Let's work with the negative image and the positive affirmation," Sharron says.

"Sure, we can do that." I didn't think I would feel to a ten, but I'd try. I envision the negative image of my father being absent. My mother working three jobs, and we're always crossing the street to *Tia* Rosi's. I imagine my father getting the same woman pregnant twice within a year and not wanting those kids either.

He wants all the fun, but none of the responsibilities. Like a teenager.

I keep repeating the mantra as those images and others float into my mind. I believe what I'm saying because I do love myself. I take care of my needs and desires, like no man or boyfriend has or could. For example, tonight we're expecting a snowfall. I want to treat myself by getting takeout from my favorite restaurant. Of course, I'm worthy of love, I have it all around me. Yes, I love myself.

"How accurate does that statement feel to you now?" Sharron interrupts my thoughts. I keep my eyes closed and say,

"About an eight."

"Great, that's wonderful! Now let's try the image of feeling loved. Repeat the mantra with the image of feeling loved and celebrated in your mind."

I begin the process again, this time with the past birthday party in my mind.

"I am worthy of being loved, and I love myself," I say about twenty times. Then Sharron asks again: "How valid does that statement feel to you?"

"About a nine," I answer, but keep my eyes closed, then peek when Sharron starts talking again.

"Alright, now let's go back to the negative image and the mantra," Sharron instructs. I begin to reinforce the idea in my mind that I am actually worthy of being loved and able to love myself.

"How sincere does that statement feel now, Joselyn?" Sharron asks.

"I feel like a ten." I peek at the facial expression that Sharron gives.

"That is excellent! Let's do it again to reinforce it," Sharron says. I repeat the exercise.

"How accurate does that feel now?" Sharron asks after I repeat the mantra about twenty times.

"I still feel like it's a ten." I feel like I'm being honest with myself. I can't see why the statements wouldn't be true.

"That's wonderful. Let's change the image back to the positive image and repeat the mantra." I follow her directions, and when Sharron asks me how true it feels, I repeat that it feels like a ten. Very true.

"Alright. That's really good. We have a few more minutes. Are their other things concerning you that we should start working on?" Sharron opens up a dialogue. I sit and think for a moment.

"No, my grandmother and father are the big ones."

"In our next session, we'll work on your grandmother."

"Sounds good," I say with a smile. I get up and put my jacket on. "Thanks!"

She opens the door. Oh yeah, snow is coming. It's in the air. Tonight is Halloween. Halloween drink?

36

Writing Guidelines

It's a Saturday in the beginning of November. I'm at home mixing vanilla non-dairy creme into my coffee.

After tasting my coffee, I walk down the dark hall to my room to check emails on my laptop. I let in a little light by pulling up the cloth blinds less than halfway. It's about eight a.m., and the sun has broken over the mountain.

There's an email from the lady I'm going to take a book writing workshop with, Georgina. I met her through Laina. She and Laina live in the North Valley near the Rio Grande River. They're fellow beekeepers. She's offering us this workshop and it starts in a couple of months. It's something I've always wanted to do, and the opportunity just presented itself. It's not some big workshop with a convention-full of people that I don't know. It's just the three of us.

On the first day of school, when Laina introduced herself as the Special Education Teacher and a beekeeper, I knew I wanted to be her friend immediately. I thought she was so cool. Laina's about fifty, has medium length wavy brown and white hair that she wears in a bun. She's about 5'6," wears glasses and has a flurry of happy brown freckles on her face. She doesn't wear makeup; she's an 'au-natural' kind of hippy chick. She takes care of herself by being active physically and mentally. Her ten-year-old son keeps her busy too. Laina's the most patient and down-to-earth person on the planet. She can genuinely work with any kid. I have so much to learn from her. I've never seen her get upset with a student. I attribute most of it to her personality. She's really easy to talk to. I love her because she has a hilarious sense of humor. Laina has her son, bees, chickens, ducks, two small dogs, a hedge-hog, and a few turkeys.

Georgina has about a hundred different plants and flowers in her yard. She has bees, chickens, two big dogs, and a husband. A tall guy with a chiseled face who is a computer programmer for work and a carpenter, for fun. They have a small adobe structure with "His and Hers" art rooms, separate from the house. One side is for her husband to do woodwork, and the other is Georgina's writing den. Georgina is about 5'5, with a slim build. She's probably in her mid forties and has a creamy, soft complexion. She has straight blonde hair and almond-shaped blue eyes.

Georgina gave Laina and me guidelines, a schedule, and a list of supplies to bring for the workshop. It read:

"To access the right/whole brain, it is better to not have coffee in your system. Coffee puts the brain into a beta brainwave pattern. Beta brain wave is the left brain, strategy, and doing aspect. We want to be in theta, gamma, or alpha states. This allows us to relax and access our body's wisdom. It helps us reach into our creative, and multidimensional aspects. The reason I'm sending this email to you weeks before our first meeting is to allow yourself to wean down. If you are unable to, or don't want to wean yourself from coffee, please inform me when you get here. I can adjust the day accordingly."

"No coffee?!" I think to myself. I don't know how true this is, but it's worth a try to get the creative juices flowing. My first reaction is slight panic. Then I tell myself I can do this. *Si se suede*! I've already weaned myself down to one cup of coffee a day for the past two years. It should be no problem to quit now... Well not *right now*. I had already started my cup today. I take another sip and savor it as it warms my belly.

Death to the Cell Phone

Today is Monday. First and second periods go fine, except for not finding coverage to go to the restroom. I hold it until after second then run during passing period.

Third period, Jayson asks me for a pencil. It's an everyday thing. I don't bother to ask where the last one I gave him is. It's useless. Jayson does this snorting sound as he wipes his hand up from his nose and into his hair. Sometimes I see him pick his nose. I feel like I work in a middle school with a bunch of mocosos. Jayson is't working and is on his phone. I tell him to put his phone away. He refuses to put it away and refuses to do work. I ask him if he wants to charge his phone in Charlie's office, but he tells me 'Oh hell no,' again. I tell him that it's not appropriate language. He ignores me so I send him to ISS.

"And you lose your participation points for the day, okay." I remind him.

For fourth, Fabian glances at his phone about a hundred times.

Fifth period Gilbert comes to me with a permission slip for a field trip. I explain that I'm not going to sign it because he's still working on an Incomplete for last quarter and his attendance hasn't been good. After a couple of minutes he grabs his backpack and walks out of the classroom. I ask him where he's going. He says,

"Home, fuck it." Way to rise to the occasion. He's too far to talk to and I don't want to yell, so I shake my head and go back into my class.

Lunchroom - What's That App?

As soon as I walk into the workroom for lunch, Ms. Baker starts tells me:

"Mohsin gave me a pass from the Speech Therapist in the middle of class today. I couldn't help but think, 'Well, if you'd stop talking in a Russian accent, they wouldn't put you in Speech Therapy!' But I knew I couldn't say that!" Ms. Baker admits, and we laugh.

I'm washing my hands when Mr. Jones and Mr. Leblanc come in.

"My observation went well. I mean, no one got in a fight or anything," Mr. Jones says. "Not like last year."

"Oh yeah, you had a fight last year!" Mr. Leblanc remembers.

"Yup! I'm always on my game, and my game is always off," Mr. Jones says.

Jim and Mr. Ridgeway walk in.

"We're going to have to check the cameras," Jim says.

"Check the cameras for what?" I ask.

"Come in the bathroom, smell this!" Mr. Ridgeway says, smiling while waving me over to the hallway.

"What? Which bathroom?" Ms. Baker asks, already knowing they're talking about marijuana smell.

"The *teacher's* bathroom!" Mr. Ridgeway and Mr. Lombardi say together.

"Oh, no," I say. "Pam and I were wondering if we smelled that from the teacher's bathroom the other day. We were joking about it!" I say.

"What are we supposed to do if we suspect that a student is high?" Ted Chavez, the new special education teacher asks me.

"Tell Jim," I say.

"He'll put them in his office. Lets 'em cook in there for a while," Mr. Jones explains. "Then he comes back and smells the room."

Ted started eating with us in the lunchroom again because no one went to his "tutoring hours" for lunch. I knew that would happen.

I'm munching a carrot with ranch dressing.

"Do you guys follow Owl Kitty on Tinder?" Mrs. Doyle asks.

"WHAAT??" I say with a perplexed expression. Mrs. Doyle is married. Explosive laughter bursts. She corrects herself,

"Not Tinder, I mean Insta!"

"Little Freudian slip there!" Lombardi chuckles. "Do tell!"

"Are you on the Ashley Maddison?" Mr. Leblanc asks Mrs. Doyle.

"What the hell's that, Joe?" Mr. Jones asks.

"That's where people go to have affairs if they're married," Mr. Leblanc says, proud of himself because he knows something regarding technology that the younger teachers don't know.

"How do *you* know that, Joe?" Mr. Jones asks.

"In L.A., I swear, billboards advertise 'Ashley Maddison', can you believe it?" I ask rhetorically. "The picture is the back of a woman and the front of a man in a hotel room."

"Ugh, is it Friday yet?" Mrs. Doyle laughs, her hand on her forehead.

"Nope. It's only Tuesday, my friend,"Mr. Leblanc says.

"Is it going to be Committee Friday or PLC Friday?" Ms. Baker asks.

"It's Potluck Friday," Mr. Ridgeway lies. He tries to trick people into bringing in a hot dish on Fridays.

"Nooo, it's not. Those are at the end of the month." Mr. Leblanc was on the "Sunshine Committee" for years. The Sunshine Committee is in charge of birthdays and potlucks.

"Can you pass the salt, Joselin?" Mrs. Doyle asks me. The salt is always by either one of us.

I finish my lunch, grab a corn chip from a bag on the table and start munching. I peer out to the student lunchroom.

"What's Charlie giving out in the Commons Area?" I ask, to no one in particular.

"Pictures. Pictures came in," Mr. Jones says. Then Mr. Jones changes to a Brooklyn accent and says, "'Heya's ya ugly mug, kid,'" while pretending to hand out pictures. Lombardi and I chuckle.

November IEP Meeting

It's fifth period. Tonantzin, the new educational assistant that I have for 1st says she's here to cover me for an IEP meeting. It's for special education students. It stands for Individualized Education Plan. I often go to these meetings to report on how a student is doing in my class. The special education teachers, I came to realize, are usually not in the classroom with you. They are too busy with meetings, IEPs and documentation.

I run down the hall since I'm already late. I found the meeting in Mr. Ted Chavez's office. He's a Chicano from Taos. He's in his 50's, with a receding hairline. He's medium height, dark-skin and dresses professionally. When you're near him, he smells like cologne and cigarettes and sometimes gum.

I gently knocked on Mr. Chavez's door and let myself in. I shake Mr. Akbar's hand and introduce myself. I say hi to my student.

"I have a chair right here for you, Ms. Martinez." Mr. Chavez motions toward the chair.

I always like to start these meetings with a parent on a positive note, as our principal does.

"Well, Mohsin is doing well in my class, he..." I start to say but get interrupted as I put my elbow on the table.

My student's father dumps on him.

"No, no. He's not doing good. His reading scores have dropped, dropped, dropped the last few tests he took. I don't know what he's doing. Reading books that are easy for him. He needs to advance in English. He's in, I don't know what math he's in. I teach Algebra in high school, and he's not doing Algebra. He's doing general math. He measures areas and circumference. I don't know. He should be in Algebra 2. I don't know what he's doing. He's playing around."

Mohsin has his head tilted down and sometimes nods to agree.

"Well, Ms. Martinez has some things here that she wanted to share," Mr. Chavez says to us and hands me the survey we had gone over together. "Go over the things you marked 'Sometimes A Problem.' He nudges me. I feel like a deer in headlights. How am I supposed to go over problems, after an emotional beating like that?

"Well, umm... You know, we should make a goal to raise the score by finding some books with higher reading levels to challenge Mohsin. What do you think?" I turn to Mohsin. He still has his head tilted down, nods yes. He usually reads comic books. "We'll find a more challenging book, and we plan to test you again next quarter. But other than that, Mohsin is usually on task. I don't have to redirect him," I try to reassure the father.

"He needs to try harder. I don't know. I don't care. It has to come from you, you understand?" He glances at Mohsin. "I don't know, he wants to be a movie producer, I don't know. He needs to be reading a book a week, something like that," Mr. Akbar spits out.

"Maybe we can put some time limits? Like a book every few weeks or something?" Mr. Chavez suggests.

"We can make goals, sure," I say and face Mohsin. Then I look at Mr. Chavez like I'm pleading 'Please get me out of here!'

"Well, thank you, Ms. Martinez. She has to get back to her class." Mr. Chavez read my mind! Thank you, Mr. Chavez!

I walk back to my classroom. That was so hard to hear. I know it comes from a place of concern, but it's hard to listen to parents say stuff like that.

I excuse myself, but when the bell rings for the end of the day, I peek back in there, and the dad is still tearing into his son. It's a hard call. Most kids need some of that and don't get it. These kids are respectful and kind. It's not my call. Even though I'm pretty sure I'm going to have a little conversation to help Mohsin process it. It may not be my place, but I kinda feel like a conversation should be had. I don't know, I'll mull it over the weekend. My job never ends.

BUT, now I can have a glass of wine when I get home! ...Ugh, and think of another Bell Ringer.

Sibling Phone Call

Felipiano and I first emailed, then texted. We agreed to FaceTime on the Wednesday before Thanksgiving. I want to do it from my mom's house, I'm not sure why. I text him first to ask if it was a good time to talk. He texts back, yes. I'm a bit nervous, so I pace the backyard. It's a sunny day for November, but still a bit brisk. "What if this opens up a Pandora's Box of some sort? What if he's crazy?" I think to myself. I FaceTime my half brother in Irvine, California, anyway.

"Hello, Sister!" Felipiano's friendly face beams through the phone. He has bushy black eyebrows, a welcoming smile, and dark hair, slightly balding. His eyes and smile remind me of my sister Joselin's.

"Well, hello," I say in a friendly tone.

"Nice to meet you over the phone and hear your voice!" Felipiano says pleasantly.

"Likewise! How are you doing?" I ask. "How are Taryn and Angus?" I ask. He had already told me his wife and son's names over email.

"They're good! They're here," he says.

"Say hi to them for me."

"I will!" Felipe answers and winks over to someone.

We talk about everything from the weather, his job is, where he grew up, and about his brother. We also talk about our diets and medical issues. When he tells me he has hay fever,

"Oh, you get that from dad." It was the first time I had referred to our mutual father as "dad." It felt weird but bonding at the same time.

"He suffers from severe hay fever, like every morning. He's complained about it a lot," I say.

"Oh, that's interesting," Felipiano comments. "Are there any health issues that you have? If you don't mind me asking," Felipiano asks respectfully.

"Not at all, other than asthma, I had some sort of bladder operation as a child. I was about three years old. I was a patient at Bernalillo County Medical Center, where Joselin's mom worked for a long time. That was the second or third time I had ever seen our father. He visited me in the hospital after the operation and brought me a stuffed animal. It was a big rat. If only I had known what 'foreshadowing' was back then!" We laugh.

"It was the first time I had met Joselin's mother," I say.

"Oh yeah?"

"How did you and Joselin end up with the same name?" My brother finally asks.

"I'm not sure if we chalk that up to keeping secrets or having a big ego, or both. Both of our mothers named us after our father, Jose. But Jose never told my mom that he already had a daughter christened Joselin, so my mom named me after him too. Except, I spell my name with a 'y,' and she spells hers with an 'i.' And Joselin's mom named her after him out of love. Mine named me after him out of hate and resentment, so he couldn't deny me. I'm his clone," I admit. "Did you ever see that 80's sitcom 'Bob Newhart?'" I ask.

"Um.. no, that might be before my generation," Felipe laughs. I sound like I'm off-topic.

"Bob Newhart ran a hotel on the show. And three hillbillies came looking for work, but only one would talk. When the hillbilly would meet someone, in a hillbilly accent, he would say: 'This is my brother Daryl, and this is my other brother Daryl.' It always reminded me of Joselin and me. I hate introducing myself to people when I'm around her. She hates it more. I should find a video clip of it and send it to you," I say, afraid I'm not making any sense.

"No way, that sounds great!" Felipiano laughs.

"So tell me how it was that you were adopted." I walk all around the quarter-acre yard, in various patterns, like a bee.

"My biological grandmother asked her best friend if she knew anyone who would want to adopt a boy. The friend asked her daughter because the daughter and her husband couldn't have kids and they said yes. So about a year later, my biological mother was pregnant again by Jose. Again, my biological grandmother asked my adoptive parents if they wanted another boy. They explained I was a full brother to Alvaro, and they agreed!"

"I'm grateful to Jose and my birth mother for whatever paperwork they signed or whatever they did to get us adopted. Al and I had a good life growing up," Felipiano says in a way that I believe him.

"That's good! It's even better that the two of you were not separated," I say while kicking at some dead grass.

"Totally," Felipiano agrees.

"So, you have no idea who your birth mother is?" I pry.

"No, I don't know much about that at all," Felipiano admits. "Just that she's from New Mexico."

"Well, I don't know if Joselin has mentioned to you, but Jose may have twins that are still unaccounted for. We don't know who they are or where they are, but we think they ended up being given up for adoption too. Our father's ex-live-in girlfriend, Jean, found a letter to Jose from a woman named Maria. In the letter, she said, "Jose, the *twins* look like you,""

"Oh, wow," Felipiano says, with an expression of surprise.

"Yeah, there's been no confirmation from anywhere else that these twins exist. And I'm not sure when the letter was written. It was around the time when Jose drove a pink Cadillac." I crack a smile.

"Oh, yeah! I've heard of this pink Cadillac! Haha!" Felipiano laughs.

"Have you spoken to Jose?" I ask.

"No, I haven't," Felipiano replies, still, in a lighthearted tone.

"Are you going to?" I feel a slight panic coming on.

"I don't know. I haven't really decided. I haven't been completely closed off to the idea of it either. But only if he would feel comfortable with it. What do you think? How do you think he would react?"

"Uh, well... *I* don't talk to him. I haven't spoken to him in about three years. No, I'm lying. I saw him at Joselin's mom's funeral. He said hi to me, and unexpectedly hugged me after the service, but I was trying to avoid him. I planned on offering to shake his hand to say 'sorry for your loss,' but he hugged me before I could get anything out. In the church I saw that he sat separately from everyone else, with the musicians. To be honest, I was so annoyed by that. Why couldn't he sit and mourn the loss of his daughter's mother, like everyone else? No, he had to show how special he is, off to the side with the musicians. He has to show off his voice any opportunity he gets. It couldn't just be about Joselin's mom. He had to bring attention to himself. He does have a damn good voice, but I was just a little annoyed by that. Anyway, I haven't spoken to him because he... I don't think he ever wanted to *be* a father. I can't force people to do something they don't want to do, so I gave up."

"Aaahh, I see."

"What are your hobbies? What kind of music do you like?" I ask.

"I listen to all kinds of music. My wife has been producing film shorts, so when she's done, she'll give them to me to score. I've been having a lot of fun with producing the music for them. I've been using a computer program called Nuendo to produce some sounds," Felipiano says.

"NO WAY. Shut the front door! That is fantastic! I do something similar. I used to work in radio production for many years. Then, my music-producer friend, he produced Richard Marx's "Right Here Waiting" song. He convinced me to get Logic Pro. It's a Mac-based program. I used it for about two years for radio production. Then started playing with the music production side of the program. I've had so much fun with it!" I was bursting to share this with my new friend. Felipiano shares the excitement.

"Cool, cool! I've heard of that program."

"Yeah, it is a lot of fun."

"At what point in your life did you find out that your biological father was a musician?" I ask.

"Well, our mother had always told us that we were adopted and that our father was a famous musician from New Mexico."

"It's so amazing you found us!" I say excitedly.

"Yeah! Someone had given me a DNA kit as a gift one year and soon after, someone else gave me another one. Would you like the second one?"

"Really? Wow, uh... yeah! Thanks!"

"Alright, text me your address and I'll send it to you," My brother says.

"Amazing! I've always been curious to find out my exact genealogy! Thanks so much!"

"Yeah, sure! Hey sis, so my battery is running low. But before I let you go, I wanted to tell you that my wife is showcasing a short at a film festival in Las Cruces. It's next month in December, and we plan to go. I don't know if you would be able to, but it would be great to meet you in person!" Felipiano says, smiling.

"Ooh, fantastic! When is it, December what?" I ask.

"Twenty-seventh through the first." Felipiano sounds like he's scanning a calendar.

"Oh, that's during our Winter Break, it's perfect!" I say excitedly. "I'd be glad to go!"

Before I hang up with my kindred brother, we agree to keep in contact via email and to send each other some sample music and videos until we see each other.

I report everything back to my mom. I can't believe I can have so much love for someone I had never met before! He felt like a long lost twin!

When I get home I pour myself a glass of wine.

I'm happy about having siblings. It's just sad to know our father abandoned seven of us.

What scares me the most, is how much I'm like my father. I don't leave children, I've just been more careful than him. But I'm in my 40's. It's not going to happen now. But, like him, I've never wanted them. I'm terrified of being a parent. First of all, I'm not sure if life is such a wonderful "gift" to give to anyone. Second of all, I can't find a decent enough man to trust with being a good father. There's the fear of abandonment by whomever I chose to be a dad. All I saw around me, single mothers. Even when women are married, they are often parenting alone. All the guys I've dated have been beautiful liars. I obviously need to stop being so vain (like my father). I have too much fear. Fear of what the environment might be in the future. Fear of making mistakes. Fear of losing my temper. Fear of losing their life. Fear of them having difficulties. Or even fear of being lazy, like my stupid uncle. There are too many variables that are uncontrollable.

"I just don't know how to get out of this funk," I say out loud to myself and take another sip.

Writing Workshop

It's the weekend of Thanksgiving Break and our writing workshop finally arrives. We had agreed on a vegan potluck lunch.

We meet at ten in the morning and would have lunch around one.

It's late November so Georgina lights a fire in the small fireplace and we talk about what we want to write about. Then Georgina has a right-brained exercise for us to do, and a writing exercise. We work seamlessly for hours then stop for lunch.

Our lunches are nourishing to the body and the soul. I cherish those private conversations.

As time moves on in our writing processes, Georgina says she will give us guidance on where to go next. Georgina has tools for us to get started and ways to stay on track. I won't give away the things women do when women create, but it's one of the most empowering things I've ever done for myself. This is healing my pain.

American Medal

Jarrod walks in with a paper bag. He's the new math educational assistant. He's a tall, thin Native American man, about 5'11". He's very kind and extremely helpful.

There are people gathered when he pulls out a few envelopes and a blue box with gold insignia. Inside of it, was a second box, a blue velvet one. Jarrod opens that one and pulls out a thick round shiny coin that is about 7 centimeters in diameter.

"It's my father's." We all gasp. He places the coin in my hand, and my hand is weighed down by it. It says "Navajo Code Talker" across the top. Imprinted on it, is an insignia. It's what's on the famous photograph of two Native American men, Code Talkers. Between them, an old radio. On the back of the coin in the middle, is a shield, which represents twins, Jarrod tells us. The shield has two tablets next to each other, one with horizontal lines across it and a frame with feathers coming out of it. Across the back states, "WWII" and "USMC." Across the bottom, in Diné, it says that the Diné language was used as a weapon.

There's a letter and a booklet published and signed by Senator Heinrich of New Mexico. It said how honored he was in playing a part in getting Jarrod's father the medal he deserved. I read the booklet and started crying. Jarrod's father never saw the book or the coin. He was supposed to receive it in 2001, but due to health issues, Jarrod's father, Adolf, couldn't attend the ceremony. About a year later he passed.

The book said the government kept the code and the Code Talkers a secret until 23 years after the war. Imagine, 23 years later! The booklet went on to say that the senator had first called the U.S. Marine Corps to find the medal. They confirmed that Adolf was in the service, but did not have the coin and referred the Senator to the U.S. Mint. When the Senator's office called the Mint, they said they didn't have it. The senator's office then tried to find who the curator was for the ceremony when the government first distributed the medals. Someone had the last name, but no first name. They finally found the organizer, and he said that it should have gone back to the mint. They called the mint again, and fortunately, they found it! Awarding the medal could only be done by the President of the United States or the Speaker of the House. The Senator worked with Speaker Ryan to get the medal issued. Senator Heinrich had to go to the mint, under armed guard, and sign for the emblem. He was under strict orders to personally give it to Jarrod, and that's what they did in 2008.

Jarrod also has a picture that was hand-drawn by his father. It's a replica of the photo of the U.S. Military men lifting the flag in Iwo Jima, except he made the features on the men appear more Native than can be seen in the photo. What a treasure!

Jarrod let me share all of this with my students.

I shared the story and let them hold the medal. I told them that they'd never see a medal like this for the rest of their lives. There are only a few Code Talkers who are still alive.

Jarrod said that he had never known that his father was in the war. His father had the traditional Native way of thinking and living. When a man is in war, he is in war, and when he is not in combat, he leaves war behind and does not talk about it. Jarrod said his dad never joined any Veterans groups or went out drinking with his war buddies. He only spoke of it once. Adolf said it was his first time in Okinawa. He saw a Japanese man, face to face for the first time. He yelled at him to get out of here. Jarrod's father wondered whatever happened to that man; if he had a family, or if he survived the war.

43

Lunchroom - Math Lesson: Six Divided by Zero = ?

Mr. Jones is talking to Lombardi in the lunchroom when I walk in. I get my lunch bag out of the refrigerator and listen in. Mr. Ridgway, Ms. Baker, Mrs. Doyle, and Mr. Leblanc are in the room.

"We're saying that anything divided by zero is the number you started with," Mr. Jones says.

"What's six over six?" Lombardi asks.

"Six, over six? Equals, one," Mr. Jones responds.

"Okay, so how can six over one equal six over zero?" Lombardi asks.

"Because zero would be one!" Mr. Jones responds. "I've been trying to tell you this for two years," Mr. Jones tells Lombardi while throwing his hands up.

"Last year you said dividing by zero was Jobin," Lombardi says.

"I know mathematically that six divided by zero is zero, but I think six divided by zero should equal six," Mr. LeBlanc says.

"I'm not going as far with the theology that zero equals Jobin. But I don't think that grouping by zero equals the whole of what you are asking to group," Mr. Ridgway puts his two cents in. I stay quiet, it's math.

The other math teacher, Mrs. Doyle, walks in.

"Run, Linda, run!" Ms. Baker warns her immediately.

"Linda, either help or run," Lombardi says as he covers his mouth with a napkin and chews his bite of a turkey sandwich.

"Well, you could use help because you're not doing a very good job," Ridgeway tells Lombardi.

"I'm doing a fantastic job!" Lombardi says.

"I think there's more of us on Jobin's side," I chime in.

"Just 'cause he's charismatic and thinks quickly doesn't mean he's correct," Lombardi protests.

"Doesn't it?" Mr. Jones retorts with a devious smile.

"If you have Jocelyn, and you divide her zero times, you still have *one* Jocelyn." Mr. Jones gives another example.

"It makes so much sense!" Mr. Ridgeway says with his eyebrows up.

"No, it does not." Lombardi still disagrees while shaking his turkey sandwich at Jobin.

"Drink the Kool-Aid!" Mr. Ridgeway pushes. "It's cold, blueberry ... with *a little bit* of bleach." We all laugh.

"Is it going to be Committee Friday or PLC Friday?" Mrs. Doyle asks, scrolling on her phone.

"It's Potluck Friday!" Mr. Ridgeway lies and smiles. We eat quickly and soon, the bell rings.

Mr. Leblanc taps me on the shoulder and then throws his wadded up napkin into the trash can.

"What?" I ask.

"You're not even going to watch?" Leblanc asks.

"I don't care!" I exclaim. He thinks I care if he makes his trash in the wastebasket.

"You're supposed to be cheerleading. That's your gender role," Mr. Leblanc says jokingly, trying to get a rise out of me.

"Oh, please!" I protest.

"Oh my God, I can't believe you went there!" Pam says, putting her phone in her pocket. Mr. Ridgeway laughs.

"You'd better ask Lombardi to cheerlead for you," I say. We go to class while Lombardi stays behind to finish his sandwich. Lucky brat has a 4th-period prep, which means he can take his time eating.

New Girls

Two unfamiliar girls walk into my 4th-period class after lunch. It's my Leadership class.

"Hi, are you two new?" I extend my hand out to one student and then the other to shake their hands.

"Yes," the half African American student responds and shakes my hand. The European American girl with freckles squints and shakes my hand. She barely touches me, like she might get germs.

"What are your names?" I ask.

"Dina," the half African American girl says. Dina is short and petite. She has curly hair that she wears in a pineapple ponytail, above her head.

"Brianna," the European American girl responds. Brianna is taller than me, about 5'7". She has long, straight pumpkin-colored dyed red hair past her shoulders.

"Well, nice to meet you. I'm Miss. Martinez. You're starting a few weeks before the end of Quarter Two, but any work you do now will count towards Quarter Three, okay?" I say. They nod their heads. "Go ahead and sit where you want. If you need any notebooks or folders, there are some up there on that table. Feel free to take what you need." I go back to my post at the door. The two whisper with each other and giggle.

When the bell rings, I facilitate the group's work on their projects. Students get busy.

In the middle of class, I overhear Brianna using abusive language towards Dina. She's telling Dina that she's stupid. I tell her we don't use that language in the classroom.

Brianna raises her voice at me and says,

"I can say whatever I want to her!"

I tell her that if she can't be respectful, she's going to have to leave the class. She snaps back that she can say whatever she wants to whoever she wants. I tell her to leave.

"No. I'm not leaving," she says, staying in her seat.

I scramble to send Jim an email. I'm not going to physically try to remove her, so I tell her then she'll have to be kind and continue on. I'm hoping Jim will come to save me. I ask Dina to move to another seat so they would stop touching and slapping each other. Dina complies. I write up a disciplinary referral for Brianna for non-compliance and being argumentative.

It's Wednesday and we have a guest teacher from a local health care organization.

When our guest came, Brianna put her earbuds in and put her head down for the rest of the class. Headphones are not allowed. But I'm willing to make an exception for this demon child who doesn't know how to behave on her first day of school.

Therapy Session 5 - Emotional Abandonment

"How was your week?" Sharron asks while sitting in her comfortable reclining chair across the love seat.

"It went well," I say as I sit as usual on the maroon velvet love seat with the hand-sewn pillows on it.

"That's great! So, where would you like to get started?" I rock my head and shift my legs to get more comfortable. Sharron pulls out a file that has two papers in it.

"I should work on my grandmother. I feel kind of bad that I didn't see her for Thanksgiving last week. But I didn't feel bad enough to *actually* go see her for Thanksgiving, you know?"

"Alright, tell me why this is a tender spot for you."

"Well, when I was in the third grade, I remember telling my mom that my *tio* Carlos had touched me. You know, 'down there.' My uncle Carlos was my grandmother's sister's husband. Soon after, I told my mom. Then my grandmother started telling me to go hug and kiss my uncle Carlos when I saw him.

"I do remember my grandmother telling me to shake hands with people when she would introduce me to her friends, at a party, or wedding. She would tell me to say hi, but she never told me to hug and kiss anyone other than him. Looking back, I wonder why she would say that to me. We lived right next door to them. Why would I hug and kiss them every time I saw them? I saw them every day... and that's the other thing.

She didn't say 'them,' she said 'him.' Was she intentionally throwing me to the wolf?"

"My mom told me she told my grandma and asked her what to do. And the matriarch of the family told me to show affection toward my abuser! I don't know if my mom or my grandma ever told my grandpa. Our family is so hush-hush over everything. According to my grand-mother, I wasn't to speak against an adult. I was only supposed to obey."

"That's a good thing to work on, considering she exposed you to more abuse. Now think about the worst part of that. Was it the abuse itself or that she didn't protect you?" Sharron asks.

I sit and think about it.

"The abuse was disgusting, but I think not being protected was worse than the abuse," I say, staring ahead blankly. "I needed the person taking care of me to take care of me. Later I heard he had done this to many people in our family and no one did anything to him or reported it to the police."

"Picture in your mind, the worst part of not being protected. What would that look like?" Sharron digs in.

"The worst part would be my grandmother telling me that I had to go hug and kiss my uncle." Tears roll from my eyes, and I reach for a tis-sue.

"Is there anything that you tell yourself now about your grand-mother?" Sharron presses.

"I tell myself I should see her and take care of her."

"Alright, now do you know that you have every right *not* to go see your grandmother?" Sharron says simply.

"Well... no. No one has ever said that to me. I was raised that it was something I'm supposed to do. It's something family does."

It's hard to explain essential Hispanic culture when you have to.

"Well, who would want to?" Sharron says, waving her hand in front of her face once as if something was stinking in the room. I laugh so hard! I want to keep that image in my mind.

Seriously! Who *would* want to visit someone who did that?

"Now, we can talk about forgiveness later, if you want to, and you may want to treat her as someone who is ill," Sharron continues.

"And I do think she *is* ill, somehow," I say while nodding my head. "I don't know what she would be diagnosed with. Being anti-feminist isn't exactly an illness. She changes her mind a million times before making the wrong decision. Women and children are supposed to be seen, not heard. Men are always right. Something is not right with her, besides her being illiterate and uneducated," I say.

"She's crazy, and she lets Crazy live with her. She babies my sixty-two-year-old uncle, Michael, who never went out on his own. He either lives with my grandparents in their home in Albuquerque, or he'll go to their house in Pecos when he has temper tantrums and gets kicked out. He can't hold a job and always argues with everyone. Michael can say anything from his throne. My grandma always protects him. I had an experience once when Michael was trying to bully me. As I was sitting, he was towering over me, yelling, waving his arm. So I stood up, in case I had to defend myself. My grandmother told me to leave, instead of telling Michael to stop. I went to my grandmother's less often after that. Michael seems to have some sort of mental illness too. He's a wild card with his behavior. I'm not the only one who visits my grandmother less when he's there."

"Alright, now let me give you another card to write a new mantra. How do you feel about 'I have every right not to be involved with my grandmother?'" Sharron asks while handing over a flashcard and a pen.

"Sure, that sounds legit." I write it down.

"For the next exercise, you are going to have the negative image of your grandmother in your mind. You are going to say the mantra: 'I have every right not to be involved in my grandmother's life,'" Sharron instructs.

I close my eyes and think of the time we lived on Broadway in Albuquerque. I was in the third grade in the mid-eighties. Broadway, south of Gibson is a very industrial part of town with one block of houses in the middle. My grandmother's sister, *tia* Feliz, and her husband, *tio* Carlos, owned their home, and the house next to it. They had recently evicted the people in the house next door for too many people living there. The people had trashed the place. My mother, grandparents, and I moved in without putting money down for a deposit. We were grateful because my mom had just gotten out of an abusive relationship and had to move in a hurry. *Tío* Carlos had lent my mom money so she wouldn't miss her car payment. She was worried it was going to get repossessed.

I sit and picture myself at the house on Broadway. When my sick uncle Carlos snuck up behind me and put his hand down my pants he said, 'Do you like it?' I froze. He asked me again. I was terrified to get him mad. What if he stopped helping my mom and kicked us out of the house if I said no? I reluctantly and slowly nodded my head yes. He calls me a '*sin verguenza,*' - someone without shame. That dirty pig had no idea how much shame I had. I was just trying to protect my mom and our well-being. Then I see myself in the bathroom at home, and my grandmother is saying, '*Y cuando ves a tu tío Carlos, abrazarlo, bezalo!*' ('And when you see your uncle Carlos, hug him, kiss him!') Oprah Winfrey says that if someone was touching you, that you should say something to an adult you trust. Abuelita's timing was odd in saying this. Why would *Abuela* want me to hug and kiss a man Oprah said was abusing me?

I focus on where I am, sitting in my therapist's chair, and on my breathing. I hold the image of my grandmother selling me out. Then I repeat the phrase:

"I have every right not to be involved in my grandmother's life." I repeat the phrase while holding the image and the feelings it brought with it. Listening to my own words, "I have every right not to be involved in my grandmother's life." But do I? My grandparents are old and could die any day now. "I have every right not to be involved in my grandmother's life." What if my grandmother needs me? What if one of my grandparents needs to go to the doctor? "I have every right not to be involved in my grandmother's life." Do you really, Joselyn? Could you live with yourself? You know what your grandmother's sisters are saying about you now that you don't go visit. "I have every right not to be involved in my grandmother's life." Yes, they probably do say bad things, but I don't care for my grandma's sisters at all. "I have every right not to be involved in my grandmother's life." Where am I with this? Do I believe the statement I'm saying? "I have every right not to be involved in my grandmother's life." I think my grandmother gave me up. "I have every right not to be involved in my grandmother's life." Why did they let him do this? Because *tio* Carlos was a man and the breadwinner? "I have every right not to be involved in my grandmother's life." That reason isn't good enough. "I have every right not to be involved in my grandmother's life," I say with more certainty.

"Now on a scale from zero to ten, how true does that statement feel to you?"

"It's about an eight," I answer.

"Okay, let's do it again."

I think about how my grandmother was there for me when I was a child.

"I have every right to not be involved in my grandmother's life," I say. I'm trying to hold the picture of her telling me the words. That I need to hug and kiss her sister's husband, but I keep drifting to when they would buy me a coat every winter. I think about what a horrible person I am to not be there for my grandparents in old age. "I have every right to not be in my grandmother's life," I repeat. I remember taking my grandparents to doctor appointments. Something Michael can't do because he doesn't have a valid driver's license or registration. He can't get his life together. It reinforces the idea that my grandmother chooses Michael over me, even though I do more for them and care for them better. I go back to the image on Broadway. "I have every right not to be involved in my grandmother's life." I think of my grandmother feeding me to the wolf. She's crazy. She must be mentally ill. "I have every right not to be involved in my grandmother's life." I really start to believe I do have every right not to be in her life.

"Now, how does that feel on a scale of zero to ten?" Sharron stops me, and I stare at her.

"About a nine," I respond.

"Great, let's go back to the image and the phrase," Sharron says, scribbling something down. I begin to repeat the phrase, putting my hands on each side of me and closing my eyes.

"I have every right not to be involved in my grandmother's life," I say. I remember how my grandmother allowed her sister to pull down all the pictures of her grandkids from her walls. Someone replaced them with images of my grandmother and her sisters. My grandma is too frail to do it herself. "I have every right not to be involved in my grandmother's life." The anger builds in me, and I begin to believe it is true. "I have every right not to be involved in my grandmother's life." She betrayed me to a known sexual predator. "I have every right not to be involved in my grandmother's life." They all protected that sexual predator for decades. My grandmother and her sister. *Abuela* must be insane. "I have every right not to be involved in my grandmother's life."

"How true do you feel that statement is?" Sharron asks and looks up at me.

"A ten," I say.

"Good! Let's reinforce it." Sharron has me repeat the exercise again. Without a doubt, I could believe the statement: "I have every right not to be involved in my grandmother's life." I keep holding the image of my grandmother protecting a child molester. Telling me to hug him. What the hell is wrong with her? Why does she always side with the wrong person? She always sides with my dad.

"I have every right to not be in my grandmother's life," I say. Sharron is right. I don't have to see someone who didn't protect me. I don't know why she didn't defend me, I guess, to guard the livelihood of her sister? My great-aunt who never worked. They were part of the generation where the women stayed home. This was before the Baby Boomers. Is that it? She protected her sister's lazy-ass lifestyle?

"I have every right to not be in my grandmother's life," I say. That woman *is* crazy, and I need to stay away from her, I decide.

"How true does that statement feel to you?" Sharron asks between mantras.

"A ten," I say, definitively.

We finish up the session, and it feels so good to go outside and breathe in the late November air.

I wonder if I'm just telling myself that I have every right not to be in my grandmother's life (literally). There's a lot of relief with the actualization that I don't have to see my grandmother. But I think I just lost my Mexican card.

I assess the session to see if it was worth the money. What Sharron said plays back in my mind when we were talking about seeing my grandmother...

"Well, who would want to?" she said.

It was worth every penny, just to hear that!

I go home to make a gin with ginger beer drink with a squeeze of lime and plan for the next day's lessons.

Debate

For fourth period I have a group discussion planned. We're going to debate what class project we'll be doing. Generally in my English classes no one speaks. It's like pulling teeth. My English students are reluctant to talk out loud in front of others. It's good practice for them to come out of their shells and gain more confidence. But this is my Leadership class, so maybe students will actually discuss the subject.

The students are thinking about doing a project either on domestic violence or the environment. Everyone except Brianna and Dina have been briefed on class discussion expectations before, so I skip them. Big mistake.

The students begin debating on why they want to do each project. Dina and Brianna start yelling at the other team about why their project is stupid and sucks. I think of intervening, but my headache only allows me to cower behind my desk and hope the attitude changes. When it doesn't I cut in and tell them to write down their vote on a piece of paper. The class seems like it will never end. I take deep breaths.

Finally the bell rings.

Lunchroom - Work on the Farm

Leblanc, Ridgeway, Lombardi, Jones, Smith and Ms. Baker are in the workroom when I walk in for lunch.

"Oh, there's Miranda. She suuuucks," Mr. Ridgeway says while peering past the window. "She's coming like once every two weeks now and making a big stink about, 'What am I missing?'" He mimics her.

"Well, she has 20 absences in my class," Mr. Leblanc says, unpacking his lunch.

"Yes! Kick her out! Kick her out! Make her work on the farm." I chuckle.

"Yeah! I so wish we could do that! I wish I could say to them, 'If you're not going to behave, you're going to work on the farm!'" I say.

"We need a farm. So we can send 'em out there." Mr. Ridgeway mixes dressing into his spinach and chicken salad.

"Go pull some weeds!" Lombardi says while licking mayonnaise off his thumb. Then he wipes his thumb on his sweater. He adds thin pickle slices that are cut long-ways on his turkey sandwich.

"Yeah!" I say. while taking out my homemade vegetarian potato soup.

"Yeah, go break rocks!" Mr. Jones says and waves his fork to our imaginary outdoor farm.

"Wouldn't that be cool?" I say. "Let's *do* it."

"Yeah, really," Ms. Baker agrees while scrolling on her phone with her left hand and holding her fork with her right.

"Go build a rock wall," Lombardi adds. Mr. Leblanc stares at Lombardi and smiles.

"That's the best idea you've had all quarter!"

"Well, let's bring it to a vote," Mr. Ridgeway says, "at the next staff meeting," but Mr. Jones wastes no time.

"Here! Here!"

"Yes!" I yell.

"Here, done!" Lombardi yells.

"Simone, can you sit down for a minute, we need to vote on something," we all chuckle.

"I don't know about a rock *wall*," I say.

"It's not authoritarian..." Mr. Jones says. "It can be student-led! If you don't want to pull weeds, you can build a rock-wall." We laugh.

"When you say it like that, it sounds *very* student-led!" Lombardi says.

"I understand how you're feeling," Mr. Jones pretends to talk to a student. "If you don't want to do this work, why don't you take a step outside, pick a few weeds, think about it, and come back and let me know," Mr. Jones demonstrates.

"Work in the gulag!" Mr. Ridgeway says.

"Aaaand we're in prison," Lombardi says, and we all laugh.

48

Meditation Apps

The Bell rings for my 4th-period Leadership class.

"Good afternoon, everyone. Your Bell Ringer question reads: 'Are you making changes to your life, since choosing this project? How?'" I walk toward my desk to take attendance, but turn and glance back. I see Brianna lean into Dina.

"We should have another fight," she says with a sly smile. I know she's talking about the disastrous discussion we had a couple of days ago.

"Noo... Oh, that reminds me to hand you your feedback on that last discussion." I walk toward the back, where I have graded papers. I begin to pass them out. I get to Brianna and give her the rubric with harsh but honest feedback.

"WHAT? I want to see... Let me see what you got?" Brianna grabs Dina's paper. You got argumentative too? What did you get? Let me see what you got," Brianna turns to the girl sitting behind her.

"If you have an issue with your grade, talk to me about it later," I say. I put back a stack of papers for students who aren't there.

"Oh, no! I don't want to talk to YOU," I hear Brianna say.

"Alright, but no one's obligated to show you their grade. Just get started on your Bell Ringer," I say while walking behind my desk.

Brianna still pesters students. I ignore it, hoping she'll quiet down. I take attendance.

"I don't even care about that grade," Dina retorts to Brianna.

"Hey, dude, what did you get on this?" Brianna is *still* persisting.

"We are going to continue with our class projects that you chose about domestic violence or the environment today. What's the scope of the problem?" I turn toward Dina, and Brianna swings her arm and hits Dina in the stomach with something. Dina cringes and doubles over in her chair with a cry.

"What was that? That's enough. Leave the classroom," I say while swinging my finger toward the door.

"No. I'm not leaving!" Brianna says with a smirk ...I walk to my desk and write an email entitled "HELP" to the Principal and the Dean of Students with a "!" delivery.

"You need to stop throwing things," I say. "Dina, will you please sit over there." I point to some empty seats.

I announce to the class that they may use their phone, a desktop, or an iPad to do their research today.

The students get busy working, but at some point I hear Brianna loudly whisper to Dina, "If she talks to me *one* more time, I'm going to *kill* her."

I conducted the class as I usually do, and no one came to get her. She ended up putting earbuds in, which are not allowed, and not bothering anyone.

Finally, the bell rings.

"Tomorrow, we'll look for collaborators for your projects. Who else in the community is already working on this issue? Nice job, folks," I announce as the students walk out the door.

Why do I not like this child so much? It's because she's rude, she's a bully. She tries to mess with my favorite students, and if anyone messes with them, I will crush her! ...Ah! How can I suddenly be so mean to a student? I can't do anything to her, but I kind of wish someone else would knock some sense into her. Jesus, who am I? Am *I* the bully, or is she?

I search for the Principal or the Dean of Students. I find them both in Jim's office.

"Can I talk to you guys about Brianna? We had a bad class discussion the other day, and I gave the students their grades back. I heard her say if I talked to her one more time, she was going to kill me," I tell them.

My boss nods her head and lowers her eyes.

"Have you tried having a conversation with her outside of the classroom?"

"Yes, we talked after I had sent her to ISS the other day for sleeping. I asked her if there was anything I could do to make the class better for her, and she said no. I asked her if she wanted to see a social worker, and she said she already was. Then I told her, 'Well, we just can't have our heads down in class.' She rolled her eyes at me, so I left."

"Nice. Okay, well, maybe you can talk to Brianna about cues for when she needs a break from class to reset. Or a note for you to indicate to her that she needs to take a break?"

"Alright, I can try that." But inside I'm screaming, 'I want her OUT of my classroom!!!' I don't know if this child really wants to kill me or not.

"Yes, try that and see how it goes. I've seen Brianna with her friends, and they do have some aggressive actions, but they do have a sweetness to them too. They kinda look out for one another." I have no idea what she's talking about, but I nod and smile. This woman can see the best in everyone. It is why I like her.

"Thanks. We'll see how it goes." I stand up.

"You know, it's going to take some time. Brianna will have bad days. Let her know you're willing to work with her. Be as clear as possible of what the expectations are," Simone says. Jim smiles. I know he's sick, so he's preserving his energy.

"Alright, I'll try it." I slip out of the office, take a few deep breaths and I go into the lunchroom to relax. I don't know how I'm going to handle this. I seriously question what I'm doing with my life.

Catalina walks in.

"What's wrong," Catalina asks me. I must have had a certain expression on my face.

"Oh, I'm just having a hard time with Brianna," I say.

"Which Brianna, the new kid?" Catalina asks.

"Yes! She's a nightmare!"

"You know what was weird? When she came with her mom to register and Brianna was taking her reading test, her mom said to me, 'You should probably know, Brianna has a son.' So I said, 'Oh, okay. We'll see if she wants to be a part of the G.R.A.D.S program. It's for students who are parents.' but then when I asked Brianna about it later, she said, 'Yeaaaah, about that, that's not my son, it's my mom's.' Isn't that weird?" I make a face.

"VERY weird," I say. "I'm going to mention it to Jill. Brianna is on her caseload."

"Who do you think is lying?" I ask Catalina.

"Brianna. Just the way she said it. And why would her mom mention it at all if it wasn't Brianna's?"

"But she's only fourteen! Could she really be a mom so young?" I ask.

"Oh yeah," Catalina answers.

"Maybe this is why she has so many anger issues. Maybe her mom made her have it. If she's denying the kid is hers, she obviously doesn't want it," I say and Catalina nods. "That's fucked up. And who could have gotten her pregnant? Either some little punk or an adult. That could potentially be *really* fucked up." Now I'm starting to feel sorry for her.

I search for Jill. She's the new social worker. When I find her I ask to speak with her in her office. I brief her on what Catalina told me. She tells me that Brianna said the reason she moved in with her grandmother is because her mom was making her take care of her baby brother. That her mom would take off and leave her with the baby. Hmm, this story just keeps getting weirder. It's very possible the mom is nuts. Well, I'm going to have to use as much patience and empathy as possible with this child. She either is a teen parent who does not want to be a parent, or she's got a nutty mom. Jill suggests that I be consistent with her. Stick to my rules in protecting the students from physical and emotional harm. Follow through with whatever the consequences are...

"Kids need adults to be consistent," Jill tells me.

I go to my classroom to download a meditation app. I don't care how much it costs. It was less than a $70 therapist session and I need something now.

49

Books and a Reunion

It's a Saturday in late December, and I'm at home packing to move into my own apartment when my phone rings. It's my sister Joselin.

"Hello, Gorgeous," I answer from my bedroom. "Hey Beautiful, are you home? We happen to be in the neighborhood. I just got back from travel. I was in LA, and Felipiano sent me with gifts," my sister says.

"I *am* home," I respond with a smile. I move the cloth shades to see out of the window. I see my brother-in-law driving into my roommate's driveway.

"I'll be right there," I say. I grab the clicker for the garage and dart down the hall. I meet them outside. It's an overcast day, and the air is cold. My nephews are in the back of the SUV on their iPads. My sister opens the passenger door, with a small, sturdy brown bag with twine string handles. She reaches out to me with her left arm and hugs me. I say hello to Francisco and the boys.

"Felipiano gave us these." She hands over the heavy bag. I can see from the top.

"Books?" I ask with excitement and a little puzzled. I love books. I guess he got us some novels to read? There is one huge book, about three inches thick. Then two smaller volumes are about one and a half-inches thick each. Joselin helps me hold the bag to get the books out and pulls the gigantic book out first.

"52 Stories in 52 Weeks" by Felipiano McCullum," I read out loud. "Felipiano wrote these?" I ask.

"Yup. He just published them. They are hot off the press and wanted us to have a copy!" My sister exclaims. "This big one is what is in these two small ones, plus his writing process. It's a collection of short stories," Joselin explains while pulling out the other two books.

"He writes?!!" I state, shocked. Joselin nods her head and smiles. "I didn't know he wrote!" I say, shocked. It's incredible that he writes, and even more impressive, he's published three books! But I'm excited that we have another interest in common! "He never told me he wrote!" I feel like he's a twin! "Wow, that is amazing," I say. We're both beaming.

"Yeah, isn't that so cool?" Joselin says and nods.

"Truly!" I respond, examining at the books in amazement.

"Have you gotten to read any of them?" I turn up to look at my sister.

"I started reading them to the boys, not sure if I picked the most appropriate one for them. It had some cussing in it." Her eyes laugh as she chuckles.

"Ooh..." I say and glance over at the boys. "It's so amazing. I'm floored," I say to my sister.

"Isn't this amazing?" I say louder to Francisco, holding up the bag. Francisco has his sunglasses on, but I can see his eyebrows peak up from behind them, and he smiles.

"Yeah! Shows a lot of discipline and creativity!" Francisco nods.

"Did I tell you that I'm taking a book-writing workshop right now?" I tell my sister.

"Uh, NO," she smiles.

"So weird," I say. "Thanks for bringing these by! I'll thank him for sending them to us!"

"Yeah, no problem! Tell me how the book writing goes!" Joselin says as she hops back up into her white Toyota SUV. I open the back door to kiss each nephew on the head. They glance up momentarily to say hi, then go back to killing and blasting on their tablets. I turn back toward my sister, she closes the door but has the window down, and leans forward.

"Oh, another thing, is it okay if I give our cousin Amber your email address? She wants to organize a family reunion."

"Yeah, that's nice. Would dad be there?" I say flatly.

"I think so... he *is* Amber's uncle," Joselin reminds me with a sarcastic smile.

"Mmm..." Joselin knows what I mean by that. It means that I would consider not going if our father went. "And Felipiano?" I follow up.

"Yeah, she's inviting him, for sure," Joselin says with her eyebrows up.

"Interesting..." I say, dazed, trying to imagine Jose and Felipiano meeting. "I see. Well, you came to drop a few bombs, didn't you?" I laugh. My sister smiles. We wave to each other, and Francisco backs up.

I would want to go to see Felipiano, but not Jose. I'll go if Felipiano goes.

I go back inside to keep packing.

50

Lunchroom - Break Up a Fight

It's a Wednesday and the bell rings for lunch. I enter some tardy slips into the computer then hurry to the lunchroom to get my food in the microwave. Ridgeway is there talking sports with Leblanc.

Catalina walks in.

"So, I told Simone that you all requested hand sanitizer, in case the pipes freeze again. She gave the okay, so I'm going to order each class-room one bottle!" Catalina announces, and we all cheer.

Mrs. Doyle walks in and I hear loud voices. I turn towards the student lunchroom to see one of the students show teeth in anger and a fist goes up.

"Oh shit! Oh, shit!" I dart out to the commons area. The principal and Mr. Jones are trying to pull two boys apart. There is a lot of commotion.

"Stop!" The principal yells.

"Whip that niggas' ass! Whip that niggas' ass!" Alberto, a tall boy with a mop of curly brown hair on his head, yells. He's been nothing but trouble since he got here. He's egging on the fighters and blocking Mr. Ridgeway from breaking up the fight.

"Stop IT!" I say, trying to pull the two boys apart.

"Bitch, whassup? Come on, BITCH! Come on! You wanna fuckin' bully me?" The kid who said that lands about three hard punches. One to the face and two to the body. Tony, the caseworker, pulls one of the boys, but they're locked, holding on to one another. Someone keeps repeating "Joey, stop! Joey, stop!"

"Bitch whassup? Wassup bitch! I ain't no pussy! Wassup? What's up, bitch?" There's blood on the floor, and the two are holding on to each other. I pry off one hand off the other's jacket, and the two come apart. Tony picks up Joey over his shoulders and carries him into another room. "Let go of me! AGGGHH!"

It takes the principal and the history teacher to pull the other student into my classroom. I couldn't get the key in the door at first, and he was fighting back pretty fiercely. Once I get the door open, the kid holds on to the door frame, but the blood makes it slippery, so I pry his hand off the corner.

"Go in the room! It's over! It's over!" The principal yells. We close the door on him, like a caged animal.

There was still excitement and energy in the room.

I go back to the lunchroom to calm down and eat. Ms. Baker is in there.

"Ahh." I take a deep breath. "That was a bloody one," I make a disgusted face.

"You didn't get scratched up?" Ms. Baker asks.

"No, not like you, that last time," I say. "It gets your adrenaline going though... Ew, I got a little bit of blood on me!" I say. There's one tiny drop of blood on my reddish-pink top. I rinse it out.

"You know Kimberly shouldn't be over there, breaking up fights. She could get hurt. They aren't going to see a pregnant lady there when they're enraged," Ms. Baker says.

"That's true," I say, and sit down to eat. "I can't eat. This job is too much."

"She could get hurt," Ms. Baker finishes.

"You're right. I should tell Kimberly to stay out of the way." I get up since I can't eat.

Of the two in the fight, one kid's parents came to pick him up right away. The other student's parents couldn't be reached by phone, so Laina drove to his home to tell them. The parents then came to the school to pick up their son.

Both boys will be suspended for three days. They won't be allowed to come back until their parents have a meeting with the principal. The students would have to sign a Peace Contract. The contract forbids them to have classes at the same time of day. It also forbids them to have any contact or discussions, even online about each other. If they do, they can be suspended again.

Mr. Jones goes home. His whole short-sleeve shirt is bloody.

Ridgeway reports that Alberto was pushing him out of the way so that he wasn't able to break up the fight. As a result, Alberto was sent home too, and a parent meeting will be scheduled with him too.

Ha! How ironic. The kid who complains about school, cusses all day, is rude to the teachers and staff and never does any work, now has to prove himself worthy of coming back. Good luck, kid.

51

Glitter Bomb

It's my dreaded fourth-period Leadership class again. To the teachers I secretly call Brianna "My Monster."

Soon I hear Brianna putting down people's projects. One kid spills paint, and another group of students drops glitter on the carpet. Do I work in a middle school? What am I? A glorified babysitter? Here I thought making a poster about the environment would be a relaxing exercise. I already wanted to kill someone.

When fourth period ends, I get an email from the art teacher. It said that Brianna followed Jovanna into her art room and threw glitter at her and got it all over the floor. Uh, gawd... I'm so tired of this child's nonsense. I'm so glad tomorrow is Friday and then Winter Break.

I close the door to my classroom for my prep period and sit at my desk. I know the next step is to have a meeting with Brianna's mom. But why would I want to have a meeting with the mom who didn't teach her child any manners in the first place? Seems redundant. God, please give me patience.

Now I'm probably going to spend the evening trying to figure out what to say to Brianna about her behavior.

An alert goes off from my calendar. "Meeting with Nayellie's mom." Oh, goodness! I forgot. Nayellie's mom wants to take her out of school because she's not going to graduate this year and wants her to work. I've got to rally the troops. I gather Mr. Leblanc, Martina, Ms. Baker and get her mentor file out with her transcripts. When mom and Nayellie show I have each teacher say, in Spanish, how Nayellie is doing well and she just needs more time to finish. English being her second language has been a hurdle, but one I know she can overcome.

"Tarda como diez años para aprender otra idioma," Mr. Leblanc explains. Martina nods.

After hearing all of our pleas, Nayellie's mom agrees to let her continue for another year. I'm relieved and Nayellie gives me a hug before she goes. She is eighteen, but she's still living under her mother's roof and needs her support. I was glad that ended well.

When I get home I try to relax with a glass of wine, but I keep having this conversation with Brianna in my head.

"What do you think happened to your participation points when I heard you threw glitter at Jovanna? First of all, what were you doing following Jovanna in there? You weren't supposed to be in there at all. Why are you creepily following her? Do you know what throwing glitter would be considered in less than four years? Assault! Throwing something at someone or spitting at someone is considered *assault*. That's why you need to get out of these habits NOW. This is why I keep repeating: stop throwing things, stop calling people names, stop putting people down, okay? I need to see better behavior out of you if you want to pass this class. This is a Leadership class, and you keep distracting the whole class to not do their work and be productive. That's why the behavior needs to stop. Or we'll take further measures like having a guardian meeting. If that doesn't work, we'll remove you from the classroom, and you won't get credit." I'm practicing how to respond to this kid. I don't know about that last part. I can't guarantee they will remove her. I shouldn't say it.

I rub my temples. Why does she bother me so much? Because I can't control her? Is it my job to control her? No, but it's my job to create a safe environment for everyone else. But, yes, I probably have some sort of control issues. I want to control her behavior. You can't control other people's behavior, Joselyn. You have to allow people to be themselves. How are they supposed to know how to act in life without seeing the consequences of what they do? Sigh, breathe, take note of your feelings.

But you can't control other people's behavior. I guess when you grow up in the '80s, you have certain expectations of what you should see at school. Smelling pot on students, kids taking 15 minutes on the bathroom pass, being on phones and listening to music with their earbuds in class are all new to me. All these things were unheard of in my generation. In my day, you were expected to have notebooks and pencils every day. I have at least three kids a day ask me for a pencil. Where the hell did you think you were going today? But I have to remember these kids are growing up in different home environments than me. Although we were poor, my mom was an early education teacher, she had pencils coming out of her ears. I'm surprised to admit I had a better life than most of these kids. These kids are poor but socially expected to wear $200 Jordan tennis shoes. It's ridiculous. They waste their lives on video games and social media and can't even have a conversation. What is happening to our society? I see the movie WALL-E in our future, which is conclusively dismal.

Breathe.

52

Winter Break - Holistic Health

Laina and I had another fantastic writing session with Georgina. We spaced the sessions out so that we could work on things and then come back together for guidance. I didn't get to finish the last writing exercise before leaving. Georgina said she would email it to us. When I got home, Georgina had already emailed the questions.

I decide to work on it since it's the beginning of Winter Break and I have time.

The question I hadn't finished had to do with the protagonist relating to the antagonist in our story. Well, the antagonist in my story is Jose, my father. The instructions say to assume my antagonist is "justified and right." Make their case in writing. Well, that's impossible because he *isn't* justified in what he did! I can only make the case that he was selfish. My father just cared about himself and his music. I don't think I can do this. I get a mental block and a headache.

I lie back in my bed and try to see it from his perspective. Adored by fans and women. No one told him not to. He didn't have his mom around. His dad was there, but married another woman and raised a son with her. His stepmom was abusive, so he didn't want to stay with them. Hmm... my father was abandoned more than once, a lot. That's why he didn't bond with anyone. He barely graduated high school, so having a talent in music was a godsend. I do respect that he was able to make a career out of making records and performing shows. It's kind of a wonder he didn't become a drinking-drug-addicted delinquent. The women were a byproduct of the singing, and it was too late once he got women pregnant. He didn't have it in him to be a father. He had no family bonds to begin with. I'm not going to excuse him for abandoning all of us, but I can kinda see how that played out.

My headache starts to subside. It feels like a bright light and a clean chime have made things crystal clear. It was an unexpected but welcomed feeling. I start to see my father as a product of his particular circumstances. He was a victim of not being taken in and loved by his own family. Well, except for his aunt, who did take him in.

I can see that my brothers and sisters and I are all okay, even better, without Jose in our lives as children. A light entered my mind, a weight was lifted. The sun in my soul came out. I had to consider it from his perspective. My father was parentless and has bonding and trust issues.

I had always resented it when people would say, "Things always happen for a reason." I thought that was a dumb cop-out. But it seems to be true in this case. Felipiano's birth mother was a hot mess, and my half-brothers were better off not to have grown up with her. Jose would not have been in their lives, regardless. He was out singing, recording, and womanizing while blaming the women he got pregnant. At least since Felipiano and Alvaro were adopted, they seemed to have had two good parents. The writing exercise took me from being closed and stubborn to more accepting.

I'm grateful for the way things happened, and I'm happy to have these new siblings.

I had to dance in my room like an idiot for a while. It felt terrific. Latin music is perfect for getting you moving and out of a funk.

I wonder if I should drink less? I've been drinking every day for awhile. How long has it been? From 2009 to now, which is 2017, that's eight years. Let me do the math. I'll estimate three drinks every day for a year is 1,095 drinks per year, for eight years is… 8,760 drinks! That's gotta take a toll on my body. I should do a drinking cleanse. I got up to do some yoga on my mat and began to consider it.

53

Meet The Family

In the past months I had traded in my Jeep for a Mazda. My stepdad was sweet enough to cosign for me. I appreciate him more and more all the time.

It's now ready for a four-hour drive to Las Cruces to meet my long lost half-sibling. My sister Joselin is already there with her husband and two kids. We all have plans to meet for dinner tonight.

It's nearing the end of Winter Break in early January, and it's about 48 degrees and dry when I get to "Cruces" in the evening. It's warmer here than in Albuquerque because it's about 200 miles south. I check into the hotel and take all my things to my room. I settle in and get a text of the restaurant location from my sister. I glance at the time and realize I barely have time to freshen up and change clothes.

When I get to the restaurant, I remember a little gift I got for my new nephew and grabbed it out of the trunk. I'm a little nervous. What if it goes terribly? Or what if it goes well? I fantasize about everyone having a great time and sending a picture of us from tonight to our father. The note would say, "Enjoying your family without you!" or something cruel like that. I think with a smile. I would have to send it snail mail. My father doesn't have email, is not on social media, and does not even own his own cell phone. He likes to live in the dark ages, but more because he's too cheap to buy technology. He usually borrows phones from one of his girlfriends or a friend.

I walk into the restaurant and recognize Dean, my brother-in-law, first. I walk over to the table and am unsure who to hug first. I go down the line with my brother-in-law, my nephews, my sister, then I lay eyes on Felipiano, then Angus. Felipiano has a big smile on his face. I love his smiling eyes. Angus is two years old, with sandy brown longish hair and big blue eyes and cute chubby cheeks. Felipiano is about 5'10", with an athletic build, kind of like someone who bicycles a lot. I love his bushy eyebrows.

"Hey, sis! Nice to meet you! This is Angus," Felipiano says as he reaches his arms wide for a hug. We hug, and I crouch down to say hello to my new nephew.

"Hello, Angus! I heard you like balls, so I got you some of these." I hunch over and hand over a gift bag.

"Oh, what do you say, Angus?" Felipiano asks Angus and he answers,

"Tank yoouu."

"You're welcome! Nice to meet you." I straighten up and find a seat at the table.

"Taryn is at the film festival now, she's going to join us tomorrow," Felipiano fills me in, and I nod.

The waiter comes to take my drink order, and the questions begin. Felipiano shows me photos of his brother's wedding and I start crying. He looks exactly like dad. I'm not sure why I'm crying. Maybe because he looks so much like dad and dad abandoned him? Conversation flows for hours, and we close the restaurant. At the end of the night, we take photos to commemorate the event and say our goodbyes.

We later meet at the hotel, and the adults decide to meet for drinks and to talk more to fill in the gaps in time.

"Did I tell you that in 2017 I was working in Newport Beach?" I ask Felipiano.

"You mentioned you were working there but didn't say when," he tells me.

"Yeah, I was kind of in-between jobs but had a gig selling men's skincare products at Bloomingdale's at the time. Were you living in Costa Mesa at that time?"

"Yeah, yeah, in fact, I was. I was working IT for an insurance company. It was in Newport Beach on Santa Maria Road and San Clemente," He says while I pull out my phone and look up the Bloomingdale's in Newport Beach. Sure enough, it's across the street.

"Did you ever go to Fashion Island? Like to Bloomingdales or the food court?"

"Yeah, I've been to the food court," Felipiano says and smiles.

"Dude! we could have been sitting right next to each other and not even know it," I say. My sister laughs and takes a sip of her margarita.

"Small world!" Joselin says.

We learn about each other for hours.

When I go to my room that night, I feel like we met a lifelong friend. I couldn't help but think about how my father missed out on some fantastic kids. What if Jose wouldn't have lied to me about having these kids? Maybe I would have known about Felipiano. Maybe I could have reached out to him when I was sleeping in my car in Newport Beach. Maybe he would have had space. Maybe he and his wife would have been okay with letting me crash at their place at the time. Maybe I wouldn't have gotten stopped by that police officer. I would have been safer. Maybe someone would have cared. Maybe.

54

Cold As Ice

When I first walk into my classroom, it's ice cold. It's January, and last night the temperatures dipped down to the mid-teens. My heater probably went out again. I complain to Mr. Jones and everyone. I'm hoping to get sympathy from Jim, who's in charge of maintenance. Dang, I don't have a space heater. I spend the morning with my ankles freezing, then my hands, then my nose. I hated it, but it kept everyone awake.

During passing period, I run to use the bathroom only to find there's no water. The pipes froze. I instinctually got soap and turned on the faucet, but nothing. I keep the pink foam soap on my right hand while grabbing a paper towel with my left. Using the towel to open the door, I ran out to hunt for hand sanitizer. The warning bell rings, so I run towards my class. I ask Mr. Jones if he has hand sanitizer and he tells me Catalina has some. I ran back to the front desk. No one's there, and I don't see any. I run back to my classroom and call Charlie to ask him to ask Catalina for some. He calls back to say Catalina says I can't have any, it's only for the front. I hang up and call Catalina.

"Why do you hate me?!" I whine. By now, I've rubbed the soap together and dried it with the towel.

"I don't hate you. It's for the front. I'll see if I can find you some. Bye!" She hangs up. I think she thinks I mean a *bottle* of hand sanitizer, not a blob. Oh, why do the smallest things have to be so complicated? I find some sanitizer wipes that I use for wiping down the desks in my cabinet and use them on my hands. At this point, I don't care. I wipe down everything I touched because I work at a school and I'm a germa-phobe.

In the middle of first period, a student walks in with a big bottle of used hand sanitizer. There's about two inches worth at the bottom. I smile and thank the student. I take the bottle in my hand and notice a handwritten note written on it. It says,

"I do love you!" It's from Catalina. I laugh.

I get through first through third periods with no problems with students. But I have had to take deep breaths before fourth, before Brianna gets there. I try to focus on the pleasant kids in that class, there are like 7 of them. I need to focus on the good.

I had a feeling Brianna would regress when Dina was back in class, and I was right. The last few classes had been great. I had seen her and Raya getting along and talking together. Brianna and I had even been interacting peacefully and amicably. She did surprise me a bit. She admitted to us that she got kicked out of a middle school for lighting fireworks in the hall. When Raya asked her why she did it, she simply said she didn't know. This is what I attribute to kids not having developed brains. This is the only reason I can come up with.

Most of the class goes fine, until I see Brianna throw a blunt of a pencil at Dina and hit her on the head.

"WHAT are you doing?" I ask Brianna.

"She called me a whore!" Brianna shouts.

"I need to talk to both of you. Dina?" I motion toward the door. Dina frowns, gets up and walks to the door. Before we're out of the classroom, Dina says, "Well, I was asking how you got those bruises on your neck!" I hadn't noticed whether Brianna had hickies or not, it was beside the point. When we cross the threshold, I close the door behind me.

"I want people to feel safe in my class," I say.

"I know Miss, I don't feel safe with her!" Dina fake whines.

"I don't understand this dynamic between the two of you," I say.

"I don't know, Miss, she does that." Dina still has a tinge of the whine to her voice, and she puts her eyes and head down.

"Well, I'm working with Brianna to change her behavior, but can we not name-call or retaliate? I'll have to put one of you in ISS." Dina nods her head and heads back into class.

I call out Brianna. She comes willingly, because her friend did.

"Do you feel safe in my class?" She nods her head. "I want everyone to feel safe in my class like they are not going to get hit in the head with a pencil." I put my hands out like I don't know what to do. She laughs.

"Ask everyone in that class if they feel safe," Brianna says, challenging me.

"I don't think *Dina* feels safe," I say.

"Well, except her," Brianna says with a devious smile.

"Come on, let's go over it again. No hitting, no throwing, no calling names," I say.

"Yeah, yeah yeah," she nods and heads for the door. When the bell rings for the end of class, she's inside, and I'm still at the doorway.

"I'm still going to have to write you up for it," I say.

"Write me up?" She's going to write me up for it!" Brianna lets Dina hear from across the room.

"But, I don't want to … press charges, Miss," Dina says innocently to me like she's being bullied by her abuser as her abuser stares at her.

"No, you may not be 'pressing charges,' but those are the school rules."

The two glare at each other, but I can't see Brianna's expression. Dina rolls her eyes and looks down. They both gather their things and leave the class.

I take all the time I need during my prep period by myself with the door closed and meditate. Even the bad things are not that bad. I don't feel any panic attacks coming on. I feel alright. What the hell am I supposed to learn about being in this situation? Empathy? How can I react to her in a way that is loving and productive for her? How can I even begin to bring out that side of myself when I'm so angry? There is something the Universe is trying to teach me, and I'm having a hard time hearing it. Breathe.

I see the hand sanitizer with the "I do love you" note on it and smile.

55

Sleuthing

It's my nephew's birthday so I join my sister and her family at Dave and Buster's. When I walk in I take in the various food smells while the casino-like sounds ring in the background. After lunch, everyone goes off in their separate directions to play games.

My sister and I stay at the table. She catches me up about our new siblings.

"Soo... Felipiano and I think we found his birth mother. She *is* Maria. We narrowed it down to her by searching through all her photos. We found one that Maria posted of her father. He looked *just* like our brother Alvaro when he was young!"

"What? Are you serious? You're talking about Maria, the woman who dad used to live with? *The one who wrote the letter saying the twins look like dad?*" I stare deep into her eyes.

"Yeah," Joselin answers with a smile.

"But Felipiano and Alvaro are not twins."

"I found out that when kids are born less than a year apart, sometimes people call them 'Irish twins,'" she says.

"Really? Are they going to contact her?" I ask.

"I talked to Felipiano. He says he's just happy knowing who she is."

"Wow."

"Yeah, so because I was going to leave for travel on a Sunday a few weeks ago, we went to another church on Saturday night." She fumbles through her phone for a minute, then hands me the phone with a photo of an older blonde lady in a pew.

"Uh, huh…" I say.

"We think this Maria. She was at the church we went to on Saturday," Joselin says with a smile, sort of smirk, on her face.

"Noo!" I say skeptically.

"Pretty sure," my sister nods. "She glanced back at me too! I wonder if she knew who I was?"

"Yeah, or she thought you were a creepy person, taking pictures of her in church!" I grab her arm, and we laugh.

"Have you shown Felipiano?"

"Yeah, and he thought it looked like her too," Joselin says.

"Wow," is all I can get out.

"There's something else," Joselin pulls up a web page on her phone. "We Googled her, and… she's been in trouble with the law." Joselin hands me her phone. It's a news article about Maria. It says she was found guilty of embezzling checks from Jerry Gutierrez when he was the mayor."

"Holy shit!" I say, as I read.

"Her first husband reported her, but they divorced, and she got married again and changed her name. Somehow she got her sentence delayed and when she changed names the law couldn't find her. She never ended up serving time," Joselin explains.

"What?"

"Yeah."

Joselin leans in.

"And I think your uncle is Facebook friends with her."

"What?! Nooo! That's impossible! None of my uncles are even computer literate!" I started thinking about who was technically savvy enough to use a computer or a phone.

"I'll find it." Joselin scrolls through her phone to a particular picture to read the comments. "Here," she hands me the phone. "He commented, 'Nice pic' on her photo," Joselin says. It's my uncle Samuel.

"I wonder how they know each other?"

"They might know each other from Rio Grande High School. Did your uncle go there?"

"Yes. Do you think he knew about Maria's pregnancies? ...wait, but this would have been after they were all out of high school." I start to map out the timeline. "Should I ask my uncle if he knows anything? If he knew my dad got both Maria *and* my mom pregnant.. well wait. I was born first... (we), were born first. Then they were born in the early eighties, so who knows if my uncle and Maria kept in touch during that time. Should I ask?" I crinkle my nose. I felt like I'd be doing something wrong. "Maybe I should ask Felipiano what he wants?"

"Yeah. Because if you start asking questions, it might get back to Maria," Joselin says.

"And why *shouldn't* it get back to her? What was she expecting, to keep this a secret forever?" I say with spite.

"I don't know, ask Felipiano what he thinks."

"Okay." I'd respect his wishes.

Then Joselin recounts that she got together with our father this past week. She told him that all of his nieces and nephew have spoken to Felipiano on the phone.

"Dad was confused as to how all of this happened. I had to go back and explain how Ancestry works and how we were all linked together. I told him that you did your DNA test, and we are related to each other, so that was good!"

"You had doubts?" I raise my eyebrows and smile.

"Well! You never know!" Joselin says. We laugh. "So then I asked dad if he wanted to see a picture of Alvaro and I pulled out my phone. I showed him one photo, and he says, 'No, he doesn't look like me.'" Joselin tries to imitate our father. I sag.

"He's still trying to deny us?" I say out loud.

"So I show him another photo, and he denies that Alvaro looks like him again. So I tell him, 'That's not the one I'm looking for.' I find the one when Alvaro is a teenager, and show him that. So then dad like deflates and then says 'Yeah, kinda,' then he gets up and says he's got to run to the post office."

"Ugh, deflates? Instead of being happy, he deflates? I can't believe he still wants to deflect and deny us! He's such a sad person. I have a hard time believing we came from him." I didn't expect a different reaction from my father, but that didn't mean I wasn't disappointed in him... again.

When I ask Felipiano if he wants me to dig around he tells that he's happy just knowing who his birth mother is.

Felipiano and Alvaro were better off not having Maria as a mother. AND definitely better off not having our M.I.A. father.

56

Lunchroom - Going to France

We're back from Winter break, and it's Quarter 3.

I wash my hands while listening in on the conversation between Mr. Leblanc and Mr. Jones.

Grades were due this morning.

"Do you have all your mentee meetings scheduled?" Mr. Leblanc asks.

"Um... no. I have to reschedule one for next week," Mr. Jones says.

"See, all their work is in, I finished grading it, so now we're waiting on report cards in our boxes? Because I couldn't access them on the computer," Mr. Leblanc says while unpacking his lunch, appearing a bit worried.

"I don't think Martina has all the grades submitted on her end into the new computer system. That's why we can't access them," Mr. Jones explains.

"We're expected to grade and submit grades at the same time as we are planning for Quarter 3. I don't know how we're supposed to do all of this!" Mr. Leblanc says.

"I'm fine with getting rid of the alerts," Mr. Jones says while Mr. Ridgeway is scrolling through his phone.

"I'm fine with getting rid of alerts and PDP's. I can't think of another profession that has to do something like that. We have enough to do! I seriously don't know how you all keep up with this!" I say. "I have a huge admiration for all of you." I put my hands together and bow my head.

"Oh, Joselyn, when you do the report cards, you can make comments, like "It's a pleasure to have so-and-so in my class..." Mr. Leblanc pretends to be typing on a computer in front of him.

"But, what if it's *not* a pleasure to have their kid in my class?" I ask.

"Well,... you lie." Mr. Leblanc laughs with a toothpick in his mouth as he faces me and spreads his fingers out.

"Simone wants me to give the ELL girls an English credit for Film class," Mr. Ridgeway breaks in.

"Are you going to do it?" I ask.

He shrugs. "Do I really have a choice?"

"Are we just *giving* credits away here? I mean, are we preparing them for the real world?" I ask. No one says anything. "We're going to hell," I say.

"Joselyn, we're doing the *Lord's* work," Mr. Jones says. I laugh and then change the subject.

"Did anyone see one of the old founders of Facebook on *Democracy Now* last night?" I ask. Everyone shakes their heads no.

"It was good. I don't trust Zuckerberg at all. He *knows* where all these ads were from. He's playing dumb. Like he couldn't have done anything about all of the false 2016 political ads? He *knows* who is buying ads and what country they are from. He knows what IP addresses bought the ads. He could have done something sooner. He didn't *want* to do anything or cooperate with congress's investigation. I hate Facebook and American social media culture. I'm glad I was able to boycott it. It was an addiction!"

"That's why I'm moving to France!" Mr. Leblanc interjects.

"We're all going with you," I proclaim.

"Okay," Mr. Leblanc shrugs.

"BYE, Samantha! I found someone who'll take me to FRANCE!" Samantha is Jobin's wife. We burst out laughing. "I'm gonna make some HORS-de-Vohrs and eat cheese!"

Mr. Leblanc cringes, puts his hands over his ears and shakes his head at Jobin's terrible French accent. It sounds more like Cajun.

57

Therapy Session 6 - Forgiveness

At the end of the day, on my drive home from work, the local news is on KUNM, the NPR station.

"A teenage girl was jailed for murder based on mistaken identity. An Albuquerque Public School teacher had identified the girl from a Facebook profile picture. The teenager who was named went to the police station with her lawyer. She let them know they were looking for the wrong girl, but police arrested her anyway and held her for a week. The Albuquerque Police Department is now in search of Alicia Pena. She is accused of luring a man to a location where he was then shot in the back by a man."

"WOW. Crazy ass kids." I push the button to change the station to music.

Tonight I have an appointment to revisit my therapist, to make sure I don't lose my mind. I had gone over the exercises she had given me. I know I can't control everything, and I can't get sick over what I can't control. More meditation, more yoga, more exercise, more feeding my soul to get through ... LIFE.

And that's just what Sharron says. I have to do the exercises when I start to feel pain or anxiety. I knew it, but needed to be told again.

"I want to learn how to forgive my grandmother because I do think she is not well, and never has been," I tell Sharron.

"Do you want to see if we can trigger a negative image and replace it with a positive response?" Sharron asks. I agree.

"What negative idea do you have because of what your grandmother did?" Sharron asks me.

"Well, when she told me to go and hug and kiss the man who was molesting me, I felt like I wasn't worth protecting." Tears fall from my eyes.

"Okay, and you want to forgive your grandmother for her past deeds?"

"Yes," I say.

"How about you write down your mantra." She opens up the small wooden drawer next to her and hands me an index card and a pen.

"What do I say?" I ask while holding the pen to the paper.

"You can say that you forgive your grandmother for her past deeds, because she was and is mentally ill," Sharron says.

"I agree with that," I write on the index card.

We practice the exercise. I picture my grandmother and start repeating the phrase.

"I forgive my grandmother for her past deeds because she was and is mentally ill," I say it about twenty times.

"On a scale of zero to ten, how much do you believe that statement," Sharron asks.

"Um.. about a 6. I don't forgive her yet," I say.

"And on a scale of zero to ten, how strong is your disturbance level?"

"Like how bad do I want to cry?" I ask.

"Right, how disturbed do you feel when you say the mantra?"

"Umm... I don't know, I guess like zero. I don't feel anything."

"Okay." Sharron writes it down. We do the exercise a few more times until the end of the hour.

"How about we continue this in our next session? Do you want to meet in a week or two?"

I'm rummaging through my purse.

"Can we email each other? I left my phone in the car." She agrees.

When I get home I make a gin with ginger beer and lime so I can get started on lesson planning.

I check a text that I had missed from my mom when I was in therapy. It's a news link. I click on it. It's about a man named Samuel Martinez who was taken in the back of a truck in Pecos, murdered and dumped in the river. I started having a panic attack. Why would someone want to kill my uncle in our hometown? I called my mom immediately. I check the time, she's probably in bed.

"Ah, Hello?" Yes, it sounds like I woke her up.

"Mom! Why would someone murder Samuel?" I'm still breathing in quick breaths.

"...Oh, ... no." I wait on the other end of the phone for answers. It feels like an eternity.

"No... that's a different Samuel. He's a cousin of ours on Grandpa's side.

"What?" I start to start to steady my breathing. "It's not our Samuel?"

"No, no... We have a cousin with the same name." I didn't even want to continue this conversation. I almost had a heart attack. I take another drink of my gin and ginger.

"Oh, ok. I have to plan. I thought it was about my uncle," I say and take a deep breath. I hang up and am so mad. How can my mom just send me a text like that with no freaking context! Ugh! Dive me to drink margaritas.

58

Lunchroom - P.A.R.C.C. and S.W.A.T.

Today's the last Friday of the month when we have a potluck to celebrate the staff birthdays for that month. It's the end of January, and I love these glorious days.

"There's no room to eat your lunch," Mr. Ridgway says as he glares at the massive spread on the table.

"Just eat the cake and make some room!" Mrs. Doyle rubs her hands together.

"Looks like everyone likes their thumbs!" Jobin says, and Mr. Leblanc laughs.

"What?" I say.

"Didn't you read your email?" Mr. Leblanc, who sent out the Sunshine Committee's reminder notice, says.

"I mean, I read it, but..." I say.

"Maybe you need a better hook," Mrs. Doyle suggests.

"Huh?" Mr. Leblanc says.

"Better subject line," Jobin says.

"Ten Rumors About DHHS that you didn't know!" Lombardi suggests.

"Yeah, Five things that can kill you in your classroom!" Jobin adds, we laugh.

I turn to Ms. Doyle.

"Can you pass the salt please."

Jobin turns to Lombardi.

"You know what's good? You know what's good? I don't wanna throw you off of what you're doing, but there are pork chops there," Jobin points in one direction with his fork. "There's a biscuit, with gravy on top." He gestures in another direction. "Pretty good stuff, *do it*," Jobin says as he sits with those very things on his plate.

"Normally, I'd say 'Don't boss me around Jobin," Lombardi says. He helps himself to a serving of homemade mac and cheese.

Mr. Ridgeway changes the subject to his son.

"Today Santiago said, 'See ya, suckers!'" Mr. Ridgeway's face scrunches with laughter. "This kid, man!" We laugh. "Then the other night, he was working on a puzzle on his iPad when we told him to put his game away and to brush his teeth. He goes: 'but I'm not done with my puzzle.' And we tell him, to put it away, it's time to go to bed. And he goes, 'Aaaah, FUCK it!' I tried so hard not to laugh." We all chuckle.

"Yeah, really," Ms. Baker says.

"It's so hard not to laugh when they do that," Lombardi admits. He has a three-year-old.

Laina walks in.

"Are those your famous 'slutty brownies?'" Lombardi lights up.

Everyone oohs and aahs.

"What are' Slutty Brownies?'" Tonantzin, asks.

"Oh, they're brownies with cookie dough, Oreos and chocolate lava," Laina explains. Everyone is a fan, even Mr. Leblanc, who tries to stay away from gluten and is always saying "*el trigo es el enemigo*," will cheat today.

I find a cucumber salad to pile on my plate.

"I think Tracy is coming to train us for PARCC next Friday," Leblanc says.

"What does that stand for?" I ask.

"Partnership for Assessment of Readiness for College and Careers. And all of the high school students in New Mexico have to take it."

"Our students struggle with it a lot, and it's been very controversial," Leblanc continues. "It's hard for our English Language Learners (ELL) and our Special Ed kids to even decode the questions. The vocabulary is very high and the content that they use is so ... White. The excerpts of test that they use are mostly from Anglo literature. It's kind of a biased test."

"Uhh, that sucks," I say.

"Yeah, it causes a lot of anxiety in the kids. We try to help them prepare by giving them test-taking tools," Leblanc tells me.

"Sometimes they get discouraged with the questions, or how long the excerpts are. And they get fatigued mentally because it's a four-hour test."

"FOUR HOURS? Who *wouldn't* get fatigued! Isn't this the test that a lot of students protested and walked out on last year?" I ask. "I saw it on the news."

"Yeah, but they need it to graduate, so we try to discourage them from skipping it. The other thing is, teachers aren't allowed to know what's on the test. We can't see what's on it," Leblanc explains.

"Well, how are we supposed to make sure they're successful on such an important test, if we don't know what's on it?" I ask.

"They just tell us to 'teach to the Standards.'"

Leblanc is my mentor- teacher. Thank goodness he tells me this, otherwise, I'd have no idea.

"But, word from the new governor is that they may get rid of the PARCC. They don't know what to replace it with though."

"Uh, I don't know how you teachers do all this. It's so much!" I say. "I really respect what you guys do!"

There are so many requirements for the Public Education Department. Then there's class preparation, working late on planning, paperwork coming out of our ears. It's insane. I had heard the last history teacher only made it one year.

"Hey, you guys know S.W.A.T. was here to take a student? Mr. Lombardi changes the subject.

"Wait, what?" Mr. Ridgway stops eating. We all turn to Lombardi.

"Yeah, they came to get Alicia Pena. Jim told him instead of coming in the school, and making a disruption, we'll bring her over to you. He and the security guard walked her across the street."

"Why did S.W.A.T. want her?" Ms. Baker asks.

"She is the girl they have been searching for, for alleged murder. Police had arrested the wrong girl by mistaken identity," Lombardi says.

"Whoa! I heard that on the news last night!" I say.

"Supposedly she lured some guy to a location to rob him. And when he ran, they guy who was in on it, shot him in the back," Lombardi explains.

"Wow," Ms. Baker says.

"She came to this school to hide from the police. What was weird was the first time she came to class, *nobody* would talk. The students must have known. I mean, *no one* would say a word. She walked in, and there were icicles in the room."

"No way!" I say with my eyebrows up.

"Serious," Lombardi nods.

Mr. Leblanc taps me on the shoulder before shooting his napkin in the bin.

"I don't care!" I yell and go back to searching for something vegetarian to add to my plate.

59

Cramps and Cowbells

Brianna's done it again. This student is unbearable, talking loudly about stupid things. My stomach starts to hurt. I can't censor her every word. I try to keep all the kids on track. I ask them for their work checklist. Let's get started. Round and round I go around the classroom as my stomach hurts more and more. These girls won't shut up. I tell myself not to be 'on her' and give her a little freedom.

Raya is working by herself, away from the other kids. The brats start talking about a boy who dresses like a girl.

"Oh, he's trans," Raya says.

"Nah, I don't know what he is," Dina says. Raya narrows her eyes. I go stand by my desk. "Just let it be." I remind myself not to get worked up, even though my stomach is hurting worse. I take some drinks of water. What she said was wrong, but I don't know what to say. There's more conversation between Dina and Raya, but I can't hear it. I can only hear my heart rate going up. I need to sit down.

Raya stands up.

"Uh, Miss, is it alright if I work in ISS because I just *can't* in here?" I get up toward her, nod my head in understanding. I'm not sure if she's going to have a panic attack like she did the other day. Either way, I trust her.

"Yes, of course." I wave my arm back towards the door, like if she really needs to, get out of here. "I understand, I get it," I whisper to her as she walks by. I wish I could go with her. I get another stomach cramp and sit at my desk again. What do I do? Dina has wasted 30 minutes of class time. Maybe I should send her to ISS? I write up a pass for her to go to ISS then I walk over to give it to her. I see she's written a few notes down on her notebook.

"Oooh, she was going to make you go to ISS!" Brianna tells Dina. I decide not to lie from my intention.

"I was, I showed her the pass. I'm glad you got started," I back off. Another stomach cramp. I go back to my desk.

"Miss! Dina almost cut my hair!" My Monster yells.

"She did not cut your hair, please keep your voice down," I say.

"Oh, if I would have run around with scissors, you would have written me up. And what are those write-ups supposed to do, anyway?" Brianna asks.

"They are supposed to be a reminder." I point to my head on both temples with each of my hands. It may be demeaning, but she does act like a 6th grader.

s"Oh, okay, remind me all day," Brianna scoffs. I the room. I lost one student to ISS, the others are paralyzed in front of me from listening to Brianna's conversation. One of them asked to put his earbuds in. Fatima can't talk and only works on her art. Two girls in the back are trying to do their work, but are sometimes stunned by Brianna and Dina's words. It's all gibberish to me. I don't want to hear what childish stuff these kids are talking about. I try to go about the room again and notice one kid is asleep. I whisper to him.

"Manuel, you can't get credit for falling asleep. Do you want to go to sleep in ISS?" he shakes his head.

"I'm just tired," he whispers.

"You are going to have to end up making this up later in lunches if you don't do it in class," I warn, but he shrugs his shoulders. I can't believe this shit. I start to go to my desk to make a note that he hasn't been working all period.

Suddenly Brianna yells: "MISS, WHY DID YOU SAY THAT DINA AND I WON'T BE HAVING ANY MORE CLASSES TO-GETHER? WHY DID YOU DECIDE THAT?"

"First of all, bring your voice down. That's not a conversation to be had right now. If you want to talk to me privately about it, you can." I try to say, but Brianna talks over me.

"NO. I WANT TO KNOW. IT'S NOT FAIR." She is irate, but I still try to redirect Brianna about three more times.

Then I decided to write a pass for her to take a break. I can't write it fast enough. I walk over to her and try to be discrete, but she yells. "No, I'm not leaving." I go back to my desk to draft an email.

"I'm not going to talk about this right now while you have that tone with me. It's a private matter."

I push the quick button on the phone for the Dean of Students' office. He's never there around this time. He answers!

"Can you take Brianna? She's making a stink and won't leave," I whisper.

"Yeah," he hangs up. He's at my door within seconds and waves his hand over to Brianna.

"No. I don't think so," Brianna tells Jim.

"Yeah, we're just going to talk," he tells her. She hesitates but stands up and walks to the door.

"I'LL BE BACK," Brianna glares at me and leaves the classroom. I walk over to the door and shut it to lock it. 'The hell you will,' I say to myself. And take a breath. She even tries to bully me!

Thank God, Jim kept her in his office for the rest of the period. I could finally breathe again. I sent an email to Jill, the social worker who is working with her. There are only about 15 minutes left of class, but they are peaceful with My Monster not there. Not enough for the stomach cramps to completely subside. Brianna still has to come back for her stuff after class.

The bell rings. People shuffle out.

"Have a good rest of your day, folks," I try to muster. I drafted an email, but I forgot to whom. Brianna walks in.

"Here, I gathered your stuff for you," Dina says, like a pathetic bully's victim. The bullying in this relationship is astounding. I work on my computer until they both leave, and I ignore them. I don't even go out to monitor the hallways. When the bell rings for my prep period, I lock the door and call my mom. My stomach is still not done doing its thing. I try to make the conversation short. When I get off the phone, I go check in with the Dean of Students. He's in his office.

"Thank you for taking her. I have a stomach ache from her all period long." I stand in a weird position, sitting with my hand pushing my side in, as my legs are crossed.

"Yeah, I let her sit in here for a good while because I had an emergency with another kid. She seemed to have calmed down a little." Jim shows a spark of hope in his eyes and smiles.

"I had an IEP with Dina the other day. I told her mom that my only concern was the dynamic she has with Brianna. Dina's mom said she was surprised that they had a class together. I told her they wouldn't have classes together in the future because they distract each other. When Dina told Brianna, she went through the roof," I explain as I sit on one of the two chairs in front of his desk.

"Yeah, that was what she said she was mad at. She didn't understand how one person could decide that. I told her, 'No, the principal decided, the staff decided," Jim said. "And you have to think about it from her young brain, that it would be unfair" He tries to explain to me. I nod my head and try to see it from her point of view.

"Yes, but we're six weeks into this quarter, and neither of them are passing."

"Well, does Brianna know that Dina is not passing the class?" Jim asks.

"Um... you know, I don't know." I still try to see the situation from the side of a greedy, needy twelve-year-old-mature brain. I can't share information from one student to another. Even if I were to tell Brianna that she should ask her friend if she's passing, that gives an indication that she's not. I have to be careful. "My stomach is still hurting." I squeeze my hand into my stomach from another angle.

"At least she does try to do better. I just think she's immature, and it's going to take time. Felicia said Dina is on her caseload. Maybe with both of them seeing social workers, we can wear them down." Jim smiles.

"And remember, we only have eight more days left," he adds.

"Eight? Nine!" I argue while standing up on one leg and resting my other leg on the chair.

"Look, today is already done!"

True, I only have one class with a roster of three in 6th period. "And Friday is an Incomplete make-up day, and she probably won't come." He smiles. I smile.

"okay. I only have to survive eight more days." I stand up. "My stomach is feeling a little better. Thanks, Jim." I take a breath before walking out of his office and go back to my classroom.

What am I supposed to learn from this? How am I supposed to handle these situations? Do I step in sooner to separate them? Today I didn't step in early enough, and my body was telling me. I sacrificed the emotional health of nine people so that two of them could act a fool and make us sick. I need to do better.

It's my prep period. I walk past the workroom and see the school social worker inside through the windows. I go in there, straight to the back, where the worktable is and grab the longest scissors we have. I try to angle them against the worktable and point them to my neck, so I would have to lean on the tips to stab myself.

"Felicia, I can't do it anymore. I need a referral."

"To who?" She asks me, She's searching for a pen in this room, always void of pens.

"To You! I can't do it anymore. I've lost it. I can't handle it." I'm still pointing the scissors to my neck, but she doesn't notice.

"Who is it now?" She says in a long, drawn out nasally drawl as she frowns.

"Everyone. I hate all kids." I put the scissors down and put my head on the table, exhausted. I drop my shoulders.

"Aww.. can you make it through the next few days?" Felicia asks.

"I. don't. think. so."

"You can do it, Joselyn! Mrs. Doyle says to me as earnestly as possible. Any minute now, they are going to kick it into high gear because they are all behind, and they will be busy. She offers me a little hope. I get up to take a deep breath when we hear Kimberly, the guidance counselor announce with a simile:

"I am proud to announce, our first graduate of the year... Carmen Robles!"

This is one of the school's rituals. When Mrs. Doyle went to Switzerland with her family one year, she brought back a cowbell. You can never have too much cowbell! We do it this way because our students finish their credits at different times of the year and unofficially "graduate." It's a great way to celebrate their individual accomplishment. Often, families come to witness and videotape the occasion.

Mrs. Doyle and I walk out of the workroom to the front as more and more people gather and clap, cheer, and whistle. It's a great time. Sometimes students cry. There are always hugs. This is wonderful. It's one more kid who has opened the door to opportunities in their life.

60

Lunchroom - Headaches and Bread

Mrs. Doyle and Mr. Ridgeway are in the lunchroom talking about a particular student when I walk in.

"He seems to be profoundly, profoundly sad," Mrs. Doyle says.

"Yeah, I have a hard time with him because he'll say something smart, but then he acts like '*ok*! That's enough for the week!'" Mr. Ridgeway says and we chuckle.

"I've seen that in him too," Mrs. Doyle says. "Jill has been working with him."

When Mr. Leblanc is finished with his lunch, he wads up his napkin and shoots it from across the room and misses. I shake my head.

"I was 3 for 4 yesterday!" Mr. Leblanc smiles proudly.

Mr. Jones puts his bean enchiladas with red chile in the microwave and starts talking about his son.

"Today, Dean woke up and said, 'Papa! You were in my dream! We were looking at rocks. What was that rock we were looking at?' I said, 'I don't know, Dean. I wasn't there,' and he says, 'but you were right there, papa, don't you remember?'" I had to explain that I can't see his dreams.

"Ha! That's funny!" Ms. Baker laughs. "Maybe it was an amethyst.' Ms. Baker suggests as she unzips her Disney lunchbox.

Hey, how did it go with Jose today, Lombardi?" Mr. Ridgway asks while leaning back in his chair.

"Ah, good, with the help of Jim. Yeah, we had a great conversation. He apologized for saying what he said to me yesterday. He said that there was something else that was already bothering him." Lombardi takes out the ingredients to his turkey sandwich.

"What did he say to you?" Ms. Baker asks as she swishes her cold soup around in a violet plastic container. "Oh, I like tapped him on the arm, kinda playfully, and he said

'DO. NOT. FUCKING. TOUCH. ME.' I was taken aback and didn't expect it. I felt like shit afterward."

"Oh, wow," Ms. Baker responds and gets in line to warm up her soup.

I eat some, but not all of my salad.

"I'm so glad you got that resolved. I hate to have stuff hanging over," I say as I start to rub my temples.

"Yeah," Lombardi responds and layers the pickles on his bread with mayo.

"Like right now. This headache is getting worse as we get closer to 4th." I rub pressure-points on my face. "I used to love that class, now I have to rearrange the whole class because of My Monster. I'm not going to have them collaborate and do group work anymore. I'm just going to have them work on their own and see how that works." I put my head down on the lid of my water canteen. "I didn't even have a peaceful weekend because she kept entering my mind. 'The blue sky is still there. Just watch the clouds go by,' I repeat what my meditation app says to me and turn my head to put it on the table.

"I totally know which HeadSpace App episode that is!" Lombardi chuckles with his index finger out. We both use the same meditation app on our phones. I get up and walk to the work table, still rubbing my temples.

"What did I do to deserve these children?!" I say, feeling desperate. I see a half-loaf of bread. I put it down and press into my eyes with my fingertips. Ms. Rivera notices me.

"Awe, I'm sorry, dude. I hope 4th goes better today," Lombardi says with a tilt in his head.

"You should put your face into that bread," Ms. Rivera suggests.

"You... you think I could do that?" I stare at her face for approval.

"YEAH, that's a *thing*, Jocelyn. Have you heard of Bread Face on Insta?" she says with a smirk.

"What?"

"She squishes her face in bread, and she has about a million followers." Ms. Rivera's makeup is always done so nicely. She's a little quirky, all art teachers are. I smile.

"You're joking. Would anyone care if I put my face in this bread?" I look around. No one objects, so I do it. It feels so good.

"Ahhh... that feels great. No wonder she does it." I left the plastic on the bread, and the bread popped right back into place. It's probably pumped with preservatives and yoga mat. I'm excited that it bounces back, so I do it again.

"Ahh, that's wonderful. Thanks for sharing that. And thank you for not shaming me while I have a mental breakdown in front of you guys.

"Can we just call this 'self-care?'" I say.

The warning bell rings, and we file out of the lunchroom.

I'm walking in front of Mr. Ridgeway when, out of nowhere, he goes, "WHOOP!" and it shakes me to my bones. My body does this convulsive-shiver while walking down the hall and Mr. Jones happens to see it and laughs.

"What the hell was that!" I turn back and ask.

"I have no idea," Mr. Ridgeway admits. "It just came out."

I see the students I love and smile. I should remember how wonderful they are. I should focus on them.

"Sergio, I wanna thank you for being solid. You know what I mean?" I say to my student who didn't do well at Sandia High School and got no attention from his teachers. He smiles at me.

"You know it, Miss," Sergio says and I smile.

61

Valentine's Day Betrayal

This morning Mr. Smith entered the lunchroom with a cardboard box of Valentine's Day goodies.

"Happy Valentine's Day! Have some!" Mr. Smith holds the box open in front of me. There are Mint Chocolate Oreos and other chocolate cookies. I decline.

"Thank you, I'm fine. Happy Valentine's Day." Mr. Smith moves on to Mr. Jones.

"Would you like some?" Mr. Smith holds the box in front of Mr. Jones as he's seated at the table.

"No thanks, I'm about to eat a breakfast burrito." Smith sets the box down on the free food table and unpacks the sweets.

"Oh, I hate Valentine's Day. It's like my Friday the Thirteenth. I've gotten in car accidents, had seizures. I'm a little weary," I say.

The bell rings for first period. I get the class going on their assignments and have to use the bathroom. I call Charlie for coverage.

"Charlie, can you come watch my kids for a second while I run to the restroom, please?"

"No." Charlie thinks he's funny.

"Come on please. Don't make me pee my pants in front of all these people," I beg.

"'M'kay, be there in a minute," Charlie says and hangs up.

I wait, and wait, and then glare down the hall. I don't see him. I can't take it. I study the students in the class to calculate how likely this group of kids would get into a fight. There are only six kids in the class.

"Karen, Charlie is coming to watch the class. I'm running to the bathroom." I tell my good kid. She nods. I do my thing and come back. No Charlie.

Second period is disrupted with Valentine balloons and flower deliveries. I was about to get frustrated when my door opened for the third time. I blurted out: "Getting disrupted by balloons is better than getting disrupted by a shooting."

"There was a shooting, Miss?" One of my students asks me.

"Yeah, don't you remember, last year at Marjory Stoneman-Douglas in Florida? It was on Valentine's Day. The shooter pulled the fire alarm, and everyone went out into the halls and he started shooting."

"Hm, good way to pick off your bullies," another kid responds.

"What?" No! That is NOT the way to deal with bullies." I start to freak out and don't know what to say.

"I saw my brother shoot someone in the head," Christian volunteers. My eyebrows go up and my mouth drops.

"That's traumatizing," I say and blink. I'm about to start to cry.

"Go ahead and start on your independent reading. I need to use the restroom." I leave the room and don't make it to the bathroom. I hide in the supply closet and break down. Ms. Baker goes in there.

"What's wrong," Ms. Baker asks, but I'm weeping.

"The-kids. The-Valentine's-Day-shooting. I, I..." I just cry.

"Do you want me to watch your classroom?"

"YES!" is the only word I can get out.

"Don't worry, I'll watch them." Ms. Baker walks out and sees Felicia. She sends Felicia into the supply closet.

"Joselyn, what's wrong?" Felicia asks. I manage to catch my breath and make better sense when I explain.

"Were there a bunch of boys in that class?" Felicia asks.

"Yes," I say, confused.

"You know, Joselyn, boys will often try to one-up each other and try to be masculine and tough by talking like this."

"They do?" I wipe my tears.

"Yeah, I wouldn't worry about it. Boys talk like that in front of each other," Felicia explains.

"That's awful," I say.

"I know, but they do." Felicia has an empathetic expression on her face.

I get myself together enough to go back to class and am able to get through third.

For lunch, I share my experience with whoever is in the lunchroom.

"That shooting was awful," Mr. Leblanc's shoulders dropped like he lost his appetite. "I think it's the fucking video games," his body wakes up and looks around.

"No, they've done studies," the math teacher begins to explain but gets interrupted.

"And the guns, these kids have access to too many guns!" Mr. Leblanc gets heated.

"Paige has lots of guns." I know Ms. Baker is talking about play guns and her three-year-old grandson.

"Where does he go to school, so I don't send my kids there," Lombardi says.

I start to say, "Toy guns," but Ms. Baker, with all white hair, puts up a real "W" gang sign and says, "Westside!" Everyone howls at the sight of this grandmother throwing up a gang sign. I cry with laughter. Only these people could make me laugh after crying.

Lunch passes quickly as usual.

At the end of the school day, my mom invites me over. I take the family a balloon and some chocolates. The balloon is for the cat, Prince. He likes to chase the string.

While at my mom's house watching the news, a friend's face flashes on the screen while the reporter speaks:

"As a result of processing some cold case DNA kits, an Albuquerque man has been charged with two cases of rape." The reporter continues to talk, but I can't hear her. Did she say rape? Noo... not Vashon! There's no way. These have to be false accusations. There is no way. I tune back into the reporter. She says one Albuquerque rape case dates backs to 1998. Another charge from California dates back to 2004.

This is not happening! This can't be true ...but it's DNA and in *two* states! Not Van, he was always respectful! We were such good friends, he gave me my first copy of Malcolm X! We hung out together all the time after high school in 1994.

I feel like I have to hold on to something. After the news report, I leave my parent's house to be alone to process this.

Driving home, I think of stopping for something alcohol. No. Do I need to go back to therapy?... No, I should feel the feelings. It's okay. I let the tears fall down my face.

When I get home I try to think. There was *zero* indication of violence. I've known Vashon since we were 17. We met at CEC, the Career Enrichment Center, at Albuquerque High. Casey introduced me to him. He was tall, kinda lanky, with a big smile. Vashon seemed cool. He was always caring and kind, a leader.

I remember he wanted a relationship with me, but I couldn't do it. I was resistant to anything that could remotely work out. We were good friends. He let me have his brown leather beret. How can this person that I've known for... let me do the math... twenty-eight years? How could he have done these things and showed me something else? Was he raping people all that time? Was he on drugs? Should I reach out to him? I'm his friend. Am I not his unconditional friend?

But Joselyn, it is rape. Who is he? I used to greet him with open arms! I would have trusted him with my life. I need to breathe. I let myself cry. Why did he have to do that? Why would anybody do that? Who... who... is he? Who is anyone? Who can you trust anymore? I take deep breaths and cry. Did his monster only come out sometimes? Why did he never show signs of disrespect? All this time that I've seen him lately, he's been doing good things in the community. I loved it. Oh my, was it all fake? I do a search for the Ted Talk he did on the Internet...

In the Ted Talk, he's talking about how you have to know a child before you can teach a child. Well, that's true. He talks about doing volunteer work at his child's school. He talks about making friends with someone who didn't have friends. How he helped the kid come out of his shell, and how the student started writing and participating at school. Is it all bullshit?

I feel so betrayed. I remember he once wrote a note to me on two sides of a piece of paper and gave it to me. One side said, "Will you marry me," and the other, it said, "in ten years." we were like 17 at the time. Is he a shell of a good man? A fake? Did he change after high school and then fake his trustworthiness? Would he admit to me what he did if I wrote him? Would he tell me the truth? Would he have an explanation? Would he deny it? What does it matter if he admits it to me or not? It matters because I've survived rape. I know what it's like, and I can't imagine how or why he could do such a thing.

I pull up another article on the cases on my laptop. The accuser from California said he raped her in the alley outside of a party. He allegedly told her if she said anything, he'd kill her. I can't imagine those words coming out of his mouth, but perhaps I never saw that part of him. That's such a violent thing to say and do! Maybe I shouldn't open the door or a window to a person who can be so Jekyll and Hyde' ish? I thought I had that unconditional love for him but, rape? I just can't. Is all love conditional? See, this is why I can never have enough trust to marry someone. I would have trusted my own children with him. Not anymore.

I lost a friend today. It's like he died. He was never who I thought he was. Opening your life to a sociopath can be very dangerous. Maybe I just need to put him behind me. He's going to have to figure out his own life while I figure out mine. Forget about him.

Now I have to think of a good Bell Ringer.

62

Equine Therapy

My Leadership class and I are on our way to Loving Thunder Horse stables in Rio Rancho. It's mid-March before Spring Break and we're on a field trip with First Nations Community Healthcare. The school partnered with the non-profit organization to teach this class. First Nations offered equine therapy as a leadership learning experience.

I had been worried about how I was going to bring my student who uses a wheelchair. Laina would have had to bring her in her car because she has office approval to transport students. But it turned out that the student didn't show up. I kind of expected it. She only comes to school half the time.

Brianna and Dina didn't make it either, which is sad. They could have really benefited from this experience.

While we pile out of the van Noah, from First Nations, pulls out some pool noodles from out of the van. We're all wondering what they're for. Nearby is a small horse arena, sectioned off by a gate made of white metal pipe. There are some stables in the back and stadium seats between the arena and the stables.

"When we think about leadership, sometimes that means listening. So I'm going to ask you to listen now and think, how do we define leadership? If you were to guide someone somewhere, how would you do it? How would you lead? Or, what if someone wanted to lead you, but they seemed to be unsure. Would you want them to lead you? Would you feel safe? See, this is all about safety and trust. I want you to stand with a partner and put this noodle between you long-ways. Put it shoulder to shoulder and walk in the same direction. Choose one person to be the leader and decide the direction you'll go in. Now, can I use you as an example?" Noah asks Joshua, and Joshua stands about five feet away from Noah. Noah places the noodle between them.

"See, there has to be a certain amount of tension between you. If there is no tension, the noodle falls, if there is too much tension, the noodle pops out, right? So you have to physically communicate with this other person to do something. So, go ahead and try it with a partner." We start to perform the challenging task of walking, holding the pool noodle between us.

After the exercise, Noah explains:

"You're going to go into the arena. You're going to take the horse by the rope and lead the horse to walk in the direction that you want to go in. The horse will follow you. You have to develop trust and communication, whether it is with your body or your voice."

"Now, Shayna is going to talk with you while I get the horses into the arena." Noah walks off.

Shayna takes over. "So I want you to take a few breaths and notice how, when you are. You are creating a new experience in your mind," Shayna says. "I want you to take in the sights of the beautiful Sandia Mountains, over here to the east and the smells. Some people don't like the smell of horse poop. But for me, it reminds me of being a little girl and always being around my grandfather's horses. For me, that smell brings a sense of safety to me. Use your sense of touch, let the horse smell you. Pet the horse, talk to them. If you are feeling uneasy or afraid, they will sense that. So, be honest. You will be meeting Laramie, the male horse, and Belle, the female horse. Horses respond to what you are feeling, so be honest. They're our friends. And be open to what you hear." A horse neighs in the background.

"Take the experience and take it all in," Shayna continues, "We're going to go over to the arena, and you'll meet the horses. Let them smell you, introduce yourself. Let them know that you're not a threat. It took thousands of years to foster a positive relationship with the horse. It took time and trust for us to have a friendship. Let them know who you are. Then those of you who have signed consents forms from your parents can put the helmet on and go into the arena. You'll go from one side of the horse, introduce yourself, go around the back of the horse and go to the other side. Horses have eyes on both sides of their face. So they're aware of what is going on all around. It's like a panoramic view from each eye. Then, when Noah gives you the rope, you will be walking the horse around the arena. This is where you're going to use your leadership skills and lead the horse. If you don't lead the horse, the horse will do whatever it wants, so you have to be direct in your path and your speed. I want each person to walk each horse at least one time. You'll see how you have to communicate with the horse. They will read you. Alright, let's walk down over there, where Laramie is." Shayna leads us down to the arena.

We walk around a little dirt trail for vehicles. Off the path where there is stadium seating, Shayna goes over to Belle and says hello to her. The horse sniff her hands, then Shaina pets the horse.

"Go ahead, come along, one by one, to introduce yourself to Belle." The students are hesitant, trying to let someone else go first. Joshua goes ahead and allows the horse to smell his hand. One by one, they introduce themselves, then Noah passes the helmets out. Each student takes their own time leading the horse, with a partner on the other side.

Basma gets Belle to gallop for a little while! Sometimes they would get stuck, and the horse wouldn't move. So then they would have to take the initiative to firmly guide the horse in the direction they wanted to go in.

"It's not mean," Shayna explains as she helps Sergio. "You're letting the horse know where you want to go. You're taking the initiative. They'll go straight to the salt rock or to the fence if you don't take the initiative." I can hear Sergio talking to Belle and then take steps to guide her forward and then in a curve around the arena. They go at a slow and steady pace, and Sergio does a great job. I see each student has their moment of being stuck with the horse. The horse will either not want to move forward, or it goes in another direction. The student works it out and leads the horse. It's adorable.

I introduce myself to Belle. I let her sniff me, and I go around to the other side and introduce myself again and let her sniff me. I take her rope.

"Come on, Belle." I walk with assertion and in a direction that I know is not going to be obstructed. It's a little bit of a struggle to turn her, but she complies. It's awesome. I take in the smells, the sights, and the feeling of the rough, dusty coat of the horse.

After each student has taken their turn with both horses, we go back to the van.

Before leaving, we stop for a few group photos. It was a wonderful day.

63

Bad Fall

My grandparents' children in order:

1. *Jesse- A Marine who was killed in Vietnam in 1968.*
2. *Andres - A retired welder who is widowed and has one adult daughter. He now has dementia.*
3. *Marcy - A married Christian woman who lives in Taos, New Mexico. She has three adult children.*
4. *Tony - Used to do a lot of drugs as a young man and suffered from mental illness as an adult. Passed away a few years ago.*
5. *Samuel - Retired HVAC worker at Sandia Labs. Is married with an adult daughter. Refinanced his home to live in a nice neighborhood in Taylor Ranch.*
6. *Michael - Never made anything of himself. Has lived with my grandparents all his life. He lives in Albuquerque or will stay in their home in Pecos when he gets kicked out for having temper tantrums.*
7. *Clara - My mother, a retired kindergarten Educational Assistant. She had me at 18 and my half-sister at 40 with my stepfather.*

"My dad fell last night, and they took him to UNMH in the ambulance. He broke his hip," My mom tells me over the phone this Saturday morning. She never phones unless it's an emergency.

"Shit," I respond. "That's not good." My grandfather is ninety-five years old and has severe dementia.

"No," my mom agrees. "It's not."

"That's when they really decline." I remind her. We've both worked with the elderly in the past, we know.

"Yup," my mom replies. I hear a sniffle. "He's supposed to have surgery today at noon. The hospital will call me first."

"Okay. Let me know when they do."

"Alright,"my mom says and we hang up.

My grandfather's surgery keeps getting postponed for life-or-death situations. He's "stable" and they're not.

The next day I go to the hospital. I park in the parking garage. When I get out of my car I step carefully. The parking garage is disgusting. There's a black film on the floor and vomit stains everywhere.

When I finally find my grandfather he seems uncomfortable and antsy. He's trying to move, but his arms are restrained; he's wearing puffy white mittens. I already know he would try to escape if he could. He's been known to take off, due to his severe dementia.

"Grampo?" I say. He stops to listen. "What are you doing?" I ask him.

"Oh, I wanna get out of here," he says in his quiet but gruff voice. He has an oxygen mask on his face and he's wearing boxing mittens and they are tied down.

"Well, you can't leave yet. You had a fall, and now they want to give you hip surgery," I explain.

"Oh no, I didn't fall," My grandfather says with his eyebrows up.

"Yes, grampo. You fractured your hip, and you need to stay right here until the surgeon works on you, okay?" I try to explain.

"Oh, alright," he says. A nurse walks in.

"Do you know when he'll be able to go into surgery?" I ask.

"Well, his oxygen was low, so the doctor had postponed it. It's pretty good now, so he's ready to go into the operating room. We're just waiting for the OR to free up."

"Can he have some water or something to eat?" I ask.

"He's on a no-eat, no-drink restriction until surgery, by the direction of the surgeon," the nurse says.

"Oh, okay. His mouth just looks dry," I point to my grandfather's mouth.

"We have some mouth sponges that can help with that. I'll get some," the nurse promises.

"Thank you," I reply.

My grandfather starts to mumble.

"I can clear off that bed for you, if you want to stay with him." The nurse points to some big metal contraption that is used to pull yourself up while lying in the hospital bed.

"Alright, I'll go home to get a few things and be back."

I go home to eat and gather a light blanket and my laptop. By the time I return, the sun is beginning to set.

I check in with the nurse's station first.

"How's my grandfather, Jesus, doing in 315?"

"Oh, well, we just took care of him because he pulled out his IV. We had to find a new place to reinsert it, and I wrapped it," a young male nurse reports.

"Oh no," I cringe. "Thank you," I say and then keep walking to my grandpa's room.

"Samuel! Samuel!" My grandfather's yelling for his son. I don't know why he'd be calling for him. He barely visits my grampo. According to my grandmother, he hasn't seen him for Father's Day for the past six years.

Samuel considers himself the most successful of my grandparent's seven children. He and his wife live in a big beautiful home in Taylor Ranch, a suburb of Albuquerque. Growing up, I didn't really know what my uncle did for a living. I knew he worked for Sandia, which is an esteemed government employer. Recently, I realized he went to community school for HVAC. HVAC, really? He acted like he was some sort of engineer and like he was better than the rest of us. Samuel has always been cold and quiet, even with his daughter.

"Abuelito, Abuelito, what do you need?" I say while walking over to him.

"Quiero salir de aqui," my grandfather tells me.

"Grampo, tienes que quedarte aquí para operarte de cadera. You fell and broke your hip. Can you relax in this bed for a while longer? They are going to take you to the operating room."

"Oh," he says. "But I've gotta use the restroom."

"You can go right there, grampa, it's okay. You really shouldn't get up right now with your hip like that. You can go where you are, it's okay." I hope he understands.

"Oh, alright," he says. A woman in scrubs comes into the room.

"I'm here to take your blood pressure, Mr. Martinez." A petite woman with caramel skin comes in and gently takes his blood pressure.

"He keeps saying he needs to use the bathroom," I tell her.

"I'll let the nurse know. She may be able to check if his bladder is full and he's not able to urinate," she says.

Soon, the nurse comes in.

"I'm going to check to see if his bladder is full, and if it is, we're going to have to insert a catheter," she tells me.

"I'll give you guys some privacy," I respond. The nurse says I'm more than welcome to stay in the room, but my family is very modest, so I leave.

When I come back, I find my grandfather asleep. They did have to insert a catheter. He must feel so much better now. I start to watch "Fixer Upper" on my laptop to distract me from where I am, but realize I'm too sleepy to care. I fold my laptop up when someone comes into the room. It's the nurse.

"Hi! Yeah, I just got the call, they want to take him in for surgery right now."

"Now? Wow." I fumble out of the cot-size bed. The hospital orderly comes to transfer him and allows me to go with him. It's 10:30 p.m.

The orderly fastens the catheter bag and the oxygen tank on his bed, and we're off to the 5th floor. My grandfather gets parked in what seems like the "runway" for the operating room. We're in the hallway, in front of monitors that note information about patient's surgeries. A man comes to check if my grandfather's hip is already marked. We check, and it is. My grandfather has his eyes closed. The man uses an iPad for an ultrasound to check his heart. The man comes back to me to tell me grampo is clear for surgery. He will be next, after the patient before him comes out. Then, the curtains in the corner bed open up, and they wheel out a man who is heavily sedated.

"So although your grandfather appears to be a good candidate for the surgery, there *are* risks. Do you have any questions?" He stares at me with his hands folded.

"How long do you think the surgery will take?"

"This woman here will take your phone number down and call you when it's over. The whole thing, including some time in recovery, can be two to three hours," he estimates.

"Well, thank you for what you do." I don't know what to say. I turn to my grandfather.

"Grampo?" His eyes open. I rub his shoulder. "Te van a llevar a ciruguia ahora." He nods. "They're going to replace your hip, so you can go dancing again, okay? You're going to be fine. It's going to take a few hours. I'll be here when you come out." He nods his head. I kiss him on his head and rub his shoulder again. They wheel him off; it's a little after 11:00 p.m.

I gather my things. I'd rather rest in my bed than in the hospital.

When I get home, it's almost 11:30. I have so much anxiety. *I'm* the one who's going to get the call if he doesn't make it. I lie there, with my thoughts floating in so many directions.

My cell phone rings, and I wake with a start. It's almost 2:30 a.m.

"This is Surgeon Patel. Jesús just got out of surgery. The surgery went well, he's stable and in the recovery room," he reports.

"Oh, thank you!"

My mother and I spent the next three days in and out of the hospital, making sure my grandfather ate. It's good this is happening during Spring Break so I didn't have to plan for a substitute.

As the days pass, I'm surprised at how none of his sons are at his side to help. Michael hasn't been here at all. Word is he's at the house in Pecos. Samuel and Andres came to visit, but none of them are here to *help*. Uncle Andres has an excuse; he, like my grandfather, has dementia and needs help himself.

And why am I here? Jesus, my "grampo," or "gramps," as I call him, is, in my eyes, is the most perfect man there is. He's the father of six children. He worked from dawn to sunset every day to provide for them and his wife. How he's put up with my grandmother for 74 years of marriage, I will never know. She's a difficult woman.

Gramps gave me my best memories. When I was very young, my mom and I lived with my grandparents at their house in Pecos. I remember my grandfather taking me on his tractor. He would sit me in front of him on the metal seat with a large metal spring underneath that creaked. He made the seat comfortable with an old flat chair pillow. He would operate the gas and brake pedals and would let me steer the wheel. We would only go one to two miles an hour, but I felt like I was on top of the world! We would pass the house, and my grandmother would come out of the dining room to wave her dishtowel.

"*Abuelita! Abuelita!*" I would call, "I'm driving the tractor!" He would take the wheel. We would go to the *terreno*. That's where he grew lettuce, peas, carrots, tomatoes and radishes. There were apple trees, and a cherry tree that gave us yellow cherries. Best cherries on the planet! I would get lost in my wonderland of trees and vegetables for hours, playing with dirt. The land in Pecos was my favorite place to be as a child.

My grandpa never brushed me off. I would "help" him fix the cars and change the oil.

He had lost his hair when he was young, and I always made it a habit of rubbing his head and kissing it. He never pushed me away when I wanted to be affectionate or hug.

When I cried about the aliens on Sesame Street, he told me they couldn't get me. They weren't real. I didn't know that, at three years old! That meant something. He helped me shrug the monsters away. He taught me to read and would quiz me on addition and subtraction.

For all my life he called me "Shoshone," which is an Indian tribe here in New Mexico. I think he called me that because I was a little darker than most of the family. And for most of my life, I thought I was Shoshone. What did I know? When I took my DNA test, I found out I'm 30% Spanish and 30% Native American. The rest is little bits of "other." I was disappointed that Ancestry couldn't tell me what tribes I was.

Grampo was a religious evening news watcher, Walter Cronkite, then Tom Brokaw. He also liked The Lawrence Welk Show and Bob Ross on PBS. Everyone should know about "pretty little trees."

I didn't know I was missing a father until my mom asked me when I was about three. I didn't know what she was talking about. If my grandfather hadn't been around, I would never have had a good experience with a male. I started distrusting men from the age of nine. After my grandma's sister's husband touched me inappropriately. I got nervous any time I was alone with a man after that.

My grandpa was a small but strong man. An honorable man who was always there. A man who would never let you down, like a father should be.

Once, my idiot ex-boyfriend got his trailer stuck on a cement post at a gas station. We were moving from Chicago to LA. He couldn't figure out how to get it out. Luckily we were in Albuquerque, so I called my grandpa. My grandpa hammered the shit out of the metal and somehow got him loose. That was my D.J. boyfriend. For all his thinking that he was a genius, all he could do was D.J., couldn't fix or build anything. No one compares to my intelligent and resourceful grandpa.

The night after my grandpa's surgery he begged me to take the brace off of his leg all night. I couldn't get him to go to sleep and I hadn't slept in three days. When I got hives and couldn't take it anymore, I told the nurses I had to get some sleep and the nurse told me they would take good care of him.

In the next few weeks, I made new enemies and new alliances in my family. I wouldn't trust my uncles with my life, that's for sure. My mother and I made sure my grandpa ate at least twice a day while my aunt came from Taos to take care of my grandma. My cousin Marisol is a manager in eldercare. She advocated his care by phone from Las Vegas, New Mexico.

My grandpa was released from the hospital. He was taken to a rehabilitation center in Taylor Ranch. I found bedsores on my grandpa's backside while he was staying there. After a few days, he tried to get up to leave, and had another fall. I took a photo of the mark on his head. The care at the rehab place was terrible, but my grandmother wouldn't listen to us. I told her she should have my grandpa taken to Las Vegas where Marisol and her staff could watch over him. She did the opposite. Instead, she listened to my uncle Samuel, who told her to keep my grandfather there in Taylor Ranch. She always makes the wrong decisions. It's so hard to see bad decisions being made and not being able to do anything about it.

One weekend Marisol and I were with our grandpa at the rehab place during lunch time when Samuel showed up.

"Quieres sandia?" I ask my grandfather. I'm feeding my gramps some watermelon and Samuel yells at me,

"Cut it in pieces! He's going to choke!"

"He's *not* going to choke, it's WATERmelon," I say back. My grandpa is eating just fine. He has good teeth, and the watermelon dissolves in his mouth.

"You're a fucking idiot! You stupid bitch!" My uncle yells at me. Samuel has the nerve to keep gramps in this hell-hole of a place, barely visiting, and then yells at *me*?

"Don't talk to her like that!" Marisol rushes closer to my uncle and he flinches. My uncle has the nerve to disrespect us like this? I've been here every day. I have experience caring for the elderly. For this guy to waltz in here to act like I'm the shitty person sets me on fire, but I don't want to show it.

"You haven't even *been* here. You think you know what you're doing? *YOU* feed him."

"You're a bunch of stupid idiots," Samuel says.

"Get out of here! You don't talk to us like that!" Marisol points to the door.

"*You* get out of here!" Samuel protests.

"*I'm* not leaving. *I've* been here the whole time," I say. I hand him the bowl of watermelon. He grabs it from my hand, cutting the pieces in half and putting a piece in my grandpa's mouth. I see his hands shaking with anger, or fear, I can't tell. Samuel notices he's shaking too, and puts the bowl down and leaves. We notice one of the workers at the door.

"Is everything okay in here?" she asks.

"Yes, better now," I say now that Samuel has left.

"I can't believe he called his nieces that!" Marisol says.

"He's no longer my uncle. Uncles don't talk to their nieces like that."

My cousin Marisol checks in with the doctor to get him released to home care.

He went from the hospital, to rehabilitation, and then home. But then he ended up back in the hospital because he pulled his catheter out.

Now the doctor wants to have a family meeting about hospice.

Three doctors meet with eight of us family members. We're all around my grandfather's hospital bed, and Grampo is sitting up. I combed his wiry hair before everyone got there.

"Well, thank you all for coming. It's nice that Jesús has so many people who care about him. We want to ask you, since Jesús is not able to make decisions for himself. We're here to ask what do you think he would want for himself now, hospice at a nursing facility, or hospice at home?" We scan around the circle at each other and then finally settle on focusing on my grandmother.

"*Abuelita*, ¿Crees que Grampo querría estar en un hospicio con enfermeras o en casa durante sus últimos días?" My cousin, Cynthia, asks my grandmother in Spanish.

"*Pues, en la casa*," she responds.

"And are you okay with him going back to the house to spend his last days?" The female doctor has her lab coat open and is wearing a dress and short cowboy boots.

"*Sí, yo lo acepto con todo mi alma*," my grandmother says. The women immediately start to tear up.

"What? What did she say?" the male doctor asks.

"She said she will accept him with all of her soul," the second female doctor interprets,

Jeez, that's the most beautiful thing I've ever heard my grandmother say. All the women grab tissue and cry like babies. I was feeling so much. I knew this was the beginning of the end and I just had to wait it out.

After our meeting, my grandfather got released from the hospital and sent to home hospice. He was sent in an ambulance and I soon followed.

When I got there the ambulance workers had already set up his hospital bed in one of the extra rooms. I go over and rub his bony arms and his bony back. I can feel his spine and ribs through the sheet.

"Grampo?" His eyebrows move slightly. "I love you," I say.

"I lo- you," my grandpa whispers back. Those were his last words. He couldn't talk after that.

64

Horse Therapy in Action

Over the next few days of the Leadership classes, Brianna hadn't given me many problems.

I sometimes get anxiety before class, because I know she's coming. But I just tell myself to "Let It Be." I can't control her. I can only administer praises or punishments after the fact.

I need to think of this more like horse therapy. I remind myself you can't force a big-ass horse to move. It weighs more than you do. Introduce yourself to the horse, talk to it, create trust. Then you can move on to leading the horse on a walk. You have to not lead them into obstacles; it's part of the trust-building. Create a bond, then you can go for a jog. It takes time. It takes a specific tone and a particular pace.

All I can do is create an environment for students to feel safe in my room, even from me. I remember how my thoughts went to bullying the bully. Wishing someone would beat her up and put her in her place. But what was needed was a few conversations in different classes.

In Mr. Ridgeway's class, they discussed bullying. He said Brianna seemed to have come to a realization that she might be a bully. Hey! Admitting the problem is the first step, right?

At the end of my day, during my prep, Simone came to my classroom to ask me if I want to be a part of a "think tank" for the state. She asked me to be part of the Equity Council. She told me the council came about because of the Martinez-Yazzie lawsuit. Two families sued the state for inadequate education for their Latino and Native American children. I proudly agreed.

When I get home, I make myself some calabacitas, a New Mexican dish of zucchini, yellow squash, onion, garlic, green chile, and corn sauteed together. I add a side of pinto beans for protein.

My Leadership Class and their environmental project have me more aware of my waste at home. I'm buying less processed food, eating more whole foods and reusing plastic bags and jars.

After I ate, I called my mom to tell her about me being on the Equity Council and the Martinez-Yazzie lawsuit.

"Our cousin Dolores is part of that lawsuit," My mom tells me.

"What?" I say.

"Pretty sure. You should call her and ask."

"I think I have her number. Let me call you back," I say.

I hang up with my mom and call my cousin.

"Yeah, that lawsuit started ten years ago. My grandson was not diagnosed as Special Ed for many years and did not get the accommodations he needed," my cousin says.

"TEN YEARS AGO?" I ask.

"Yes, we've been in litigation forever. Now my grandkids have already graduated. But we won the case and I'm losing steam. I'm just afraid that the state will give schools some boxes to check and call it a day," my cousin explains.

"Well my principal asked me to be a part of the Equity Council and we have a conference in a few weeks," I tell her.

"Hmm. No one told me about it," Dolores says.

"I'll text you the information, if you want to go," I say.

"Will you, please? I'll meet you there."

"You got it. I'll see you there cousin," I say before hanging up.

After texting my cousin the information, I text my best friend Betty in L.A.

"Hey, you wanna do 30 days, no alcohol? See what happens?" I text.

"Yes!" she replies.

"Really? SWEET! Okay, we'll start tomorrow," I text her back.

It made me think about why I've been drinking this whole time. It started as little daily celebrations in L.A. First, it was like 'Yay! We made it to L.A.!' Then every small accomplishment was a drink celebration. People drink for lunch or dinner every day. But I think for me it turned into a coping mechanism after I got laid off. I had one therapist tell me that I should do things that 'feed my soul.' My homework was to write some ideas down. I put activities down like yoga, running, swimming, writing, dancing, making digital music. I need to go back to all that stuff. I'd like to cook more for myself and cut out the processed foods completely. I feel better when I eat whole foods for meals.

Mmm... food. I'm going to rummage for a snack. I make a drink and crack open my laptop to plan for tomorrow. I work until ten, like every night.

65

Too Tough

We're back at school after Spring Break and the warning bell for first period beeps. I start walking down the hall to my post outside of my classroom.

"Miss, Miss," Darlene, who's in my Leadership class, calls from behind. "I'm sorry I missed the field trip. I was with my therapist. And she was like," Darlene makes her hand like a mouth opening and closing. "On, and on, you know? And I just, I just ended up missing the field trip."

"Oh, that's alright, Darlene. I mean, we missed you, but I understand." The bell rings. "Okay, see you later," I say and turn to go into my classroom.

"Okay, Miss." Darlene smiles, walks backward, and then pivots around to go in the opposite direction.

"Miss, the cops are across the street," another one of my students says.

"Yeah, the police are always in this neighborhood," I say.

"No, Miss. They're here for us," she says. We both keep walking. I roll my eyes.

"Okay."

I walk into my classroom and get the class started.

"Happy Friday, everyone. Today we're going to start with independent reading, and then you're going to turn in your reading logs. For fifteen minutes, you can choose to either catch up on your workbook or work on your computer lessons. For the last fifteen minutes of class, we're going to play Kahoot on the class book, alright?" I turn around to start organizing things on my desk when my classroom door opens. Jobin is in my doorway. He never interrupts my class.

"Ah, Miss. Martinez, can I speak to you out in the hallway?" He's staring at me in a strange way. I drop my things on the desk. When I get to the doorway, the Attendance Coordinator, Charlie, is there.

"Do you know where Tonantzin is? I ask Charlie. I have a meeting scheduled with Simone, but I need Tonantzin to cover my class." I glance around but don't see anyone.

"Oh, she's in her office, comforting a kid who was pretty upset about something," Charlie says.

Jobin interrupts.

"There's a bullet that came in from the outside, went through Mr. Leblanc's room, into mine, and is lodged in my display board."

"WHAT?" My eyes get big. I put my hands on his shoulders and stare at him.

"Are you okay? Is everyone okay?"

"Yeah, I'm alright. I'm not sure how Mr. Leblanc is." I lock eyes with Charlie, the attendance director.

"Can you watch my class for a second?" He nods his head. I walk down past Jobin's classroom and search for Mr. Leblanc, but he's not there. There are two students in there, one is sitting, the other taking off his backpack. I walk all around the school, but I can't find him. I circle back around to the commons area.

"Bye!" Ms. Bell says to me. All her students wave to me and say, "Bye, Miss."

I try to whisper to Ms. Bell, who's gathering her students for a field trip.

"I don't think you're going on a field trip," I say.

"Yeah, we're leaving now," Ms. Bell says and continues to march her kids down the hall. I shrug. It's not my place to stop her. I'm sure we're on lockdown.

When I get back to Mr. Leblanc's room, he's there.

"ARE YOU OKAY?" I say to him.

"Yeah," he says with raised eyebrows while wiggling a toothpick in his mouth and shrugging. His expression says, 'Okay, considering the situation.' I give him a hug. He points in front of him to the wall. I turn to see a column of papers stapled to the wall, at the bottom of them, there's a black hole. I walk closer.

"Oh, no." I get about three feet away. Mr. Leblanc walks forward and points to the adjacent wall. There's an angular circle, where the bullet entered the sidewall. "WOW," is all I can manage to get out and put my hand to my mouth. I know I have to get back to my class. I walk out of Mr. Leblanc's into the commons area. I see Jobin outside of his classroom, still talking to Charlie.

"Oh, man. " I glance down the hall and see Jim, the dean of students. I ask Charlie if he can keep watching my class. I have a meeting with Simone, but I can't find her. Jim makes eye contact with me from down the hall.

"Do you know where Simone is? " I ask him.

"She's in a meeting with Felicia, in her office, but the police are already here. We're on lockdown. A few of the kids were on the outside and saw the car drive by. They saw the gun out, and someone shooting. They're pretty shaken up about it."

"Oh jeez," I say. "Well, I guess my meeting with her is canceled."

"Yeah, pretty sure," Jim says. I see the back of the security guard at the door.

I walk back to my classroom to find Tonantzin there instead of Charlie.

"Hey, hi," I whisper to Tonantzin.

"Hi," she says.

"Did they tell you what happened?" I try to say, as not to alarm the children.

"Yeah, I was the one who called 9-1-1," Tonantzin says with her forehead wrinkled in worry. "Yeah, they said they would send someone when they could."

"What?!" I whisper-yell.

"Yeah, and I said, '*Did I mention we're a school*?'" she says with her hand on her face like it's a telephone.

"What the hell?" I can't believe it.

"Yeah, and I had Amber and Marcella and Roberto in my office. They all saw it from the outside and a bullet whizzed by them and hit the building above the entrance," Tonantzin explains.

"Are they okay?" I turn to her and say.

"Yeah, but they were shaken up about it, you know?"

"Yes, of course." I'm still whispering.

"So, are we on a lockdown?" Tonantzin asks.

I nod and my timer goes off. It's time to start our game.

"Alright guys, log off of the computer, we're going to play a game." We played our game until the bell rang for 2nd period.

In the middle of 2nd period, the principal comes into my classroom.

"Hi, guys. I'm coming in to announce that we are no longer on a lockdown. The police gave us the all-clear. Police said there was gunfire down the street in an unrelated incident. We're in the clear, BUT, to be on the safe side, today for lunch, we are going to have lunch inside, okay?" I hear one of my students groan.

"Ah, that means I can't play basketball," he says with a frown. He's another one of my ankle-bracelet-wearers.

"Yeah, I know, it sucks, but it's just for today. Thanks for being understanding." I'm shocked that anyone would *want* to be outside, but then again, this kid recently got out of juvenile detention. He's unfazed by these things. The principal leaves. I get engrossed in the skit that the class is putting together. The class flies by and the bell rings.

"Have a good weekend, guys. Please be safe. I want to see you Monday." Second period shuffles out, third-period students shuffle in. I go out to stand by my door. Jobin is by his door and Mr. Ridgeway walks closer to us.

"Why are we not closing down?" Ridgway whispers to us. I twist my face and shrug. "If this was Truman, we would have been shut down by now." I take a deep breath, shake my head, and glance around. "Kids are over there taking pictures of the bullet hole," Ridgeway says. I turn, and there are three students in Mr. Leblanc's doorway.

"Sheesh. Yeah, that's an excellent question." I feel my anxiety rising.

"Beep, beep, beep," the warning bell rings.

"One minute, folks, get to class," Jobin announces to the students in the commons area.

"Are the police here?" I ask.

"Yeah, they've been in and out of Mr. Leblanc's room all morning," Jobin whispers. The bell rings.

I start my routine and get the kids working so I can take attendance. They have fifteen minutes to read a book. I sit on my chair and take attendance. I start to think about what happened. Someone just drove a car and shot at our school. Could it be an old student? A current one? A random shooting? I scan my walls. These stucco walls are not protective, huh, for a bullet to go through two walls? I sit there. My classroom is on the same side as Mr. Leblanc's. It faces the street side. Someone could come back and do it again. I could be sitting here like this, and anyone of us could get shot through the wall. I start breathing harder. Wow. I put my elbow on my desk and my head on my palm. Mr. Leblanc's bullet-hole is what, fifty feet away from me? I feel cold. I start to tremble. What are we still doing open? I click on my emails. There is one from Simone. It said a text message was sent out to parents that reiterated what she had said when she came to my classroom. I take a deep breath and observe my students. I see one student that Tonantzin said had witnessed the shooting.

I went to the student and whispered in their ear.

"I just heard you were outside when this happened. Are you okay?" She nodded her head and I rubbed her shoulder.

I stood up and went toward the front of the class.

"Hey, I want to say to you all, if anyone is shaken up by what happened today, you can see Ms. Felicia. She's available to you all." Some of the students nod their heads, yes, and I start to walk back to my desk.

"What happened, Miss?" Rodrigo asks.

"Uh, there was a drive-by shooting." I don't know what I should say.

"Ah Miss, you afraid of a little drive-by?" Rodrigo says while slouching in his chair and holding his phone against his tummy.

"When the bullet goes through our building, yeah, I get a little shaken up." I nod and kick my foot forward to walk to my desk.

"What was it .45?" my student asks.

I'm a bit taken aback.

"I, I don't know. The police are taking it out of the wall right now, Rodrigo," was all I could say. I sit back at my desk and check my emails. Nothing. I still don't understand why these kids are here, why any of us are here. Maybe they're used to this kind of stuff? How does anyone know the shooter is not coming back? I take a deep breath. 'Joselyn,' I tell myself, you are going to have to remain calm until the end of this class. I started to picture if there had been more bullets. Thank God there wasn't! Any four of my kids could have been killed. They were sitting right at the computers that face the front wall to the street. I take another breath.

Before I know it, it's lunchtime, and I'm about to have a full-blown panic attack. Simone finds coverage for me, and I go home. I found out that it was two cars speeding down the street shooting at each other.

I don't think I'm tough enough for this job.

66

P.A.R.C.C. Prep.

PARCC testing was coming up and at our staff meeting we were given instruction for how to prepare with our classes for a week or two. The game plan for us teachers was to go over some declassified test questions. We were to review them with our students. Declassified test questions are questions from past tests that were no longer being used. But as we did so, we made the mistake of not checking one of the answers. We all assumed because we all had agreed on one answer, that it was correct. When I went over it with my students and confirmed with the answer key, I realized the answer the teachers selected did not match the answer key. The question then became, was the answer wrong? ...And was that why they were no longer using this question? ...Or are we all just stupid teachers?

I was now sharing the frustration my students had for this test. Especially because as teachers, and schools, we are accountable for their test scores. Our grades as teachers from the state include how well our students do on these tests. We have known for years that students from the poorest states don't do well on these tests. When you break down the real reasons why they don't do well, it often comes down to the fact that these kids don't come to school. How can teachers be responsible for that? I asked my colleagues more questions about why parents aren't held more accountable for their children coming to school. Jim said that the state doesn't know what kind of consequences to give parents.

"It's child abuse to not allow or make your child not come to school! You are robbing them of an education and a future!" I called out.

"Yes, but the state doesn't want to put them in jail. Then the parent or parents are not working and not able to sustain their family and pay taxes, Jim replied.

"So I guess giving them fines would be just as unfair to an already poor family?" I ask.

"Right," Jim responds.

"A lot of these kids go out with their friends, day or night and don't get up to go to school," Leblanc says.

"If I ever not wanted to go to school my mom would take me by my *grenas*!" (would pull me out of bed by my hair), I say.

"Well, you can't hit kids anymore!" Leblanc points out.

"Why don't they take their phones away? Then they're either not staying up late on their phones or meeting up with their friends?" I counter.

"How are you going to physically take a phone away from a kid?" Leblanc asks.

"You don't have to, you just stop paying the bill." I think I know everything, and I'm not even a parent.

"Well, phones are a way that parents use to know where their kid is, you know," Leblanc says. All the more reasons for me not to want to have these potential problems. I would not want to be a parent in to-day's world.

"Jeez. How do we fix this?" I say desperately.

"We can't. All we're really allowed to do is help them prep for the exam. If the students have technology questions, we can help them with those. But we're not supposed to look at the questions on the test," Leblanc says.

"Wow, okay," I say, defeated.

"The other frustrating thing about this test is we don't get the results back until the summer. When we try to go over the results with the kids in the fall, most of them don't remember what was on the test," Jim says.

"Oh, wow. Learning from mistakes is where our best learning comes from," I say.

"Yeah," confirms Jim.

"We may be able to request breaking up the test into smaller chunks so they don't get so mentally fatigued. And maybe having smaller testing rooms. The larger the testing room, the more easily students are distracted by others," Leblanc offers. "But the kids hate it and they get really stressed out. We just give them test-taking strategies and try to make it more comfortable for them with water and snacks. We also try to show a positive attitude."

It makes me wonder if testing defeats the purpose of why we're all here.

I go to my mom's after work to talk to her about this. She tells me that the school she worked at got 'D' or 'F' grades for several years. The district's solution to that was to change the principal. I told her that sounded reasonable.

"Yeah, and the first thing she did was spend money on painting the school and getting new furniture."

"What? That's just cosmetic! That's not going to cause better learning! Why didn't she get a better staff, or more teachers, or more social workers?" I ask. My mom twists her mouth down and puts her hands up with a shrug.

"I remember when I was living in Chicago, they started closing down the failing schools. I thought it was stupid because it's not the *building* that's failing the students, it's the people. Now you're just going to make other schools more overcrowded and with bigger classroom sizes. Those kids are still going to fail because they're behind on the basics. It causes overcrowding, and it's going to pull down the test scores of schools that had decent test scores," I say with frustration.

When testing day came, we told the kids ten million times that phones were not allowed. They had to turn them in, or else their whole test could be invalidated. Jayson, of course, kept his phone in his pocket and I caught him pulling it out. This kid should be in Special Education and reads at a third-grade level. ...And he wants to graduate early, hay-yai-yai!

67

Sister Secrets

My grandma's full siblings, judgments included:

1. **_Grandma_** - *Is the oldest. She only went to school for one year. She was about 14 years old when their mother died. After she died, she took care of her older half-sibling's children and her younger siblings. She is illiterate and mother of six. She grew up in Pecos and was a busy homemaker. She's an amazing cook and used to make the best bread and tortillas on the planet. She was my primary caregiver as a baby and child.*
2. **_Angela_** - *Is an uneducated lazy mother of three who lives in Colorado. She married a man who went to the Korean War. He's the cook of the family.*
3. **_Feliz_** - *is an uneducated, fat, lazy mother of three who sits around, eats all day and watches T.V. Her husband is Tio Carlos who molested children in our family for generations. He died from his diabetes. She is terrified of being alone.*
4. **_Beatriz_** - *Is a mother of three. When her husband died of cancer, she took care of children in her home child care and abused them. She wears an ugly old red wig now.*
5. **_Edwardo_** - *Became a barber and successful business owner. Like Feliz, he also can't be alone. After his first wife divorced him, he lived with a woman for 20 years before marrying her.*

They divorced two years later. He married his third wife after dating for a few months.

Over the last week my grandpa went from eating, drinking, and talking, to nothing, not even a whisper. It's torture to see him like this. Part of me wants his suffering to end. The other part of me aches at the thought of him actually being gone forever. This is what purgatory must be like. Watching someone you love, suffer. I expected "the call" to come during his hip replacement surgery, then any day after that. My life now is just waiting for this damn call. He was never one to give up. I guess he feels the same way now. I've gotten sick with a cold and puffy with hives from all the stress.

***

It's a little after 6 a.m. on a Monday in March. My phone rings. I see it's my mom.

"Oh, no. This is it," I say to myself while picking up the phone. Before I even say hello, I hear my mom sobbing on the other end. I'm about to ask her how she is, but clearly, she's not well.

"Mom?" I delay saying something stupid.

"He's.. gone!" She sobs. "My.. dad.. is.. gone." I barely make out what she's saying.

"When did it happen?" I still don't know what to say. "I.. don't.. . know," she cries.

"Where are you?" I sit up in bed.

"I'm... going... to... my... mom's," My mom barely gets words out.

"Alright, I'll meet you there."

"Okay," she's still sobbing uncontrollably. I don't want to cry because if the floodgates open, it's going to be howling and boogers. I have to get sub plans ready for work before I go to my grandma's.

I drove to my grandmother's to say goodbye to my grandfather. Later my grandmother's sister, Beatriz, arrived. I have a particular hate for this aunt. When my mentally ill uncle Tony died, she told my mom we shouldn't have a service for him. Her reason was because my grandparents don't have the money. I wanted to poke her eyes out after I heard she said that. She later apologized to my mother for it, but I never forgave her. No one has the right to say that. It was none of her business. We had a particularly beautiful service for Tony, and my grandparents didn't have to pay a dime.

My grandfather's death had my heart in a tender mood. I extended my arms to this stupid aunt and she gave her usual porcupine hug. She puts her arms out, but moves her head far back, like you have porcupine quills that will poke her.

"My sister," was all she could say. I motioned to her that my grandma is in the living room. Beatriz goes straight to her.

After about an hour, many of us ended up together in the kitchen. My aunt Marcy is washing dishes. My mom, Beatriz, my cousins and I are seated at the table. The phone rings.

"Oh, I hope it's not Feliz," my aunt Marcy says. My grandma's other sister, Feliz, can't stand to be alone and wants to come over every day. She calls non-stop. No one likes to have her over because she expects to be catered to hand and foot.

"You know, she has," Beatriz makes a circling movement with her finger around her temple, "lost it."

"Well, I wonder why? She has to face up to what she's done in life," I say.

"What do you want her to do? She can't handle it!" Beatriz shakes her head, and her old red-orange wig swings from side to side.

"She had to have known that her husband was molesting children?" My mom tries to get to the truth, but doesn't really get an answer.

"Remember those sisters that were whores? The Sanchez sisters? Carlos would get up early before work to visit them. She knew about that," Beatriz says assuredly.

"And then that damn dog, Pancha, do you remember her? Carlos loved that dog. I mean, he *loved* that dog. He had a special relationship with that dog," Beatriz says with her eyebrows up.

I can see the meaning of what Beatriz is dawning on my aunt Marcy. Marcy is drying a dish, but her face and jaw drop. She stands there frozen, holding a pot in one hand and a towel in the other.

"I.. don't.. think I.. can handle... what you're saying," my aunt Marcy says. We're all surprised by what Beatriz has revealed. In sister rules, she broke the number one rule.

Later that night when I was home, I was thinking about my aunt Feliz and uncle Carlos. They used to take me to prayer meetings all the time. Those prayer meetings were for nothing. Those two sickos couldn't enter the gates of heaven if they both spoke in tongues and fainted all day long.

I have a flashback memory of me at eight or nine years old. I remember going over to my aunt Feliz's house at about 7 in the morning. My grandma sent me to drop off some freshly-made tortillas. My aunt opens the door in her bra and pants and lets me in. She walks back through the living room and down the hall to the bathroom to finish getting ready. As I go to the dining area to put the tortillas down. I glimpse down the hall and see her husband in their bedroom in a robe, holding the dog over the bed. I keep walking into the dining room and kitchen. After a moment, I hear my uncle open the back sliding door and see him let the dog out. I wondered why the dog was inside. She was not an inside dog. Now I know why.

(I no longer call her my aunt) Feliz is so sick. She's living in her own shit. Her past must haunt her daily. That's why she can't stand to be by herself. She can't stand who she is. She literally can't live with herself. Here I wanted to punish her. She *is* her own punishment. She is now, and she will forever be living in her prison sentence. If there is a hell, she's going straight to it. She was an accomplice in her husband's crimes. She's lucky to not be in prison right now. All this time, I didn't realize how free I am. My conscience is free from hurting children. I live freely. Feliz lives in hell every day, the one she created with her husband. Nothing is more satisfying than justice.

In all honesty, I'm glad I'm on this 30-day drinking cleanse right now. My grandpa's death would be an excellent excuse to drink myself into a void.

68

Equity Council Conference

I was pumped up about being on this committee. I anticipating see-ing how hundreds of people would make education better for New Mexico. I met my cousin Dolores there. We had breakfast, then listened to how people in the Public Education Department wanted to make a difference. They handed us out some workbooks and reading material - a lot of it and we did some of the exercises in groups.

By the end of the second day I was disillusioned. They turned it all back on us. It felt like a shit-ton of busy work for people on the coun-cil to do. No word about funding or a redistribution of funds to help these disadvantaged kids. They wanted us to create a committee at our school. We are supposed to define equity for weeks, raise expectations, use culturally sensitive materials, do intervention plans, improve out-comes, and blah, blah, blah. We already do all of those things. They're only asking us to reverse systemic racism and move mountains with no policy changes or funding.

I see one of our biggest problems is getting these kids to school. How are we supposed to discuss a novel like *The Absolutely True Diary of a Part-Time Indian, Journey to* Aztlan, or *Night*, if the kids don't come to school? They don't know what's going on in the book! They cant' get to a deeper meaning if they are embarrassed about not knowing the plot? How are schools supposed to learn their students' names when their class sizes are so big? Talk about problems with classroom manage-ment.

Dolores was right. The state was giving us boxes to check and lots of hoops to jump though.

When I discussed this with Mr. Leblanc, he recommended I read *Shame of the Nation* by Jonathan Kozol and I started to. It's eye-opening. It talks about how schools are still segregated, despite the Brown vs. Board of Education lawsuit. It talks about how schools are so underfunded and what message that gives to the minority students. The book discusses how everything revolves around testing and about how schools have cheated to bring their test-scores up. They get rid of low test-takers to bring the school's test scores up. Or fudging numbers to get their graduation rates up.

Since I started reading that book, how we can fix the educational system is always on my mind.

69

Lunchroom - Mmm... Nachos

Jobin ate quickly and was finished when Mr. Lombardi came into the lunchroom to make his food. Lombardi is not in a rush because he has a 4th period prep. When Lombardi finishes making his turkey sandwich, all the seats are taken at the table.

"Here you go, sir," Jobin stands up and offers his seat to Lombardi.

"Are you sure?" Lombardi asks.

"One hundred percent," Jobin nods. Lombardi sits down.

"Wow, this feels weird. It feels like I'm sitting in dad's chair."

Lombardi's lanky frame appears small in the chair, compared to Jobin.

"Your younger, much better-looking dad?" Jobin suggests.

"One of those two." Lombardi winks and smiles.

Mr. Ridgeway walks in with a bag from the burrito spot next door. I recently had to give up dairy. I discovered I have a sensitivity to it, which is a shame because I'm vegetarian, and cheese has been a big part of my diet.

"Dude, now I'm totally craving nachos." I drool when Mr. Ridgeway reveals his big colorful pile of heaven.

"Eeee," Ted laughs between bites.

"You can't have nachos!" Jobin reminds me.

"I can have nachos... without the cheese! .. That's... not... going to taste good," I say out loud.

"It's called CHIPS," Jobin tells me. Everyone laughs. "'Can I have a cheeseburger, hold the cheese,'" Jobin mimics me.

Mr. Ridgeway is engrossed in his nachos as Jobin starts talking about his two-year-old son.

"Pam, you know that story I was telling you the other day about Dean? It *was* an amethyst," Jobin tells Ms. Baker.

"Really?" Ms. Baker asks.

"Wait, did he say 'amethyst?'" Ms. Baker asks.

"No, but the way he described it. He probably could say amethyst," Jobin says. "He says 'am-buu-laa-nce,'" Jobin imitates, and we laugh.

Mr. Ridgeway finally glances up from his nachos.

"Are you making fun of somebody?"

"Yeah, one of the students," Jobin quickly lies.

"Oh! David finally joins us!" Mr. Lombardi calls out.

"His son," Ms. Baker says.

"I was thinking 'which student does that?'" Mr. Ridgeway says.

"I wish I could stay home with Dean," Jobin says, with a sad expression on his face.

Mr. Leblanc begins pounding on the table and chanting.

"MAKE SAMANTHA WORK!" Jobin joins in on the second round, "MAKE SAMANTHA WORK! MAKE SAMANTHA WORK!" They both pound their fists on the table and protest. I shake my head and smile. The others laugh.

"I saw one of your comrades yesterday," I cryptically told Mr. Ridgeway.

"What are you talking about?" Mr. Ridgeway crunches into another nacho.

"They were marching up and down the street with a huge United flag. I was like, 'Oh, there's one of David's people.'" Mr. Ridgeway usually doesn't associate with any group, but he loves the new soccer team for New Mexico. We're all proud of the name "United." Unity is precisely what is needed during this time.

"Yeah, the stadium was sold out yesterday for the first time! It was so much fun! The crowd was into having a good time, you know? There were no drunken assholes, it was great!"

Lombardi's staring at his phone. "Ah, the Muller Report was leaked."

"What was leaked, number one or number two?" Ridgeway asks.

"Why does it sound like you're talking about poop?" I wrinkle my nose.

"'Ain't nothin' gonna happen." Mr. Jones says.

"Stop saying that! I don't want it to be a self-fulfilling prophecy!" Lombardi says.

When Mr. Leblanc finishes his lunch, he takes a series of vitamins. Today, as he takes each one, he lifts it and says,

"Cyanide!" and swallows it. "Arsenic!" and swallows that.

"Hand it over!" I say.

"And old lye!" Mr. Leblanc lifts his last vitamin and downs the last pill. I shake my head and smile.

The bell rings.

"I want nachos!" I yell. We all shuffle out to the south hallway.

"Oh, by the way, Jim said we can't be 'whooping' loudly in the hallways anymore.

We have a new student that's sensitive to loud sounds," Ridgeway says.

"What? You're the 'whooper,'" I accuse.

"I know, I started it. I take full responsibility," Ridgeway says.

"Good, cause I have PTSD from that bullet coming through the wall."

70

Funeral Services

"Do you know where your grandma is?" My second cousin, the preacher, asks me. It's 11:30 on a Saturday and my grandpa's funeral service was supposed to start at 11:00.

"She wanted my uncle Andres to bring her, but Andres has dementia," I say apologetically. "Let's have Olivia call him." I turn to my first cousin Olivia.

"Can you call your dad?" I hand her my phone. She dials the number by heart. I turn up to her. She's tall with black wavy hair and fair skin.

"Dad, where are you? Oh, you're on Fortuna? You went too far, turn back until you get to Ilis." She winks at me from the phone. I whisper to my preacher cousin.

"They got lost, they'll be here in five minutes. I'm sorry. I know you like to start on time," I say apologetically. He can't get mad in front of a hundred family members.

When my grandma and uncle get there at 11:45, my uncle laughed about being late.

We slowly walk her all the way to the front. It felt like it took two days. My grandma moves very slowly.

By the time we got to our seats, our cousin, the pastor, was waiting on the stage. My grandmother cried at the urn and the large photo of my grandfather. First, Pastor-cousin said a few words, then a lady from the church sang a song. My first cousin Cynthia gave the eulogy. Her sister, Marisol, sang. I said a few words about "What My Grandpa Taught

Me." My cousin had it printed on the back of the leaflet that was passed out.

I noticed my uncle Samuel in the crowd with his wife, his daughter and her rugrats. He had recently called my grandma after my grandpa died. He said that grandpa died because we took him to Las Vegas. I made a few secret jabs at him when I spoke, and I moved my head in his direction when I said it. He didn't stay for lunch, which I was glad of.

My loser uncle Michael didn't make it. Hmm... I know he's at the house in Pecos, but you'd think he'd come to his own father's funeral. Maybe he thought he would be emotional? I mean, Michael lived with my grandpa all his life. It's a bit strange that he wouldn't show up.

The day was exhausting. We split up the leftovers and went home.

I have no more bereavement leave left. I have to plan for Monday.

71

Lunchroom - Wieners and Waffles

Mr. Ridgeway is talking to Mrs. Doyle In the lunchroom.

"Yeah, so when the bell for first rang, I see Jamie walking into Pam's room, and I tell her, 'Hey, where are you going? You have this class for first.' She says, 'Yeah, well I'm either going to work in here or in ISS from now on,'" Mr. Ridgeway says while pulling out a packaged sausage from the refrigerator. The teachers gasp at what Jamie said.

"Excuse me?" Mrs. Doyle says rhetorically to Mr. Ridgweay.

"What were you guys doing in class today?" I ask Jobin. "It sounded fun."

"Oh, we were playing games, building rapport." he says.

"'Building rapport?'" I ask.

"Yeah, you know the kids won't do any work until they like you, right?" Jobin asks.

"They won't?" I didn't know this. "I'm always down-to-business," I say.

"Try it," Jobin suggests.

Lombardi walks in and starts to make his regular turkey sandwich with mayo.

"I've got a bone to pick with you, Lombardi," Mr. Jones says.

"Oh, come on, I haven't even made my sandwich yet!" We all know Lombardi likes to shake his sandwich at whomever he does not agree with at the lunch table.

"I'm so glad you don't eat wieners," I mumble.

"Hey!" Mr. Ridgeway says while proudly shaking his sausage. I shake my head.

"Would you like to put your wiener in my bean juice?" Mr. Jones asks Mr. Ridgeway, and Jones puts a bowl of beans in front of him. We guiltily laugh.

I honestly could not survive this job without these amazingly weird people. I would not make it through without the support and the laughter of our twisted little minds.

The jaded comments that Jones always checks us on. He'll check white people on their white privilege, he corrects me on my sexism. He checks us on our biases and hidden discriminations. He'll lie to keep us on our toes. It's nice for us to get a real dose of ourselves.

The guys are great with wordplay too. I'm trying to learn from them to join in.

"What should I bring for the next potluck?" Mr. Ridgeway asks.

"You wanna do waffles again?" I ask.

"Waffles? How about French toast?" Ridgeway asks.

"Waffles, French toast, same thing," I say.

"What?" Mr. Ridgeway says while he, Mr. Jones, and Lombardi whip their heads toward me. "No way," Ridgeway argues, and then Walt, the new Educational Assistant, walks in.

"Walt, where do you stand on French toast?" Mr. Ridgeway asks him unexpectedly.

"What? What do you mean?" he asks.

"Do you stand on the crust, or...?" I ask while motioning with my hand. I get a chuckle.

72

Grandma's "Deal"

"Mom wants you to call her," reads a text from my mom.

I'm at home in my living room, working on lesson plans.

Aunt Marcy has been staying with my grandma since grampo passed away. I call my grandma, and in Spanish, she lays out this deal for me to live with her, rent-free, until she dies. When she dies, I can keep her house. She says we'll do it all on paper. She tells me to think about it and to figure out how much is owed on the home.

I ask my mom how much she thinks they owe on the house. She thinks it's about $60,000. Great, my grandmother wants to give me a heap of debt. Even if I got a loan to upgrade the house, it would all take so much work and time, time that I don't have as a teacher.

Throughout the next few days I call my grandma on a few different occasions to tell her that me living there isn't going to work out. But for some reason, I it's not sinking in.

***

"Mom wants you to call her," reads a text from my mom a couple of weeks later. I call.

"*Que has hecho?*" ("What have you been doing?") My grandma asks.

"*Nada mucho. Ayer fui a comer con la Shandi.*" I had dinner with my cousin last night.

"*Ahh, no debes de comunicarte con ella.*" You shouldn't talk to her. "*Ella 'sta bien wild. Es una leona!*" My cousin is wild, a lion.

"*Y tu? Que haces?*" I change the subject.

"*Que pienses de ese deal que te ofrecí?*"

"*Abuelita*, I don't think that's going to work. I just can't *quit* my job. I'm under a contract and your house is so far from school. Besides, you would still need someone to take care of you during the day. Why don't you sell the house and use that money to live in the old folks home that Marisol runs? You would never be alone."

"Aa*h, no. Ahhh... pos bueno.*" I begin to say "I'm sorry..." but the phone is already dead. She hung up on me.

Oh, no. *My grandmother just hung up on me.* She's never going to forgive me for this. Ever.

Do I tell her the *real* reasons I can't live with her? But there's nothing to gain from guilting my grandmother for her mistakes now, at the end of her life. I'd spare her of what I would give her sister Feliz, given the chance. What would I say to my grandma, if I was honest?

"Thank you for all the good things you did for me. For teaching me Spanish and getting me winter coats when I was a child. Thank you for making food for me and teaching me how to make tortillas and sopaipillas. But I can't live with you because you hurt me. I didn't understand it then, but I understand now. You sold me out to a pervert. You pushed me towards him. You told me to hug and kiss a man who was sexually abusing me. I can't go back into your home for you to start telling me what to do, how to live my life. I'd go back to when I was nine. It would be a constant reminder to me of all of that pain. I can't. My mental health won't let me. I'm sorry that it may put you in a position that you didn't expect. You didn't protect me as a child, but you protected your good-for-nothing lazy sister. I can't forgive you for that right now enough to live with you. I know you're ninety years old, but it's not possible. I know you thought I would be there for you, but I have to take care of me now because you didn't, when I needed it the most."

Should I say that to my 90-year-old grandmother? I go outside to take some deep breaths. Maybe I should go for a run.

73

Lunchroom - In Hell Together

Mr. Jones is talking about his two-year-old son Dean.

"Dean goes, 'Do you hear that, worm? It's the train.'" Mr. Ridgeway and I chuckle. He goes: 'Papa, why can't he hear me?'"

"Because he doesn't have ears," I interrupt the story. Mr. Jones puts his hand out to me palm up and nods his head.

"Because he doesn't have ears, yeah." I truly love it when Jobin talks about his family. He lights up. And his son is so cute.

"I'm going to enjoy second period today!" Mr. Jones gloats because the seniors are going to be pulled out of second period for testing. Mr. Ridgeway and Mr. Jones continue their conversation. Theresa, the math teacher, walks in. I stir my cup of tea while spinning the beaded design the Native Club students taught me how to make. I've been supervising their club every Wednesday for lunch.

"Is this yours?" She puts her hand on my little creation. I nod. "It's pretty, what is it?"

"I'm not sure yet. I was thinking of making it a hair clip," I say.

"Oh, that would be cute too, I thought it was a coaster."

Theresa takes it and spins it around.

"Oh, but a coaster would be even better!" I say and take the beaded design, tilt my head, and spin it around on the table.

"Nooo..." Mr. Jones interjects from his conversation.

"No?" I ask.

"You don't want to put shit on that, that's nice. You want to put that *on* shit," He says in a cadence that signifies the obviousness of what he's saying. I burst into laughter.

"He wants you to use it as toilet paper," Theresa says.

"Yeah.. you know, as a decorative toilet paper display holder," Mr. Jones, as usual, makes it up as he goes along.

"Display holder? What is that?" I ask.

"Turd display?" Mr. Ridgeway asks. Our conversation gets lost.

"On a separate note, the other day, I was at the park with the boys, and there was a big group of people grilling and eating," Mr. Ridgeway begins to tell. "They see my boys running around, and a lady from the group brought me a plate and the boys some juice boxes and some food. She said that they had extra and for us to have as much as we like. I said thank you, and I was really touched, that we had this, like, human-to-human moment. As I was leaving, one of the dudes came up to me. He said, 'Hey, I don't know if you have a church already, but you are welcome to come to our church.' And he gave me a flier. I was so mad. I was like, 'I knew there was a catch!" Mr. Ridgeway points his finger upward.

"There's always a catch," Mr. Jones says.

"You didn't do it from the kindness of your heart, you did it because your lord and savior told you to!" Mr. Ridgeway progressively gets louder and louder. I chuckle.

"Yeah, cause in my head I was like, 'This was a cool human-to-human interaction; sharing food.'" Mr. Ridgeway says as he leans back on his chair.

"Are they no longer humans now?" I ask.

"No," Mr. Jones answers quickly for Mr. Ridgeway.

"No!"Mr. Ridgeway answers right after and then continues with the story. He pretends to be the guy inviting him to the church. 'We hope to see you some time.'"

"N," Mr. Jones says.

"No!" Mr. Ridgeway says. "That's never going to happen. The only way that's ever going to happen is if I died and if you steal my body. Or..." Mr. Ridgeway paused to think of something.

"We're in hell together," Mr. Jones finishes, and they chuckle.

I finish my tea, and the warning bell rings.

74

Hispanic Guilt

My mom and I are at my grandmother's on a Sunday in April and I'm in the kitchen when I hear my mom from the other room,

"*Pero, MAMÁ, NO DEBE DE LLEVAR COSAS TUYAS Y DE MI PAPÁ! Porque la dejas?*" ("But MOM, SHE SHOULDN'T BE TAKING THINGS THAT ARE YOURS, AND MY DAD'S. Why do you let her?")

"*Nooo... es negocio tuyo. Si, yo se lo di*" ("It's not your business. I gave it to her.")

"*MA-MA, sabías que cuesta dinero? Dinero que puedes pagar a alguien quien te cuide!*" ("MOM, those things cost money, money that you could use for someone to take care of you!")

"*No, no. Yo puedo hacer lo que yo quiero.*" My grandmother tells my mom she can do what she wants. This lady is more stubborn than a bull.

"*Que no entiendes números?*" ("Don't you understand numbers?) She shouldn't be asking for these things. Those guitars should go to someone in the family, not your *sister*," my mom says to my grandma.

I think my grandma did it out of spite because she doesn't care for any of her grandchildren. This is her retaliation for us not jumping to taking care of her.

"Anyway, it's just material. I don't know why we have to fight about material things," my Christian aunt Marcy squeaks out.

"Grandma doesn't know what she's doing. She's not going to say no to her sisters," I say to my aunt, but my grandmother appears in the entrance kitchen. She overheard me. Her face twists.

"*Ahhh... Yo se lo que estoy haciendo. Y tu? Tu ni me cuides!*" ("Ahh... I know what I'm doing. And you? You don't even *take care* of me!") My grandmother spits out to me.

'TIME TO GO BACK TO THERAPY!' I say to myself as I gather my things. I turn to my mother and say.

"Let's go. This is not going anywhere. I don't want to keep fighting," I say. My mom asks my grandma why she let Beatriz take the microwave that goes with the oven that my mom bought her for Mother's Day. My grandma acts like she doesn't know what she's talking about, and my mom finally gets her purse and keys, and we go.

Do I really need to spend money on therapy? I know what my therapist is going to say. 'Use the method.' but how can I "See out" when all I see is red? I could use a drink... but maybe I'll do some yoga and meditation instead. After my 30 days alcohol-free, it gave me a "reset." I don't have alcohol in the house anymore. I think it's fine to celebrate when I'm out with friends, but not every day, or every other day. It had to have been taking a toll on my body.

When I get home, I write and do yoga.

75

Senior Dinner

One of the most delightful days of the year was last Friday, Family Fun Day. It's when we cut fifth and sixth period to continue lunch and have games set up. Everyone has the most fun with the water balloons. It becomes students against staff and gets crazy. When the kids ran out of water balloons, they started using bowls, pitchers, or anything that could hold water. We'd try to lure the kids into traps and vice-versa. It was fun.

Today is the Senior Dinner. It's usually on a Friday evening at the end of May.

Fridays go by fast. I gave out finals, graded, and almost everyone failed. I'm wondering if it's my fault or theirs? Most of them didn't even show up. Shows me where their priorities are! We officially have three more days of school and the little brats took vacation early.

For lunch I take out my calabacita tacos with black beans. Ms. Baker is already in the lunchroom when Mr. Ridgeway walks in.

"If I have to spend another minute with that family, I'm going to lose it," he says.

"Why? What's wrong?" I ask, popping the tops off my jars.

"They can't *talk* to each other, they all yell," Mr. Ridgeway replies. He turns around to get his lunch from the refrigerator.

"Oh my god. I'm glad you didn't ask me to interpret!" I say out loud, selfishly.

"So, is Joe going to take Tuesday off?" Mr. Ridgeway asks Mr. Jones.

"I don't know. Theresa, are you coming in on that Tuesday?" We had an extra day to work because we had a rare snow day off this year and had to make it up. Mr. Jones turns to Theresa.

"Tuesday? Probably? Yeah, are you guys?"

"Yeah." Mr. Ridgeway answers. "It will be a good day to..."

"Punch people," Mr. Jones finishes the sentence.

"Get cleaned up," I finish the sentence.

"Get cleaned up?" Mr. Ridgeway asks as he motions plunging a pretend needle in his arm. I roll my eyes.

"Get my *classroom* cleaned up, not *me*!" I correct myself.

"Did Annette ring the bell?" I changed the subject.

"Yeah, at like 4:35," Mr. Ridgeway says.

"Damn, that's late," I say.

"Oh, I felt so bad for her!" Mr. Jones says.

"Why?" Ridgeway asks.

"She had worked and worked on the test for her on-line class. When she finished, it said, 'Congratulations on completing the practice test! You can now take the real test! ... Martina had unlocked the wrong test!"

"Ahh, shiiit," I say.

"I told her, 'Anette, this is not the time to cry. You just have to do it.' I locked her in my room and... made sure none of her friends distracted her."

"You threw vegetables at her," Mr. Ridgeway pretends he knows the end of Mr Jones's sentence.

"I threw vegetables at her stupid senior face," Mr. Jones says.

"Wait, what? Did you really throw vegetables at her?" I ask, puzzled.

"No, I didn't throw vegetables at her!" Mr. Jones yells.

"Well, why did you say that?" I ask.

"It sounded funny," Mr. Ridgeway says, and I laugh.

"Yeah! Loosen up, lighten up the mood," Mr. Jones agrees.

"Is Joe retiring this year?" Mr. Ridgeway asks and takes a sip of coffee.

"Yeah, he told me himself," I say.

"Well, if Joe is retiring, then maybe we can see if the new teacher we get has a dual license in history and English. That way they can take some of the load off of you," Mr. Ridgeway proposes to Mr. Jones.

"That still doesn't solve the problem of someone having four preps," Mr. Jones counters.

"Well, I don't care about *them*," Mr. Ridgeway says while shrugging and showing the palm of his hand.

"Ah, that's the nicest thing anyone has ever said to me. I love you, man," Mr. Jones says.

"Aww, see, and you say you don't want friends," I tell Mr. Jones.

I love these guys. The fact that they can express feelings, joking or not. I've never seen such loving masculinity before.

Laina comes in to feverishly make copies for the Special Ed files. She's closing out students who are exiting out of the program since they are graduating.

"So Jayson is not coming back next year," Laina says.

"Why, because he couldn't graduate early?" I ask.

"Yep," Laina replies. I just shake my head.

"George Larima is valedictorian this year!" Laina announces with a smile.

"No way!" we say simultaneously.

"Wait, what?" Mr. Jones whips his head around twice. Mr. Ridgeway pulls his protein drink out of the refrigerator and turns toward Ms. Vogler.

"George Larima, he's valedictorian this year," Laina repeats, with the same smile, nodding. We all stop what we're doing and stare at her.

"That's insane. Is he going to make a speech?" asks Ms. Baker.

"It's up to him," Laina says and nods while smiling.

George is a long-haired kid with blondish-brown wavy hair and glasses. He could pass as a homeless person, but is not. He's into video games, AND, he has Tourette's Syndrome. We all stare at each other, stunned.

Mr. Ridgeway sits down then coughs while drinking and spills protein drink on his pants. When he stands up to clean it up, I laugh because it's milky color appears to be a... different kind of stain. Mr. Jones points to it, and Mr. Ridgeway says it's "protein drink," but the word "drink" is filled with another cough.

"Protein, huh?" Mr. Jones lifts his eyebrows and glances away.

We quickly eat and soon the warning bell rings. People groan and shuffle out.

The rest of the day is a blur.

Finally, it's time for the Senior Dinner. Catalina and her helpers decorated the tables in black, silver, and turquoise. The school usually provides fried chicken, nachos, cake and cookies. We tell parents if they want to bring a side dish, they can. Parents and seniors trickle in and set up food and drinks. People bring plenty. The DJ starts the music. There's a three-tiered cake of a graduation cap and diploma. Catalina puts it on a table of its own with decorations. There were tables and tables of food. It's a full house.

I stand by the water fountains. George Larima and his grandparents walk by. I stop him,

"Hey, George! Congratulations on getting valedictorian!" His grandmother had kept on walking before him and did not hear me. His facial expression appears bewildered. "*Oh, my God.* You didn't know?" He shakes his head. I grab his shoulder. His long-bearded salt and pepper-haired haired grandfather did hear. Grandpa's eyes get wide, and his smile is enormous. "You're going to have to act surprised, okay?" I plead to George. George nods his head. "Please, act like you didn't know." He nods his head, and I send him off. His grandfather has a smile from here to tarnation.

"I was the last of *my* class!" Grandpappy says and walks off.

I'm standing there when one of my graduate mentees approaches me.

"Miss, can I talk to you?" Leo asks.

"Yes, of course. Do you want to go into my classroom?" I don't know if he means in private or not. He nods his head. I unlock my door and we go inside. I close the door slightly to block out some of the noise.

"Miss, I just want to tell you thank you for being my mentor and believing in me."

"What? Of course! You don't have to thank me for that."

"No, it's just that I didn't think I was going to graduate. I never told you why I was out of school for a year," he pauses. "I was at the carwash over here on San Mateo about two years ago. When I finished washing my car, I moved to the vacuums. Some guy in a black truck backed up and pulled out a gun and just started spraying everywhere. I didn't realize I was shot until I felt the blood on my leg."

"What!"

"Yeah, he shot all over and then took off. I was out of school getting better, but then I realized I lived across the street from the guy who shot me. I changed the way I looked so he wouldn't recognize me. I changed my hair and started wearing glasses. I was just afraid for a long time."

I'm stunned.

"I can understand why!" I lean on my cabinet.

"Yeah, I just tried to lay low because it seemed like they were drug dealers. There were people coming in and out of their house a lot."

"Wow, yes," I try to validate his feelings.

"So, I really didn't think I would graduate. I want to tell you thank you for keeping me on track and calling me and texting me when I didn't come to school. I really appreciate it." He gets a little emotional.

"It was my pleasure, Leo. I'm so proud of you." I give him a hug.

Simone announces that she's grateful to see everyone over the microphone.

"Come on, let's go celebrate you." I hug him again and smile.

Simone continues, "Thank you to those who brought food to share. We're celebrating our 35 graduates today. We'll announce the valedictorian and salutatorian shortly. Please enjoy the food, music, and the photo booth! Congratulations to the graduating class!" Everyone applauds.

The food line is long, so I wait until it's died down. I scrounge for whatever is homemade and vegetarian. We socialize, and I eat standing up, bouncing around to the music.

Simone gets on the mic after everyone has had some time to eat,

"Okay, everybody, it's time to announce our Valedictorian and Salutatorian! The Salutatorian award goes to... Anette Espinosa!" Everyone applauds. Simone gives her an award and a bouquet of roses. She waits for the applause to die down. "And the Valedictorian of Dolores Huerta High School is.... George Larima!" Everyone applauds. George pops up (a little too quickly). He retrieves his framed certificate, roses, and balloons. He takes a picture with the principal and returns back to his table where grandpappy and grandma hug him. Grandma's in tears. Everyone is taking videos around them. There are congratulations from his mentor and two of his teachers. His family takes photos with him and his award. The social worker pats him on the back and congratulates him. They don't know! They don't know I ruined it.

Families have their fill of food. People have fun with the photo booth, and then Simone announces the slideshow. The lights go down, and the display shows all the seniors and the staff. People cheer for each other, laugh, and clap. It's great.

After another fifteen or twenty minutes, we start to clean up, and everyone goes. Simone thanks us for staying late, and we all go our separate ways.

As I reflect on today, I notice how each individual staff member is so essential. I cherish the men I work with, I can trust them. They can be emotional. They can be tender and can love. They can be fathers to their kids and husbands to their wives. They leave the toilet seats down. What more could you ask for? I love that the students see them with their wives and kids for parties and the holidays. I have to hand it to all the men there. They are a treasure, and they all care about the kids. I've never felt threatened or disrespected. In fact, I've never felt so listened to. It could bring me to tears. It's funny that we don't hang out outside of school, but we are in school quite a bit. It'd be overkill. It's enough to appreciate them even more.

I honestly could not survive this job without these amazingly weird people. I would literally not make it without the support and the laughter of our twisted little minds. The jaded comments that Jones always checks us on. Mr. Jones will tell you the truth that you didn't think you needed to hear. He'll check white people on their white privilege, he corrects me on my sexism. He checks us on our biases and hidden discriminations. He'll lie to keep us on our toes. It's nice for people to get a real dose of themselves. Mr. Ridgeway is on top of everything, makes awesome projects for his classes and is hilarious. Mr. Leblanc 'gets it'. He understands racial issues, women's issues and politics. He does his best to teach his students life issues through lessons. He's a loyal friend. Felicia can handle any emotional emergency. She is the calm in our storms and can make appropriate jokes in the face of darkness. Kimberly, the guidance counselor, is the sunshine in our days. Catalina makes a party a party, Jarrod is grounded and helpful. Mrs. Doyle makes it a point to "crack her eggs." She means when she's able to get a student to care about math, she's reached her goal. Ms. Baker is smart, artistic and has a great sense of humor. Laina is encouraging, has a heart of gold with the patience of a nun. Martina is the computer teacher that all the students trust. Viviana is the queen of memes that will make you laugh out loud. Jim is the 'Student Whisperer,' he literally whispers to the students and he's a loving father. Theresa is the short, young, but energetic math teacher, and Lombardi is loved by all. Simone is a loving and fearless leader who has more faith in you than you do. I thanked them this morning for always allowing me to vent in the staff lunchroom. Thanked them for never coming down on me or ever shaming me for losing it. I thanked them for the amusement. There's no way I could get through the stress without the humor. I must savor this moment in life. This environment has been healing for me.

When I get home, there's an email from my cousin on my dad's side, Amber. She's organizing the family reunion for the end of May. We're going to meet at her sister Linda's house in Los Lunas for a cookout. She's got a spreadsheet attached with a sign up sheet for food. According to my sister Joselin, Amber didn't invite my dad. It would be an awkward way for Felipiano and dad to meet like that. Joselin told Amber that Angelina and I haven't spoken to him in years. I sign up for chips and dip and hope no one springs my father on us at this party. I decide to meditate and explore the possibility. I'm not sure if I'm supposed to do that during meditation, but I enjoy doing it, so I do.

76

Grampo's Guitars

"Hello?" I answer when my mom calls. I'm at home on a weekend in May watching Netflix.

"Hey," my mom says.

"What's going on?" I ask and put her on speakerphone.

"I found out that Aunt Beatriz..."

"She's your aunt, not mine. I disowned her. Anyway, sorry to interrupt. What about her?" I ask, fluffing up my pillows.

"...she took one of grampo's guitars. The old one, the Gibson."

"She WHAT?!" I yell.

"Yeah, gramma let her take it," mom says.

"What the hell is wrong with Bea?! I can't even believe ...yes, of course, I can. This is just like her!"

"Oh, and Beatriz said Ron would buy grampa's truck for $500." Ron is Beatriz's son.

"WHAT?! That's robbery! What the hell does she think she's doing? What a dirty swindler!"

"And by some miracle, my mom said no to that, I'm surprised. So, I called Beatriz today. I said, 'That guitar should not have left that house. It's a family heirloom.' and she said, 'IT'S NONE OF YOUR BUSINESS.' and she hung up on me."

"SHE WHAT? How is this NOT your business? We're next-of-kin. She's nuts! I cannot even believe it, who *does* that shit? It's grimy and disgusting to take advantage of old people... and especially your own old sister!"

"Don't forget, when my grandpa died, Beatriz kept all his money and didn't split it up among the siblings. That's why Feliz didn't talk to her for five years afterward." My mom reminds me.

"I had forgotten about that. Dirty old rag. She needs a new wig. It looks like a dog died on her head." My mom laughs.

"All those years of dying her hair! Burned it all. You can see her scalp."

"Wow. So now what?" I ask.

"I don't know if there's anything I can do, my mom *gave* it to her, and she's not certifiably mentally ill," my mom explains.

"Oh, man," I say. I know from experience that calling the elderly abuse line is useless. I called it to report Michael a few times. Only the person being abused can call. You can't call for other people. It's frustrating.

"Well, I'm going to call the Adult Protective Services line to ask what I should do tomorrow," she says.

"Mmkay. I'll get my butter and popcorn. Let me know what happens."

"Okay. I will," my mom says before hanging up.

Instead of making a drink, I go outside and take some deep breaths. I got rid of all the alcohol in my home and decided not to drink alone anymore.

77

Another Fall

"Grandma fell!" My cousin Marisol's text came at around ten in the morning on a Saturday. Not a minute later, my mom calls, and I answer.

"Grandma fell. They're taking her in the ambulance now." My mom sounds a little worried. "Her feet are purple. Andres is going to follow the ambulance in his truck. Mom told me to stay here with the lady that takes care of her."

I told her I'd meet them at UNM Hospital, after they check her in and hung up with her.

I start to think about getting ready. But there is something inside me that doesn't want to rush to be there. Something else inside me feels guilty for not rushing. 'What if she dies?' I think to myself. I go to the picture of my grandfather on the refrigerator and start to cry. I'm overwhelmed, get tired and have to go to sleep. I sleep for a while, wake up, remember that I have to go to the hospital, and I go back to sleep.

I wake up to the sound of my phone ringing. It's my uncle Andres.

"Hey-ya, Joselin, do you think, when they let my mom out, you could come and pick up your grandma? She can't get up on my truck," my uncle says.

"Oh, yeah, has she been seen by the doctor yet?" I ask, groggy on my couch.

"No, no. We've been here waiting. She's been seen by some nurses, but not the doctor."

"Oh, okay. Well, let me know, and I'll be right over," I say, feeling a little less guilty for not being there already. "How's my grandma?" I ask.

"Oh, she's fine. You wanna talk to her?" My uncle asks and hands over the phone before I answer. I put my phone on speakerphone.

"Hi," my grandma says. I hadn't spoken to her since she got mad at me for not deciding not to move in with her.

"Hi," I say back. "*No te duele nada*?" (Are you in pain?).

"*No, no* más *me duerma los pies.*" (No, my feet have just been falling asleep). I tell her that I will take her home when she's ready.

"Okay, thank you," she says in English and hangs up. I go back to sleep.

Uncle Andres calls me a couple of hours later saying that they're ready. When I get there, she is being seen by the doctor at that moment. My grandmother is in a room across a hall from the nurse's station. We end up waiting another three hours for test results to come in and for her to be released.

Andres can't remember where he parked his truck. His dementia seems to be getting worse, but I don't comment on it. He doesn't want to search for it in the dark, so we take gramma home first. Then I give him a ride home.

I feel guilty that I can't live with my grandma. I can't even go through all the reasons why. She's controlling. She tells you HOW to do everything, from picking up a spill to who to hang out with. She would remind me of the many times she's betrayed me.

- Forcing me to see my dad as a child & trying to force it into adulthood.
- Having my father over, when I explicitly asked her not to. After my telling her how he's hurt me, and that he doesn't care about me.
- Throwing me to the wolf. Telling me to hug and kiss my great uncle when she damn well knew he was abusing me. She never asked me to hug any of my other uncles.

- Taking pictures down of all family from her walls, except the ones of her and her brother and sisters.
- Giving family heirlooms to her sister instead of her grandchildren.

She's tough to please. Nothing I ever do is ever good enough. I finally realized that when I was about seventeen and stopped trying. She'll yell for me and when I come running she calmly tells me to get her water. There's so much trauma, I can't subject myself to it. My every fiber says no. I have to be true to myself. Remember, gramma has always been loyal to herself and her sisters. I'm not sure if she loved or showed love to her children. I hope my mom felt loved enough. It's no wonder our family is so disjointed, not close, not communicative of their needs. Not supportive. Strangers, practically.

I was disappointed to not be the granddaughter that I expected myself to be. But I'm pretty sure I would rather kill myself than put myself through that torture.

I should meditate.

78

Gaslighting

My mom calls me on Friday after work. I just got home. I put my car in park and turned off the radio. She tells me about a conversation she had with Uncle Edwardo, my grandmother's only brother:

"I was talking to *tio* Edwardo today. He found a Mexican lady to take care of grandma. She's going to stay with grandma and grandma will pay her once a week."

"Oh good," I say, relieved.

"*Tio* Edwardo said that when my dad fell, that Michael couldn't get him up. So Michael got my dad by the collar and shook him and then threw him on the couch."

"WHAT?! Are you serious?" I say, in shock.

"She called Samuel to help Michael pick my dad up," my mom says.

"What?! Why did they *pick him up*? You aren't supposed to pick up the elderly when they fall! Why didn't they call an ambulance? ...Well how did grampo end up at the hospital?" I ask.

"Samuel and Michael put him in bed, and Samuel left right away. My mom said my dad started to change color, so she called 911."

"Are you shitting me? *That's* how grampo got to the hospital? Why are they so stupid? Everyone knows you can hurt someone more if you move them."

"Wait a minute. *That's* why Samuel has been blaming grampo's death on grandma and us! *HE'S* the idiot that made the wrong decision! He doesn't want to blame himself, so he's blaming us! WOW! He's gaslighting!"

"What I find weird is that gramma wants me to make a doctor appointment for her because she's been dizzy. She says she has pain on her left ear and pain on her left arm socket. She said it was because she got a gallon of milk, but I suspect Michael hit her," My mom says.

"Why do you say that?" I ask.

"This is the first time she has ever signed an Order of Protection against him in all of these years. Why now?"

"Why wouldn't she tell us that? Why would she protect an abuser?" I say as I realize that's what she did with my abuser.

"I guess so we don't go kick his ass!" My mother hisses.

I wondered if Michael had it in him to hit my grandmother and shake my grandfather, causing his death? I've seen him do awful things to them, showing his teeth in anger, snapping belts at them, as if he would use them. Yelling, having tantrums. He would yell at my grandfather when my grandfather was asleep. Who does that? Let the man rest! You never know when he'll be normal around company, or when he'll say something in anger. He could have been physically abusive toward my grandparents, yes. But my grandparents denied it.

"How did Uncle Edwardo know about this?" I ask.

"He said gramma told him. He told me not to say anything," my mom admits.

"Wait a minute, so if this was how Samuel and Michael treated him, who's to say it *wasn't* Michael's fault grampo fell?"

"I don't know," she pauses. "I wish I would have been a fly on the wall that day."

"That would be a good reason not to show up at your father's funeral!" I think out loud.

"True," my mom agrees.

"Oh my gosh," I say.

"Kay, I'll talk to you later," My mom always ends phone conversations abruptly.

"Okay," I hang up. I sit in my car, thinking whether this was possible, and if this was why Michael didn't show up to his father's funeral. The best father in the world.

79

Family Reunion

"Perla's been trying to figure out what order you kids were born." Amber tries to cut through all the other voices of the family reunion on my dad's side, without my dad. Most of my dad's nieces were there. Our half-brother from El Paso, Toby canceled. Felipiano couldn't make it, and Alvaro is, of course, in another country.

"So, Marcella is the oldest," Joselin points to Marcella.

"Its:

1. Marcella, born in 1970
2. Joselin born in 1974
3. Toby was 1974
4. I was born in 1975
5. Alvaro was 1980
6. Felipiano a year later in 1981, and
7. Angie in 1985

Seven kids, six moms," Joselin tells them.

"I think uncle Jose did actually love your mom," Amber says to Marcella. Marcella appears confused. She wouldn't know since her biological mother gave her up for adoption. "Uncle had asked her to marry him before he went to Korea when he was in the military."

"He did say that," I add. "But dad had heard rumors that your birth mother had cheated on him, so he broke it off," I say, recounting what he told me.

"I have no idea," Marcella says, shrugging her shoulders.

"Then he dated my mom," my sister Joselin notes. "It was me, then Toby was born ten days later, then Joselyn was born seven months after that." Joselin points to me.

My sister Angie's eyebrows go up. She's sitting on the floor on a pillow, rubbing her pregnant belly.

"I keep forgetting you and Toby are so close in age!" Angie says.

"Yes, and you're surprised by it every time," Joselin laughs.

"I don't think my uncle knew how to love. He got passed around a lot as a kid after their mom died, and he never bonded with anyone. Your dad might have been also jealous that grandpa raised Rey. There were rumors that uncle's half-brother Rey wasn't grandpa's son, but that grandpa's wife had had an affair," cousin Linda says. Joselin, Angie, and I gasp.

"I had never heard that," My sister Joselin says.

Marcella explains that one of the sons they adopted has Attachment Disorder. Apparently his mother left him for days by himself as a baby, and something just got rewired in his brain. She said they've gone to therapy, and the therapist says he will never be able to show us love.

"When I gave birth to my first child, I couldn't understand how they could have given me up. I had carried her for nine months, and I couldn't imagine it," Marcella says.

Marcella tells us that her best friend had called her one day to tell her to turn on Oprah. They were offering help in finding adopted parents. She called and the lady she spoke to said that adoptive records are sealed in New Mexico. She told her to call the records department directly. The man who answered looked up her record. He told her that her mother was from Albuquerque, but she had had given birth in a hospital in Grants. He gave Marcella her mother's name. He tells her the record said that the father did not want to claim responsibility. She ended up calling and they set a meeting, including Jose. She said it got awkward when Marcella's birth mother and Jose started mudslinging at each other and arguing. Marcella cut the reunion short and went home.

"Oh, what a mess!" I say.

"Oh yeah, it was," Marcella confirms.

"Wow," my cousin Amber says.

"Yeah, because your dad never had a stable home, I don't think he could ever trust anyone. And I don't think he could ever love anyone," Linda says.

"He lived with Jean, and I thought he was going to marry her, but he never did!" Linda says.

"Jean was a good girlfriend, and he cared about her," cousin Amber says.

"She *was* a good girlfriend. She's the reason he started seeing Joselin and me. She told him 'these are your kids, you should see them,'" I add.

"And the weird thing was, Jean asked him for a kid, and he refused! He had all these other kids. See, I don't think he ever wanted to be a dad," I say while getting up for another bowl of chips and dip.

"But he was proud of you! Every time he would come to see us, he would always talk about the two of you. He would say 'Joselin is doing good, she's working. The other Joselyn is in California.' He does love you and would talk about you," cousin Belinda interjects.

I try to explain, "Yeah, but it was so hard to bond with him. He would talk to me like I was the neighbor. He never could get to know me. I don't know. After so many years of trying to love someone and they don't show you love back. It's too hard to have a one-sided relationship, you know what I mean?"

"No, and you can't. You can't have a one-sided relationship," Cousin Linda agrees.

"Is it my responsibility to show him what love is? I don't know. It's been so hard, getting disappointed. You show someone love, and they can't show it back," I say.

"No, it's not your responsibility," Linda confirms.

I wasn't expecting all this validation! I was expecting more about how I'm supposed to respect my parents and show them love unconditionally, like it says in The Bible.

"Check this out," Amber says, and pulls out her phone. "I read this book that helped me," she shows me her phone screen. It's the cover of a book titled *Healing From Toxic Parents*.

"Hmm," I read the summary.

"Will you screenshot that and send it to me, please?" I say. I'm all about self-healing.

"I remember when your dad was dating Felipiano's mom. She told my mom that the first pregnancy was a miscarriage, and the second was an abortion," Amber reveals.

"Wait, what?" I ask.

"That's what I remember," Amber nods.

"Wait, so if Maria told our dad that, then he *didn't* know Alvaro and Felipiano existed?" I ask Joselin. "I was mad that he acted like he didn't know what Joselin was talking about. Denying that Alvaro looked like him. If Maria lied to him, that means he *would* have been surprised," I say, a bit shocked.

Two different conversations are going on about the past and our father. Joselin is in one circle, and I'm in the other. We're going to have to cross-reference later.

By the time I knew it, it was ten at night, and Joselin was getting my nephews ready to go. I gather my things and start saying my goodbyes. The hugs I receive are the best in the world.

On my drive home, there are so many thoughts circling my head. I drive into a May shower and I turn my windshield wipers on low. There's lightning lighting up the clouds. My own cousins confirmed to me what I thought was the truth. My father has attachment disorder! He doesn't know how to love. I wasn't crazy. It wasn't my imagination!

I had always loathed those sayings like "Qué será, será," or "It is what it is." Those phrases felt like excuses, but, in this case, it was true. Felipiano and Alvaro growing up together, away from their biological parents was a blessing. Their biological parents were both incapable of being parents, mentally, and emotionally. Same with Marcella. As much as I love that poor, broken man, we were better off without him. It started raining harder. I'm driving deeper into the storm.

This pain had been festering for years. The writing workshop was exactly what I needed when I needed it. Writing's been healing beyond measure. It's helping me deal with the stress of school and family. I've been comparing myself to my father. I try to distance myself from him when I see commonalities. Maybe I don't want kids, like him, but at least I take care of other people's kids. Is that my way of not abandoning kids? Not leaving them behind like our father left us? Maybe that's why I want to be there for kids who have experienced so much trauma. Is my whole life going to be proving to myself that I'm not like my father? Maybe that's why I'm a vegetarian. To prove to myself I can be disciplined and not glutinous like him.

I need to be okay with the what I have in common with my father. He does have strengths and talents. Let go of the worry that I have of being like him and just do what feels right for me.

Breathe.

For almost two decades, I had been covering up, ignoring, and not dealing with my pain. But all I had to do was face it and deal with it, write about it, process it. Ask myself the questions about what I thought and felt, like an adult. Use my words. It's okay to feel whatever I feel, but everything passes, even the difficult feelings.

I need to feed my soul. Do the things that make me happy and do those things. In my head, I promise to reach out to my friends in L.A. I need those connections, they help me feel whole.

I've changed in this journey of dealing with the abandonment of my father. I can see his point of view a little clearer. He made the best of the cards he was dealt, which was not a good hand.

I have so much sympathy for my student Raya, whose parents have both have died. Why don't I feel the same compassion for my father? I want to be Raya's mama, I feel so bad for her! Can my heart see my father in the same way?

I can appreciate what was given to me when I needed it. I'm a step closer to forgiving him, but I still don't want him in my life. He still has psychological issues, like attachment disorder and narcissism.

I'm grateful to my step-dad. I don't care how old you are, It feels good to have parent-figures in your life, and he was man enough to take on that role.

My sisters and friends have been there for me. In all honesty, I don't think I could have made it through without them. It's weird that in the process of losing a father I gained a brother. I hope the other brother can be open to connecting sometime. That would be really cool. I'm so proud of who they are. They can connect and love other people. I'm really happy for them.

My father's nieces have opened their homes and their hearts to us. They were always a close family. I want to feel that. I did feel it, tonight. I feel the love in their hugs and smiles and in their efforts to bring us all together. We exchanged phone numbers so we can get together again and more often. Amber invited us to Michigan, where she lives. My aunt's family are all lovely people. And they love us, and that's all that matters.

It's pouring as I drive home. It's hard to see through the windshield and through my tears of joy. I'm still not sure what I'm supposed to be doing with my life, but I have some things to process. The short answer is to live it. Live it with love and joy.

80

Graduation

"Do you have Noemi's phone number," Mr. Leblanc asks me. He's been pacing the foyer of the National Hispanic Cultural Center. Families are filing into the auditorium for this year's graduation.

"Yeah," I say and unlock my phone. "Why?"

"Can you call her and see if she can get a hold of Evelyn Chavez? She's still not here yet! They were supposed to be here at 3:30. They already finished the graduation practice; it's 5:00! How can you be late for your own graduation, huh?"

"I don't know." I shake my head and dial the number. Noemi answers.

"*Tienes el número de Evelyn?*"

"*Si, te lo mando por text.*"

"Okay, gracias!" I hang up.

"She's going to text it to me," I tell Mr. Leblanc. We wring our hands and shake our heads and mumble how these kids are late to everything. We continue to walk and pace. 5:20 comes around, and the staff takes their places in the back. The graduates are in a separate parallel line across from us in the same hallway behind the stage. We fidget and compliment each other on how well we all look.

Kimberly is in a black gown that is shorter in the front and flows with ruffles that are longer in the back. It has eight-inch stripes in beautiful colors overlaying the black. She's wearing princess heels, and her feet are so lovely, she could be a foot model. Mr. Leblanc keeps glancing at the time on his cell phone every two minutes and pacing.

Catalina had Laina running errands and she didn't have time to change. She's in jeans and a plaid black and blue shirt and some boots with her hair up in a ponytail. She seems like she ready to collect a bee swarm at any moment. The quirkiness of us is so perfect.

"I'm just going to text her and tell her to sit in the audience," I tell Mr. Leblanc. He scrunches his nose and holds his breath.

"Should I? We're about to go in!" I've been in a bad mood all day after doing grades. They were so disappointing.

"Try calling her and see where she is," he finally exhales. I call the texted number.

"Hello?" Evelyn answers.

"Evelyn, where are you?" I say with as much urgency as possible.

"We're right here, we're walking in the door."

"Run to the back. We're all here. Run!"

"The back? Where is the back?" she says.

"I'll go get her," Mr. Jones says and starts walking at a fast pace.

"Mr. Jones is going to go get you," I say. "Go towards the front where the table of programs and all the people are."

"Okay!"

"Wow, that was a close one!" I say. Mr. Leblanc starts to breathe again. We're all in our places. Teachers walk in first. We walk to a standing ovation. The staff walks through the crowd as they clap for us. We get to our seats in the audience. I feel like a rockstar with all that applause. I search for my parents in the crowd. We continue to stand as the graduates are announced, and the commencement song begins. Students march in and take their places on the stage.

The graduation is excellent. Author Juan Blea was our keynote speaker and talked about how the ones who are not here with us, are with us. He said being here for our graduations is his favorite thing to do and how he's proud of every graduate in the class. There were awards and scholarships given out. Then the social worker announced each student's plans after graduation. Most kids graduate with college credits from the community college, due to the dual enrollment program. There were a couple of graduate speakers. Our Valedictorian with Tourette's Syndrome decided not to speak. I was a little disappointed. We had an adorable senior slideshow and then presented the diplomas. They changed their tassels to one side of their caps to the other. The graduates beam, proud of their accomplishments

When the students walk out of that arena, they finally see at us in a new light. Like, 'Oh, you really *did* care!' It only lasts one day. But it's worth four years of struggle to see those smiles. I realize I'm where I need to be, doing what I ought to be doing, for now.

In lots of ways, these kids have saved me and help me become a better person. Here I was thinking I was busy giving them an education when they educate me on how to treat people. They teach me how to be more patient and make me think about how to respond with love. I haven't mastered it, but I'm more aware. What could be more important than educating the youth of America? They give me a reason to get up in the morning and give me a cause. They gave me a distraction from my pain. I judge them and then judge myself, and then realize how much more disadvantaged they are than I was at their age. They make me love them, even when they drive me nuts. I'd rather struggle with these kids in the classroom than see them struggle in the streets, or maybe even in a courtroom. Maybe I am a glutton for punishment. But it's gratifying to give hope to those who weren't sure they would be graduating, or to see a kid go from not giving a crap about school, to caring. I live for those graduation smiles! The students who were committed would have graduated with or without me as their teacher. I just hope I was better to them than the teachers that brushed them off. But did *I* need all this struggle? I most certainly did.

If I hadn't taken this job, I wouldn't have met Laina or taken the writing workshop with Georgina. I wouldn't have been referred to my wonderful therapist without the referral from Felicia. All of these things have been key to my healing and sanity.

I had moved away from home for 17 years to leave these problems behind. Coming back has made me face my family pain and led me to some true healing. I know I'm healing because I don't get all they symptoms of stress anymore. I'm not depressed anymore. I don't get fibromyalgia flare-ups, my hair has been growing in the bald spots, and I feel better not drinking every day.

The folks at my work are jewels. I love them. What I love most about the men I work with. They have secretly sewn together the pieces of my heart that were torn over not having my father's love. The love a father has for his child. I see the love Lombardi, Mr. Jones and Mr. Ridgeway have for their wives and children. They are all making their own steps in the sands of time, separate from their parents. New footsteps, bold ones! I worked with such jerks at the radio networking job. I was shocked by some of the racist or sexist things that they would say. The men and women I work with now are all intelligent and caring people. I wouldn't trade these folks for the world!

81

Ex-Girlfriend

I get a text from a number I don't recognize.

"Hi this is Jean. Don't know if I have the right person but I've been looking for *mi hita* for a long time. If it's you, please let me know."

Oh wow, it's my father's ex-girlfriend, Jean. The one that told my father that he should start seeing us kids, and he did.

I respond to Jean's text and we end up talking for about two hours. She tells me stories I hadn't heard before.

She tells me about how when she and my dad lived together, she would have to leave their place every Sunday. My dad told her that was his day with Joselin. Her mother didn't allow her to be around any of our father's girlfriends.

"But I found out later that he was seeing a woman named Cindy on Sundays."

Jean says Cindy got pregnant by my father in about 1986.

"Cindy was working for an attorney's office. She took the company Price Club card and started stockpiling baby supplies. She bought as many diapers and baby clothes as she could get her hands on. Soon after she had the baby, the attorney's office found out about the embezzling. They decided to press charges. That was when Cindy asked your dad to sign custody over to her, which he signed with no resistance. Then she skipped town."

"So this is the *second* embezzling girlfriend that my dad had?"

I tell Jean we found two full-blooded brothers that are Jose's on Ancestry. They are the "twins" she had read about in the letter from Maria.

"My cousin Linda said Maria told her mom the first pregnancy was a miscarriage and the second one was an abortion. I guess he didn't know they existed," I tell her.

"Oh, no, *he knew*. We got in a big fight about them. He said, 'They're not mine, the mom gave them up.'"

"Ughh," I say, disappointed in my dad's behavior. Again.

Jean thinks my father has a daughter from Colorado too, but she doesn't know the mom or daughter's name.

After we hung up I got another text from Jean.

"So was it a mistake for me to get you and your dad together?" Whoa, that's a deep question. I think about it for a few moments before I answer.

"No, I got to see who he really is, instead of romanticizing about a father that does not exist," I answered back.

I'm grateful for my stepdad. I may be in my forties, but you're never too old to have a dad who doesn't abandon you and who treats you with respect and care.

82

Ring Around the Rosie

Be a teacher, they said. Four years go by. Then in March of 2020, the pandemic hit. It was Thursday and teachers were on their way out of the building for our Spring Break when Simone called us all into the Workroom. She told us she just got off the phone with the Public Education Department. They notified her that schools will be closed for three weeks due to the coronavirus pandemic.

Lombardi, being a math teacher, knows the dangers of how a virus will spread exponentially and makes the comment, "if we come back in three weeks."

Simone responds that it will be for the governor to decide and notify us.

We leave, shocked but relieved that we don't have to be interacting with 100 plus people a day during this time.

Before the three weeks is over the governor announces that schools will not be reopened for the rest of the year. Small gatherings are still banned, so no venues for graduations.

We have a couple of Zoom meetings to keep on track of our responsibilities while we do distance-learning with the students. About 30% of our students don't have computers or the Internet, so we had to give them paper packets to work on. I wondered about getting Chromebooks checked out to those students without computers. Then I realized we would probably never get them back. Some students, parents or family members might sell them for food or something else.

In one Zoom meeting, Simone announces that we have been hit with a huge Small School Funding cut of $135,000.

"This is tough because small schools have the same operational costs of a large school to keep the lights on, except it takes more money to run a small school like ours because we have smaller classroom sizes and we need more staff," Simone says through the computer screen. I get a heavy feeling in the pit of my stomach and start to sweat. She's going to have to cut staff. Could she cut me? I don't feel well. Simone says she will be having a meeting with the Governance Council to problem-solve where to cut the budget.

I share my worry with Laina and Joe Leblanc but they both say the same thing, that she couldn't cut me. It doesn't relieve my anxiety.

A couple of weeks after that Zoom meeting I got a call from Simone.

"Hi Joselyn, is this a good time to talk?"

"Umm... well, I'm driving on my way to go walking with my sister," I say

"Oh, okay. Can you call me when you are available?" Her voice has a tinge of sadness or disappointment.

"Yeah, sure. I'll call you in an hour or two," I say.

"Okay, great. Talk to you soon," she says.

I'm in the car with my baby sister on my mom's side.

"What if she's calling to cut me?" I ask my sister.

"Oh, nooo... Don't worry about it. It's probably not that. Let's just enjoy our walk."

"Whatever it is, I can't do anything about it." I try to shrug the call off, but it's on the back of my mind the whole time.

When I get home I call Simone back. My sister is in the room with me and I put the call on speakerphone."

"Hi Joselyn, thanks for calling back. I hate to inform you of this, but due to the Small School Funding cuts, the Governance Council has to eliminate your position for next year," She says this with as much sympathy in her voice as possible.

"Ohhh.. I'm sorry to hear that," I say shocked, yet not surprised.

"Yeah, it was a really hard decision and I'm really sorry, but there's nothing I can do about it. I'm really sorry."

"Alright, I understand. Thanks for letting me know."

"Hope you have a good night." Simone hangs up.

I sit there in disbelief.

"Oh, I'm sorry," my sister tells me.

"Will you come outside with me? I need some air," I say.

"Yeah sure,"

We go out on the balcony of my apartment.

"I'm going to miss my coworkers!" I tear up. "And my kids!" More tears flow down my cheeks as I wipe them with my shirt. "Oh my god, I'm not even going to be able to say goodbye to my kids! We're not going back to school and I won't be back next year! March was it!" I'm bawling like a baby, crying so hard that I'm hyperventilating. The neighbors can probably hear me. I cry hard for at least five minutes. I'm grieving. This chapter of my life is over.

After a few days, I decide I want to continue being a teacher. I get back to work, searching for a job at another charter school.

I spent my summer writing, editing, searching for jobs and day-dreaming about my next book. My brother published a short murder mystery and it inspires me to write a murder mystery novel. I'm having fun with the idea.

Eating only whole foods that I cook has been my thing lately. No more processed foods (except for chips and chocolate)! I'm not drinking alcohol at home, which has helped me lose three or four inches on my waist. And with the state's stay-at-home order, I'm not drinking out either.

I'm keeping in touch with friends and even my grandmother. The Mexican lady is still taking care of my grandma. And I'm still working on forgiving my abuela.

As long my biological father does not reach out to Felipiano and Alvaro, I'm not interested in talking to him. I wish him well.

I'm not sure how we're going to navigate through this pandemic, but we're spiritual beings. It's essential to feed our souls with things that make us feel healthy. When our souls don't feel right, the physical part of us doesn't feel right either. So I'm building a home studio to create more music and voice narration for e-books.

May we find ways to make the world a better place and use whatever challenges come our way to move us through life. Only we can save ourselves from our own victim mentality.

I know the feelings that come with losing your sustenance. It's scary. We may be physically distancing ourselves, but I'm with you. Never let your demons win.

Annalise grew up in New Mexico, but got out of Dodge after college. Fist she moved to Chicago for five years, then she moved to Los Angeles. While living in L.A. she reached her dream of becoming a nationally syndicated radio producer. But all of that unravelled after the economic downturn of 2008. She lost her job and was living out of her car. Using a pen name, *Teacher Unhinged* is a story of her transition from Hollywood back to her hometown in Albuquerque, New Mexico. She unexpectedly gets a teaching position with at-risk students at a charter high school in a section of Albuquerque that used to be known as "The War Zone." She's jolted into the realities many students and teachers face.

Teacher Unhinged is Annalise's first book. She still resides in Albuquerque and is still teaching. But teaching online under a pandemic is quite another story...

CPSIA information can be obtained
at www.ICGtesting.com
Printed in the USA
LVHW020819041120
670669LV00004B/471